Scuba Diving

FIFTH EDITION

Dennis K. Graver, EMT, SEI

HUMAN KINETICS

Library of Congress Cataloging-in-Publication Data

Names: Graver, Dennis, author.
Title: Scuba diving / Dennis K. Graver, EMT, SEI.
Description: Fifth Edition. | Champaign, IL : Human Kinetics, [2016] |
    Includes bibliographical references and index.
Identifiers: LCCN 2016018110 (print) | LCCN 2016031644 (ebook) | ISBN
    9781492525769 (print) | ISBN 9781492542032 (ebook)
Subjects: LCSH: Scuba diving.
Classification: LCC GV838.672 .G74 2016 (print) | LCC GV838.672 (ebook) | DDC
    797.2/34--dc23
LC record available at https://lccn.loc.gov/2016018110

ISBN: 978-1-4925-2576-9 (print)

This publication is written and published to provide accurate and authoritative information relevant to the subject matter presented. It is published and sold with the understanding that the author and publisher are not engaged in rendering legal, medical, or other professional services by reason of their authorship or publication of this work. If medical or other expert assistance is required, the services of a competent professional person should be sought.

The web addresses cited in this text were current as of June 2016, unless otherwise noted.

Acquisitions Editor: Tom Heine; **Developmental Editor:** Anne Hall; **Managing Editor:** Nicole Moore; **Copyeditor:** Jan Feeney; **Permissions Manager:** Martha Gullo; **Senior Graphic Designer:** Nancy Rasmus; **Cover Designer:** Keith Blomberg; **Photograph (cover):** Dirscherl Reinhard/Prisma/age fotostock; **Photographs (interior):** Dennis Graver, unless otherwise noted; **Photo Asset Manager:** Laura Fitch; **Visual Production Assistant:** Joyce Brumfield; **Photo Production Manager:** Jason Allen; **Art Manager:** Kelly Hendren; **Associate Art Manager:** Heidi Richter; **Illustrations:** © Human Kinetics; **Printer:** Walsworth

Human Kinetics books are available at special discounts for bulk purchase. Special editions or book excerpts can also be created to specification. For details, contact the Special Sales Manager at Human Kinetics.

Printed in the United States of America   10 9 8 7 6 5 4 3 2 1

The paper in this book is certified under a sustainable forestry program.

Human Kinetics
Website: www.HumanKinetics.com

United States: Human Kinetics
P.O. Box 5076
Champaign, IL 61825-5076
800-747-4457
e-mail: info@hkusa.com

Canada: Human Kinetics
475 Devonshire Road Unit 100
Windsor, ON N8Y 2L5
800-465-7301 (in Canada only)
e-mail: info@hkcanada.com

Europe: Human Kinetics
107 Bradford Road
Stanningley
Leeds LS28 6AT, United Kingdom
+44 (0) 113 255 5665
e-mail: hk@hkeurope.com

Australia: Human Kinetics
57A Price Avenue
Lower Mitcham, South Australia 5062
08 8372 0999
e-mail: info@hkaustralia.com

New Zealand: Human Kinetics
P.O. Box 80
Mitcham Shopping Centre, South Australia 5062
0800 222 062
e-mail: info@hknewzealand.com

E6733

Scuba Diving

FIFTH EDITION

Contents

Foreword

Recreational scuba diving has progressed from its beginnings in the 1950s. Dennis Graver's fifth edition of *Scuba Diving* is uniquely designed toward a level of education that provides new divers with an exceptional level of knowledge while promoting safety and enjoyment. With our training agencies, Scuba Educators International (the former YMCA scuba program) and PDIC International, our goal is to provide a full education for new divers. This text accomplishes that goal and perhaps can also be used for advanced programs as well.

At a time when instant gratification leads many to seek recreational activities that can be accomplished with little effort in a brief time, scuba takes new divers into an environment that remains challenging. Therefore, the need for a full education has not changed. Perhaps the delivery of information will change in the future; however, the need to understand the complexities of the undersea world will not.

In addition to bringing this fifth edition up to current levels of information, Dennis has provided end-of-chapter questions that result in additional learning. This edition is among the best of texts in the scuba industry for new divers.

Dave Barry wrote, "There is nothing wrong with looking at the surface of the ocean itself, except that when you finally see what goes on underwater, you realize that you've been missing the whole point." I couldn't agree more.

Tom Leaird, CEO
Scuba Educators International
PDIC International

Acknowledgments

My appreciation includes the review of the Application of Knowledge (AOK) questions by Dr. Terry Beattie, former diving medical services officer for the Washington, DC diving unit. His physiology expertise was also helpful.

Wall diving in Haiti

Diving Into Scuba

The Joys of Diving

As a diver, you are weightless and can move in all directions. Your freedom approaches that of a bird as you move in three dimensions in a fluid environment. Diving weightless in clear water in a forest of underwater plants with sunlight streaming down is only one of many unforgettable experiences awaiting you.

Just as there are mountains, plains, and various environments above water, there are various environments for you to experience underwater. Coral reefs, kelp forests, incredible rock formations, and other natural wonders await divers in various geographical regions. In addition, divers can explore piers, jetties, quarries, mysterious shipwrecks, and other artificial structures. The variety of underwater sights is limitless. There is more to view underwater than anyone could possibly see in an entire lifetime. A range of activities—such as photography, hunting, and collecting—make diving challenging and rewarding. Scuba diving includes an activity to interest everyone.

Divers are friendly and easy to get to know; their camaraderie is well known. Diving is a sharing activity, and there is much to share. If you enjoy traveling, you will probably love diving. Dive travel is the number one business of recreational diving. Reasonably priced dive vacations to exotic islands abound. Most divers plan one or more diving vacations each year.

The sensations of diving are fantastic but are difficult to explain. Words cannot describe the peaceful solitude of inner space. Diving contributes to good health, can help reduce work-related stress, can increase self-esteem, and can make you feel great. You need to experience the emotions and sensations for yourself. You will then begin to know the joys of diving.

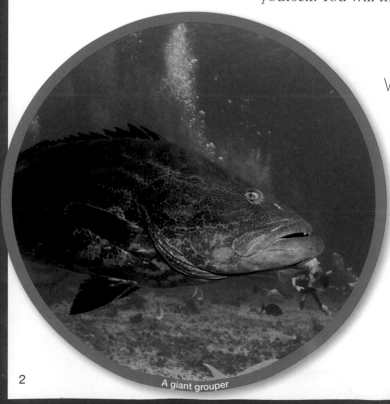

A giant grouper

When you descend beneath the surface of the water, you enter an entirely new and beautiful world. You have opportunities to see incredible life-forms that only a few people ever see. Imagine swimming in a giant aquarium, and you'll get a glimpse of what you can expect to experience in the underwater world.

How Diving Evolved

Interest in the underwater world has always existed. Driven by curiosity and the need for food, people have ventured beneath the surface of Earth's seas for thousands of years. Records exist of sponge divers, oyster pearl divers, military divers, and even salvage regulations dating back to 3000 BC. In ancient times, the two methods employed for diving were breath holding and the use of an inverted, air-filled bell (which was large and heavy). John Lethbridge, an Englishman, developed an oak cylinder diving engine in 1715 to pump air into a bell. The hand-operated air compressor, invented in 1770, allowed fresh air to be pumped into a submerged diving bell. In 1772, Sieur Freminet of France invented a helmet-hose system that permitted divers to work without a bell. The greatest early advancement in underwater equipment occurred in 1837, when Augustus Siebe (a German living in England) invented the first closed-dress diving suit, which became known as the hard-hat system. Siebe's system was so effective that it dominated underwater work for 100 years, and it is still in use today.

The origin of recreational diving can be traced to 1825. That year, William H. James, an Englishman, invented the first **open-circuit** self-contained underwater breathing apparatus **(scuba)** system. Although this system was not very practical, it did solve the problems of the air hose tether and the depth restrictions related to oxygen poisoning. Benoit Rouquayrol (a French mining engineer) and Auguste Denayrouze (a French naval officer) invented the aerophore in 1865. Their creation is considered the source of modern scuba equipment.

Later, two Englishmen, Henry Fleuss and Robert Davis, developed a **closed-circuit** oxygen rebreather system in 1878. This system eliminated the air hose that had previously tethered divers and restricted their movement. The system had great military application because bubbles were not exhausted into the water. Oxygen rebreathers were used extensively by Italian and British frogmen during World War II. However, the use of oxygen rebreather systems is limited to a depth of 20 feet (about 7.6 m) because breathing pure oxygen at greater pressures causes convulsions, which can be fatal during submersion.

Yves Le Prieur of France developed a manually controlled open-circuit scuba system in the early 1920's (year disputed); however, modern scuba diving was launched with the development of a "demand" scuba system that was perfected by Frenchmen Emile Gagnan and Jacques Cousteau in 1943. With this system, a diver could demand compressed air from a steel cylinder by simply inhaling from a pressure regulator held in the mouth. Scuba was introduced in the United States in 1950 and has been popular ever since.

The military has continued to improve underwater breathing systems that have found their way into use by recreational divers. The latest scuba systems are **semi-closed-circuit** rebreathers. These systems use sophisticated electronics to control the oxygen mixture that a diver breathes, periodically releasing only a small amount of bubbles. High levels of training, frequent use, and dedicated maintenance are required for the safe use of these expensive rebreathers. Table 1.1 outlines the basic features of each type of breathing system in more detail.

The Diving Community

The recreational diving community consists of equipment manufacturers, diving retailers, diving educators, diver training organizations, dive resorts, diving

Table 1.1 Scuba System Comparisons

Open-circuit scuba	Semi-closed-circuit scuba	Closed-circuit scuba
User inhales compressed air	User inhales oxygen and inert gas	User inhales pure oxygen
Exhaled air exhausted into water	Exhaled gases enter closed system	Exhaled gases enter closed system
Air supply duration varies with depth	Carbon dioxide absorbed within system	Carbon dioxide absorbed within system
Components simple	Oxygen added as needed	Oxygen added as needed
Unit easily maintained	Air supply duration unaffected by depth	Depth limit of 25 feet
Affordable	Components sophisticated and complex	Convulsions and death possible
Basic training required for use	Unit requires high maintenance	Components simple
	Expensive	High maintenance
	Highly technical specialty training required	Not available for recreational use
		A predecessor to semi-closed-circuit scuba

supervisors, dive guides, dive clubs and associations, publishing companies, and certified divers. Commercial, scientific, and professional diving are not considered recreational pursuits; separate communities are involved in these types of diving. This book addresses only recreational skin diving and scuba diving. A scuba diver breathes compressed air underwater, while a skin diver holds his or her breath while submerged.

Few laws pertain to recreational scuba diving. The laws that exist do not govern who may dive. The diving industry is self-regulating. The diving community realizes that it is dangerous when people who have not completed a sanctioned course of instruction attempt scuba diving. Dive businesses require proof of completion of training before they will allow you to have your scuba tanks filled or allow you to participate in diving activities. Many dive operations also require proof of recent experience documented in a diving logbook. If you have not been diving for a year or more, you may be required to complete at least one dive under the supervision of a diving professional. The supervised dive requirement helps increase the safety of divers whose skills may need to be refreshed.

When you complete your training requirements as a scuba diver, you receive a certification card called a **C-card**. Most C-cards do not require renewal, but the recreational diving community universally recommends the completion of refresher training after periods of inactivity in excess of six months.

Certified divers may dive without supervision or may employ the services of a diving guide. Just because a divemaster or diving supervisor is aboard a dive boat, you should not assume that this person is a guide who will dive with you. Guide services are not necessarily included with diving trips. If you want a guide to lead you about underwater and show you the sights, you should arrange for guide services in advance.

You will learn more about the community as your diving experience increases. Many opportunities for adventure and enjoyment can be found within this community. Get actively involved in the community when you complete your training and officially qualify as a scuba diver.

Diver Training

A national diver training organization must sanction your training. The training organization establishes standards of training that you must meet before the organization will issue a certification card. The Appendix A includes a list of national diver training organizations. Your instructor should have credentials that identify her as a qualified instructor. The instructor's membership in the training organization must be current in order for the person to be qualified to teach and certify divers. Be sure to confirm your instructor's qualifications.

An entry-level training course usually consists of a series of academic sessions, pool or confined-water (pool-like conditions in open water) sessions, and open-water training (in actual diving locations). You will learn theory in the classroom, learn skills in controlled conditions, and then apply your skills in an actual diving environment. This logical progression is common for all approved diver training courses.

The minimum requirements for your training are as follows: You should have four or more academic sessions, four or more pool sessions, and at least four scuba dives in open water. A skin dive in open water may also be part of your training.

Your initial training should involve a total of 30 to 40 hours of instruction. The instruction should occur over a period of several weeks instead of a few days. The time between class sessions allows you to reflect on your training and helps you absorb and retain the knowledge and skills better than a concentrated training schedule would.

Proficiency Testing

After you have learned and practiced the skills of skin and scuba diving, you must demonstrate your competence at a level established by the agency sponsoring your training. Proficiency testing may include diving exercises that are challenging and fun. Examples include mask recovery and clearing for skin diving, simulated boat exit for scuba diving, alternate air source breathing, buddy breathing, equipment handling, and a sequence of surface entry and equipment donning known as a bailout.

Diving Prerequisites

Scuba diving can be undertaken by anyone over 12 years of age who is in normal health and has a reasonable degree of physical fitness. People younger than this should not participate in scuba diving (even when supervised by adults) because they do not have the mental and emotional maturity to deal with the problems that might arise. Skin diving is a good activity for youngsters if they are well supervised.

For scuba diving, you need to have swimming ability, but you do not need to be a competitive swimmer. At the beginning of your training, you should be able to swim 200 yards (183 m) nonstop at the surface using any combination of strokes. There is no time requirement for the swim. Being comfortable in the water is more important than being able to swim fast. You also need to be able to swim 25 feet (7.6 m) underwater with no push-off. By the end of the course, you should be able to swim 300 yards (274 m) nonstop at the surface using any combination of strokes; you should also be able to swim 50 feet (15.2 m) underwater with no push-off. The goal is to increase your aquatic proficiency during the course.

Good health means your heart, lungs, and circulation are functional and that you do not have any serious diseases. Any medical conditions—even if controllable under normal conditions—that might incapacitate you in the water could cause you to drown while scuba diving. Some individuals with asthma or diabetes may be able to dive if they have obtained special medical approval. People with physical disabilities may also dive if they have medical approval from a physician. The air spaces in your body—sinuses, ears, and lungs—must be normal because changes in pressure affect them. Other medical conditions, such as seizure disorders, absolutely preclude a person's involvement in diving; a seizure while diving can be fatal. Women who are pregnant should not scuba dive. Increased pressure can adversely affect an unborn child. Pregnant women may choose to participate in snorkeling as an alternative to scuba diving. Many women ask whether they may dive during menstruation. Menstruation does not preclude a woman from diving if her health permits participation in other sports during that time.

You need to be emotionally fit as well as physically fit for diving. If you are terrified of water or of feeling confined, diving is probably an activity you should avoid. Normal concerns are to be expected, but stark terror is unacceptable.

You should have a physical examination before you begin your training, especially if it has been more than a year since your last exam. Ask your instructor to recommend a diving physician. Physicians who do not understand the physiology of scuba diving sometimes inappropriately grant approval to people who have medical conditions that place them at great risk in and under the water. Your instructor can likely recommend a physician who understands medical issues related to scuba.

Diving Risks

All activities present some risk. There is risk involved in walking across the street or driving a car. To avoid injury while participating in an activity, people take precautions for their safety. Precautions must be taken for scuba diving just as for any other pursuit. The level of risk in diving is similar to that of flying in an

SCUBA WISE

I nearly drowned when I was 4 years old, and I became terrified of water. When I was 8, I spent a summer with my uncle in Ohio. He would take me to Lake Erie and give me pennies if I would wade into water deep enough to cover my navel. I learned to swim as a Boy Scout at age 11. Although I completed a lifesaving class at age 16, I was still apprehensive about water. When I learned skin and scuba diving and discovered that I could actually relax in water, the water became my ally. For the first time in my life, I enjoyed water and was able to rid myself of my childhood fears. Just because someone feels anxiety about water does not mean that the person can't enjoy scuba diving. If you can swim 200 yards, you can learn to dive and to love being in and under the water.

airplane. Both are low-risk activities when done with well-maintained equipment according to established rules and in good environmental conditions. Unfortunately, both activities are unforgiving if you ignore the rules and recommendations designed to minimize the risks.

The following information (and the information throughout this book) will make you aware of injuries that scuba divers can incur. This information alerts you to potential hazards and, more important, helps you learn to avoid injury. If you do what you are taught to do as a diver, your risk will be minimal, and all of your diving experiences will likely be pleasant ones.

Pressure changes with depth. Changes in pressure can severely injure bodily air spaces if you are not in good health or if you fail to equalize the pressure in the bodily air spaces with the surrounding pressure. You will learn equalizing techniques as part of your training. Gases are normally dissolved in the fluids and tissues of your body. Increased pressure increases the amount of gas dissolved in your body. If you ascend too rapidly from a dive, the gases in your system can form bubbles and produce a serious illness known as **decompression illness.** By regulating your depth, the duration of your dive, and your rate of ascent, you can avoid decompression illness. Failure to heed depth and time schedules and ascent rates can result in serious, permanent injuries.

Diving can be strenuous at times. You need sufficient physical fitness and stamina to handle long swims, currents, and other situations that may arise. If you become winded from climbing a flight of stairs, you may need to improve your level of fitness before learning to scuba dive. Exhaustion in and under the water is hazardous. A good exercise to improve fitness for diving is swimming with fins while breathing through a snorkel.

Diving takes place in water, an alien environment. You use life-support equipment to dive, but you cannot depend entirely on the equipment for your well-being. Aquatic skills are essential in and around water. People with very weak aquatic ability can drown when minor equipment problems occur—problems that could be handled easily by a person with good water skills. To be a scuba diver, you must be comfortable in the water.

You should not be overly concerned with the potential risks of diving because the possible

Red Sea coral cave

injuries are preventable. Learning how to dive as safely as possible is the purpose of your training. You will learn to minimize the risk of injury and maximize your enjoyment of the underwater world.

Selecting a Dive Course

There are many diver training organizations and thousands of professional diving educators. Your phone book might list diving businesses that offer sanctioned courses. Many universities, community colleges, and recreational departments also offer scuba courses. (See Appendix A for a list of diver training organizations.) Ask about the qualifications, experience, and reputation of several diving instructors in your area to select the course that can provide you with the best possible training. Here are some questions you should ask:

- Is this training sanctioned by a diver training agency?
- How long has the instructor been teaching scuba diving?
- Which levels of training is the instructor qualified to teach?
- May I speak with the graduates of a recent class?
- Why is this course better than others in the area?
- Are assisting and rescue techniques taught in the course?
- How many instructor-supervised open-water dives are included?

The tuition for diving instruction is usually between $200 and $300. The lowest-priced course may not necessarily be a bargain. Find out what is included with the course fee and, more important, what the total cost will be for you to become certified as a scuba diver. You do not have to purchase all the equipment needed to scuba dive, but you need to have a mask, snorkel, fins, and usually boots and gloves for your training (see figure 1.1). Use of the additional required equipment is typically part of the course tuition.

You should find out whether the price of the course includes the costs of educational materials and certification. There may be additional costs for travel, lodging, parking, boat fees, and equipment rental for open-water training. Determine the complete cost before enrolling in a course.

When you have selected the best program for you and have enrolled in a course, you should receive a reading assignment for your first session. If you are not given an assignment, speak with the instructor; your learning will be enhanced if you read in advance about the topics to be presented in class. Good diving instructors provide a handout with reading assignments.

Figure 1.1   Required scuba diving training equipment.

Diving Responsibilities

When you qualify as a scuba diver, you assume many responsibilities. You are responsible for your safety, for the safety of those you dive with, for the image of scuba divers, and for the preservation of the diving environment. The diving community encourages divers to accept responsibility for their actions. To be part of the diving community, you need to be a responsible diver. Learn what you should do, then do what you learn.

Summary

Diving can be a source of great joy. Many exciting experiences await the trained diver. You need dive credentials to participate in diving activities. You must complete diver training to obtain your C-card and logbook. But diving is not for everyone. You must have normal health, good swimming skills, and reasonable physical fitness. Diving poses risks that a well-trained, wise, and fit diver can minimize. Compare training programs and choose the best education, which may not be the quickest or the least expensive. Remember that you accept a great deal of responsibility when you become a diver. Do not assume that you can transfer the responsibility for a dive accident to someone else. Ultimately, you control your actions underwater. Become a competent, self-reliant diver who adheres to recommended safety practices, and you will discover the joy of diving.

Application-of-Knowledge (AOK) Questions

The following questions will enhance your understanding of what you have learned in this and every chapter. Take time to consider each question before you look at the answer, which is at the back of the book in Appendix B. When you apply the basic knowledge you have learned and correctly respond to the following questions, you demonstrate understanding, which is a higher level of learning than mere knowledge. Do not be concerned if you do not have a correct response. Your analysis of the question and the revelation of the answer will increase your understanding.

1. What is your primary reason for learning to scuba dive? What do you think you will do while scuba diving after completion of your initial training?
2. Why do beginning recreational divers use open-circuit breathing systems instead of closed-circuit systems?
3. Why should you document your dives in a logbook?
4. What are the advantages of completing a 40-hour scuba diving course rather than a course that is much shorter in duration?
5. Why is a medical examination recommended for those who want to learn scuba diving? What type of doctor is the best choice for a scuba diving medical exam?
6. List three actions you can take to minimize your risk of injury when scuba diving.
7. What are some of the factors that you should consider when selecting a scuba diving course?
8. List three actions you can take to demonstrate that you are a responsible diver.

A sea fan

Diving Science

Anatomy for the Diver

Inside your body are air-filled spaces that are affected by changes in pressure. The three body air spaces of primary concern to you as a diver are the lungs, the ears, and the sinuses. Understanding the structure and function of your throat will also help you as a diver. Figure 2.1 illustrates the structure and functions of the sinuses, throat, and lungs.

Sinuses

The sinuses warm and humidify inspired air. They secrete mucus to help protect the body by trapping airborne germs. The small airways that connect the sinuses to the nasal passages are normally open. Congested sinuses pose problems for divers. In the next chapter, you will learn more about sinus problems and how to prevent them.

Throat

In addition to being the organ of voice, the throat and larynx help prevent foreign matter from entering the lungs. If something foreign, such as food or water, comes into contact with the larynx, a reflex action causes a spasm of the larynx. Coughing expels the foreign substance. You have experienced this sensation when something has "gone down the wrong pipe." Review the throat section of figure 2.1. During your scuba diving training, you will learn how to keep water out of your larynx to avoid coughing and choking in and under the water.

Lungs

Healthy lungs are essential for scuba diving. The lungs are large organs that contain millions of microscopic air sacs. Your lungs have a maximum capacity and a minimum capacity. When you exhale completely, your lungs are not empty. They contain about 2 pints (1L) of air. The air remaining in your lungs after you have exhaled completely is your residual volume. The amount of air you move in and out of your lungs is your tidal volume. When you are at rest, your tidal volume is small. When you exert yourself, your tidal volume increases until you reach both your maximum lung volume and your residual volume with each breath. Your vital capacity is the difference between the volume of air for a maximum inhalation and the volume of air for a maximum exhalation—typically about 6 to 8 pints (2.8 to 3.8L). In the next chapter, you will learn several reasons why your lungs are the most critical air spaces when diving.

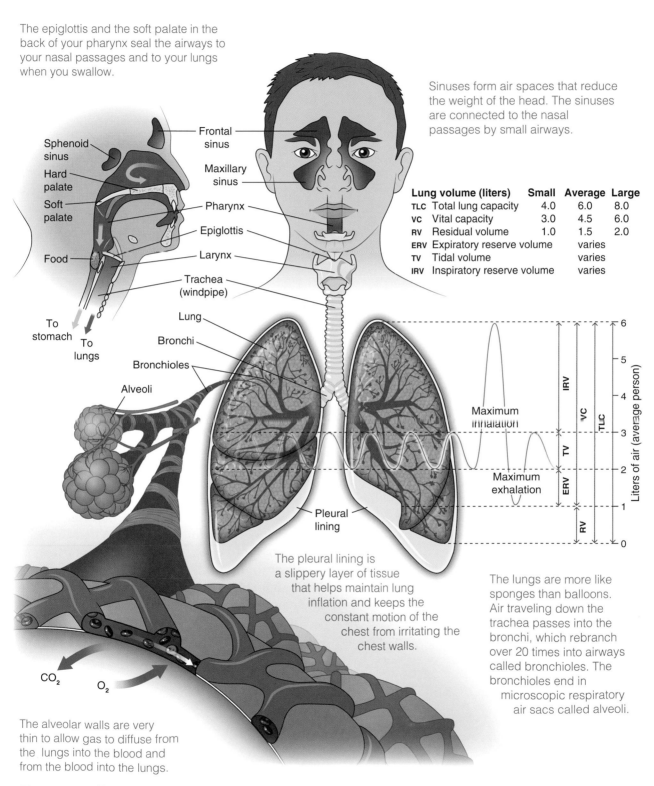

The epiglottis and the soft palate in the back of your pharynx seal the airways to your nasal passages and to your lungs when you swallow.

Sinuses form air spaces that reduce the weight of the head. The sinuses are connected to the nasal passages by small airways.

Sphenoid sinus

Hard palate

Soft palate

Food

To stomach

To lungs

Frontal sinus

Maxillary sinus

Pharynx

Epiglottis

Larynx

Trachea (windpipe)

Lung

Bronchi

Bronchioles

Alveoli

Pleural lining

Lung volume (liters)		Small	Average	Large
TLC	Total lung capacity	4.0	6.0	8.0
VC	Vital capacity	3.0	4.5	6.0
RV	Residual volume	1.0	1.5	2.0
ERV	Expiratory reserve volume		varies	
TV	Tidal volume		varies	
IRV	Inspiratory reserve volume		varies	

Maximum inhalation

Maximum exhalation

IRV

VC

TLC

TV

ERV

RV

Liters of air (average person)

The pleural lining is a slippery layer of tissue that helps maintain lung inflation and keeps the constant motion of the chest from irritating the chest walls.

The lungs are more like sponges than balloons. Air traveling down the trachea passes into the bronchi, which rebranch over 20 times into airways called bronchioles. The bronchioles end in microscopic respiratory air sacs called alveoli.

CO_2

O_2

The alveolar walls are very thin to allow gas to diffuse from the lungs into the blood and from the blood into the lungs.

Figure 2.1   Functions of the sinuses, throat, and lungs.

Colorful fish in a Florida coral cave

Your body is a marvelous machine. It performs many complex functions automatically. Your body is well adapted to an air environment, but it can also adjust in many ways to the aquatic environment. In this chapter, you will become familiar with some of the structures and functions of your body that are important for scuba diving. You will learn the differences between the air and water environments and how changes in pressure affect your body. As a diver, you face many challenges in the underwater environment, but these challenges can be managed.

Ears

Behind your **eardrum** is an air space called the **middle ear**, which is illustrated in figure 2.2. The pressure in the middle ear must equal the pressure in the outer ear; otherwise, the eardrum cannot move freely. The next chapter explains how to keep pressure inside your ears equal to external pressure. Your **eustachian tube** allows the equalization of pressure in the middle ear. The liquid-filled cochlea contains hairlike projections called cilia, which convert mechanical movement to electrical signals for the brain. The movement of the oval window by the tiny bones of the middle ear causes the liquid and the cilia in the cochlea to move back and forth. The oval window movement could not take place without a second window in the hearing organ—the round window. When the oval window moves inward, the round window moves outward, and vice versa.

If the motion sensed by your semicircular canals and the visual cues received by your eyes are not in harmony, motion sickness can result. Sudden changes in temperature or pressure in the middle ear can affect your semicircular canals

Abbreviations

✓	**ATA**	atmospheres absolute	✓ **FSW**	feet of seawater
✓	**atm**	atmospheres	✓ **ft**	feet
✓	**CO**	carbon monoxide	✓ **m**	meters
✓	**CO$_2$**	carbon dioxide	✓ **O$_2$**	oxygen
✓	**°C**	degrees Celsius	✓ **psia**	pounds per square inch absolute
✓	**°F**	degrees Fahrenheit	✓ **psig**	pounds per square inch gauge
✓	**FFW**	feet of freshwater		

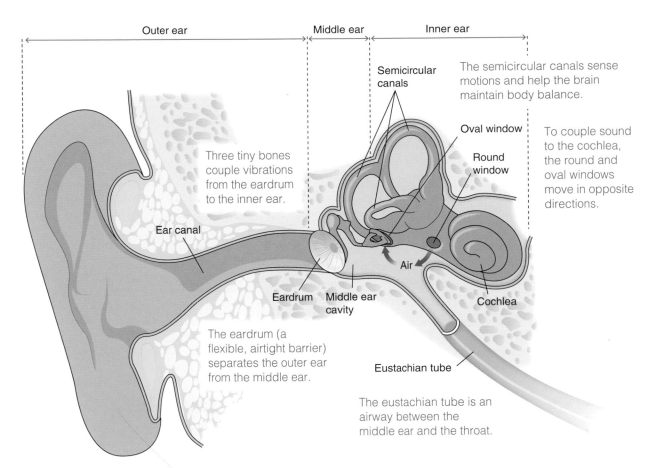

Outer ear | Middle ear | Inner ear

Semicircular canals

The semicircular canals sense motions and help the brain maintain body balance.

Oval window

Round window

To couple sound to the cochlea, the round and oval windows move in opposite directions.

Three tiny bones couple vibrations from the eardrum to the inner ear.

Ear canal

Air

Eardrum

Middle ear cavity

Cochlea

The eardrum (a flexible, airtight barrier) separates the outer ear from the middle ear.

Eustachian tube

The eustachian tube is an airway between the middle ear and the throat.

Figure 2.2 Process of hearing in air.

and cause temporary disorientation. (The next chapter presents potential ear problems for divers, how to avoid them, and how to handle them if they happen.)

Teeth

You may be surprised to learn that there are dental concerns for divers. Pressure can affect air pockets in improperly filled teeth and can cause tooth pain. If a tooth hurts only under pressure or only after a dive, see your dentist and tell him what you suspect. The roots of some upper molars extend into the sinus cavities. You should postpone diving for several weeks after you have had a tooth extracted.

Your mouth and jaws are designed for an even bite. If you bite hard on a mouthpiece with only your front teeth for prolonged periods, your jaws will become sore. Special mouthpieces designed for a proper bite can help reduce the problem. You should not have to bite hard on a mouthpiece to hold it in place. If you find biting necessary, get lighter equipment. Prolonged, improper biting that irritates your jaws can lead to serious inflammation of your jaws and ears.

Respiration and Circulation

One of the fascinating processes within the human body is your ability to breathe in air and circulate oxygen to the tissues with no conscious effort. As your level of exertion increases, your heart and lungs automatically adjust to meet the increased demands for oxygen and nourishment. An understanding of the gases involved in respiration and the basics of respiration and circulation can help you understand the effects and the demands of diving on your lungs and heart.

Gases We Breathe

Several gases affect recreational divers. You need to know about their effects on your body. About 80 percent of air is nitrogen (N^2). At sea-level pressures, nitrogen has no effect on your body. At a depth of about 100 feet (30 m), the increased pressure of the gas has a detrimental effect, which is called **nitrogen narcosis**. Excessive nitrogen in your body at the end of a dive can produce a serious illness known as decompression sickness. You will learn more about nitrogen narcosis and decompression sickness in the next chapter.

Oxygen (O_2) is the gas that supports human life. Any other gas mixed with oxygen serves only as a vehicle for oxygen to be inspired. Approximately 21 percent of air is oxygen (see figure 2.3). You need to breathe at least 10 percent oxygen to remain conscious. However, oxygen breathed under high pressure is poisonous and causes convulsions because oxygen at increased pressure affects your nervous system. You usually have compressed air—not pure oxygen—in your scuba tanks. A specialty form of diving uses a nitrogen and oxygen mixture with a higher percentage of oxygen than is found in air. The mixture, which reduces the effects of nitrogen at depth, is called **nitrox**. The use of special mixed gases, including nitrox, requires special training, equipment, and procedures.

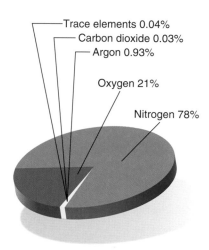

Trace elements 0.04%
Carbon dioxide 0.03%
Argon 0.93%
Oxygen 21%
Nitrogen 78%

Figure 2.3 Composition of air.

As your tissues use oxygen, they produce carbon dioxide (CO_2). Carbon dioxide is the primary stimulus for respiration. The greater the level of carbon dioxide in your body, the greater your urge to breathe will become. If the level of carbon dioxide in your body becomes too great, unconsciousness will result.

Carbon monoxide (CO) is a poisonous gas produced by the incomplete combustion of gas or oil. The exhaust from an internal combustion engine contains carbon monoxide. An oil-lubricated air compressor that overheats can produce carbon monoxide. Even a minute amount of carbon monoxide in your scuba tank can poison you and lead to unconsciousness or death. Air filling stations must take care to avoid contamination of air with carbon monoxide.

Breathing and Circulation Mechanics

When you need to breathe, sensors at the base of your brain send a signal that stimulates your diaphragm to contract and your chest to expand. This draws air into your lungs in the same way that an old-fashioned bellows draws in air when you expand it. Your diaphragm contracts and increases the volume of the chest cavity, while the muscles of your chest expand your chest cavity to inspire air. Figure 2.4 illustrates how the heart, lungs, and circulatory system work in the process of respiration.

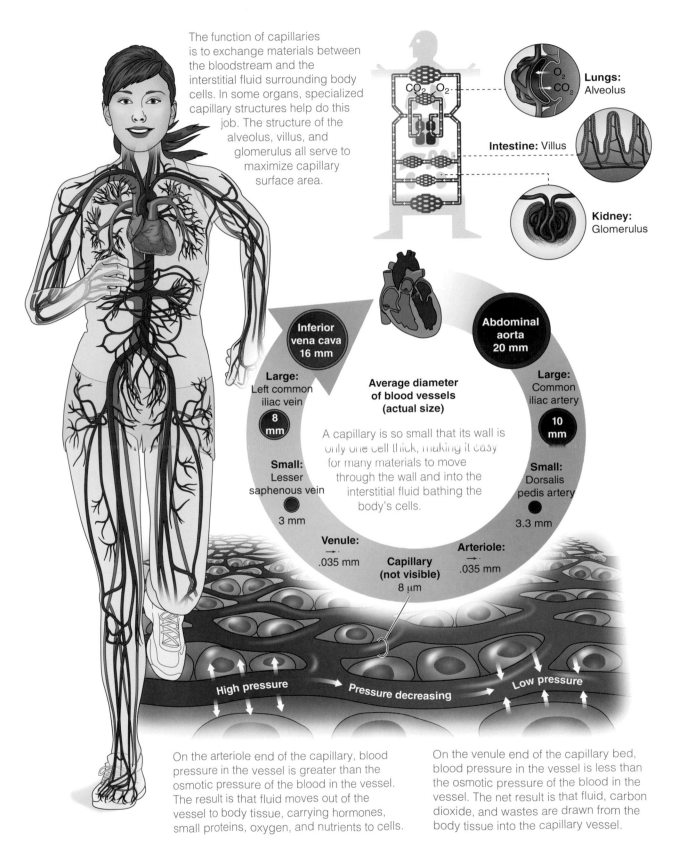

The function of capillaries is to exchange materials between the bloodstream and the interstitial fluid surrounding body cells. In some organs, specialized capillary structures help do this job. The structure of the alveolus, villus, and glomerulus all serve to maximize capillary surface area.

CO_2 O_2

Lungs: Alveolus

O_2
CO_2

Intestine: Villus

Kidney: Glomerulus

Inferior vena cava 16 mm

Abdominal aorta 20 mm

Large: Left common iliac vein

8 mm

Small: Lesser saphenous vein

3 mm

Average diameter of blood vessels (actual size)

A capillary is so small that its wall is only one cell thick, making it easy for many materials to move through the wall and into the interstitial fluid bathing the body's cells.

Large: Common iliac artery

10 mm

Small: Dorsalis pedis artery

3.3 mm

Venule: → .035 mm

Capillary (not visible) 8 μm

Arteriole: → .035 mm

High pressure → **Pressure decreasing** → **Low pressure**

On the arteriole end of the capillary, blood pressure in the vessel is greater than the osmotic pressure of the blood in the vessel. The result is that fluid moves out of the vessel to body tissue, carrying hormones, small proteins, oxygen, and nutrients to cells.

On the venule end of the capillary bed, blood pressure in the vessel is less than the osmotic pressure of the blood in the vessel. The net result is that fluid, carbon dioxide, and wastes are drawn from the body tissue into the capillary vessel.

Figure 2.4   The cardiorespiratory system.

Blood consists of plasma (which is a colorless liquid) and a variety of cells. Hemoglobin, a blood component, is the primary oxygen-carrying mechanism in the blood. Approximately 45 percent of the blood is hemoglobin. Hemoglobin releases oxygen when it reaches tissues that need oxygen.

When the tissues use oxygen, they produce carbon dioxide. The carbon dioxide diffuses into the venous system and into the lungs in exchange for oxygen. This completes a circulatory cycle, which takes about 30 seconds.

Carotid sinuses on each side of the neck sense blood pressure within the circulatory system. Excessive pressure on the carotid sinuses during exercise causes the heart to slow when it should be working hard to meet the oxygen demands of the body. Decreased output from the heart can lead to insufficient oxygen for the brain, which can cause unconsciousness. A blackout caused by pressure on the carotid sinuses (see figure 2.5) is a carotid sinus reflex. Therefore, beware of diving equipment that is tight around your neck.

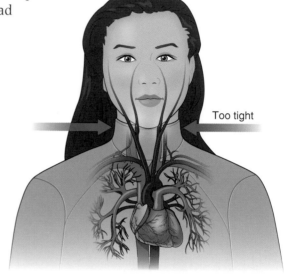

Too tight

Figure 2.5 Excessive pressure on the carotid sinuses can lead to unconsciousness.

Exhalation is usually a passive process. To exhale carbon-dioxide-laden air from the lungs, the diaphragm relaxes, and the elasticity of the chest cavity forces air from the lungs. You ventilate your lungs approximately 12 to 20 times per minute when at rest. Respiration functions automatically. The key to respiration is the level of carbon dioxide in your circulatory system. When the carbon dioxide in your body reaches a certain level, your brain stimulates respiration. When you voluntarily hold your breath, the buildup of carbon dioxide within your body urges you to breathe. Many people believe that the amount of oxygen in the body controls respiration, but it is primarily the level of carbon dioxide that regulates breathing.

Hyperventilation is rapid, deep breathing in excess of the body's needs. Limited hyperventilation—three or four breaths—enhances breath holding (see figure 2.6a). But if you hold your breath after excessive hyperventilation, you may lose consciousness without warning before being stimulated to breathe (see figure 2.6b). A breath-holding diver who loses consciousness from lack of oxygen usually blacks out near the surface during ascent. The sudden loss of consciousness near the surface is called **shallow-water blackout**. Loss of consciousness while in the water can cause drowning. You should avoid excessive hyperventilation.

If you breathe rapidly and shallowly, carbon dioxide continues to build in your system, but you do not expel it from your lungs. Inadequate breathing is **hypoventilation**. Shallow breathing is dangerous, especially when you exert yourself, because you can lose consciousness from lack of oxygen. You need to breathe sufficiently to exchange the air in your lungs.

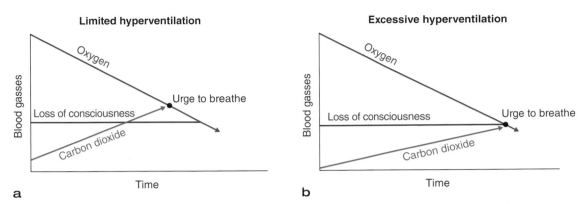

Figure 2.6 Charts showing (a) limited hyperventilation and (b) excessive hyperventilation.

Contrasts in Air and Water Environments

We live immersed in air, which is a fluid. Air has weight and takes up space. We don't pay much attention to our immersion in air because we are adapted to this environment. We have lived in it all of our lives, and we cannot see the air. The weight of the atmosphere does affect us, however.

Air weighs about 0.08 pound per cubic foot (1.28 mg per cubic cm) at sea level. As altitude increases, air becomes thinner, so its weight per volume is less in the mountains than it is at the seashore (see figure 2.7). The change in the

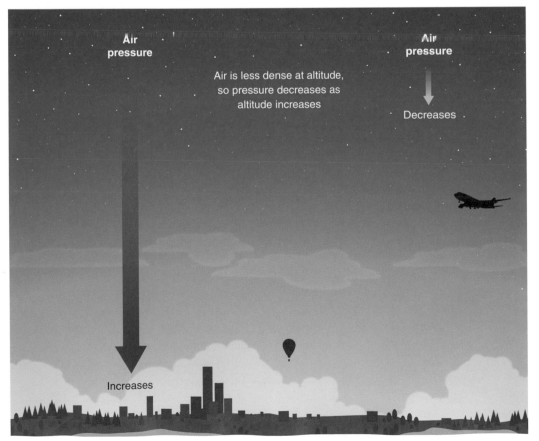

Figure 2.7 Air density and pressure are affected by altitude.

weight of air affects the air spaces in our ears when we fly or when we drive in the mountains.

Density

Density is weight per unit volume (for example, pounds per cubic foot). Water is a fluid, but it is much heavier than air. Seawater weighs about 64 pounds per cubic foot (1.025 g per cubic cm), which makes it about 800 times denser than air. Freshwater, because it does not contain salt, weighs a little less than seawater: 62.4 pounds per cubic foot (1 g per cubic cm). Temperature affects the density of water, air, and all fluids; cold water is slightly denser than warm water.

Air can be compressed, but water is essentially incompressible. Air becomes thinner as altitude increases, whereas water density remains constant throughout the water column.

Drag

Drag is a force that slows movement. Resistance to movement is much greater in water than in air. Factors affecting drag include the viscosity of the fluid, the speed of motion, and the size and shape of the object moving through the fluid. Drag is greater when the fluid is denser, the motion is faster, the object is larger, or the surface of the object is more irregular (see figure 3.9 in chapter 3).

Because of water's higher density, the molecules of water are much closer together than those of air. The tightly packed molecules affect the transmission of light, sound, and heat (see table 2.1). Light travels about 27 percent slower in water than in air. Sound travels about 4 times faster in water than in air. Still water conducts heat nearly 25 times faster than air does and moving water can

Table 2.1   Water Compared With Air

Property	Air	Water	Comparison	Effects
Density	0.08 lb/ft³ (1.3 kg/m³)	62.4 to 64 lb/ft³ (1,000 kg/m³)	Water is 800 times denser than air.	Resistance to movement
Compressibility	Yes	No	Air density varies; water density is constant (at dive pressures).	Affects body & attached air spaces
Speed of light	186,000 mi/s (300,000 km/s)	140,000 mi/s (225,400 km/s)	Light travels 27% more slowly in water.	Affects vision
Light absorption	Low	High	Water absorbs color quickly.	Light & color loss
Speed of sound	1,125 ft/s (340 m/s)	4,900 ft/s (1,400 m/s)	Sound travels 4 times faster in water.	Unable to determine source
Conductivity	0.17	3.86 to 4.12	Heat loss is 22 to 24 times faster in water than in air.	Rapid loss of body heat
Heat capacity	0.24	0.94 to 1.0	The heat capacity of water is 4 times greater than air.	Absorbs heat quickly

conduct heat hundreds of times faster than air. Water has an enormous capacity for absorbing heat with little change in its temperature. The higher density of water affects you in many ways when you dive. The next chapter explains how to deal with the effects of water density.

Buoyancy

An object's ability to float in a liquid depends on the density of the object compared with the density of the fluid in which the object is immersed. Water exerts pressure equally in all directions, even upward. You can feel the upward force (**buoyancy**) of water when you try to push something under the water. Buoyancy results from the difference in pressures on the upper and lower surfaces of an object. The weight of an object plus the weight of the fluid (air, water, or both) above the object exert a downward force. Fluid pressure pushes upward from below. The difference between these two forces is the buoyancy of the object.

Archimedes, an ancient Greek scientist, discovered that the force of buoyancy acting on a submerged object equals the weight of the water displaced (this is known as **Archimedes' principle**). A hot-air balloon floats in air because the hot air inside the balloon weighs less than the volume of cooler air the balloon occupies. A diver is buoyed upward with a force equal to the weight of the water that the diver displaces (see figure 2.8). If you and your equipment weigh less than the weight of the water you displace, you will float, or have positive buoyancy. If you and your equipment weigh more than the water being displaced, you will sink. An object that sinks has negative buoyancy. If you and your equipment weigh exactly the same as the water displaced, you neither float nor sink. Instead, you remain at the depth where you are; you have **neutral buoyancy**.

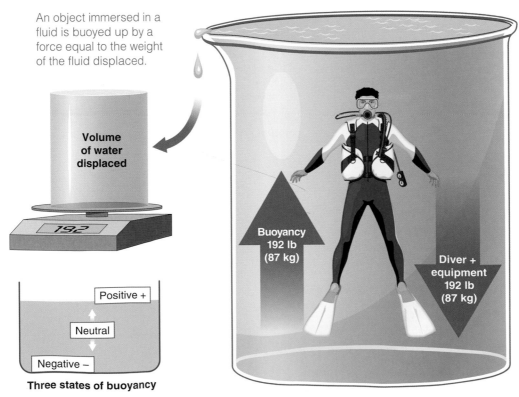

An object immersed in a fluid is buoyed up by a force equal to the weight of the fluid displaced.

Volume of water displaced

192

Buoyancy 192 lb (87 kg)

Diver + equipment 192 lb (87 kg)

Positive +

Neutral

Negative −

Three states of buoyancy

Figure 2.8 Principles of buoyancy.

As a diver, you can float at the surface, sink to the bottom, or hang suspended between the bottom and the surface. If the volume of an object increases with very little change in its weight, buoyancy increases. This happens when you add air to an inflatable jacket or vest. The next chapter addresses the factors affecting buoyancy and the principles of buoyancy control.

Pressure Measurement

Force (often weight) per unit area—such as pounds per square inch or grams per square centimeter—is **pressure**. The envelope of air surrounding the earth is the atmosphere. The weight of one square inch of the atmosphere at sea level is 14.7 pounds (1.03 kg per square cm), or 1 atmosphere (atm) of pressure. As you descend in water, the weight of the fluid—the pressure—exerted on each square inch of your body increases. One square inch of saltwater that is 33 feet (10.1 m) in height weighs 14.7 pounds, 1 atm, or 1.01 bar. One square inch of freshwater 34 feet (10.36 m) in height also exerts a pressure equivalent to 1 atm. Because 1 bar is almost equal to 1 atm, we'll consider them identical in this book. Because water does not compress (at the pressures involved with recreational diving), it follows that water pressure increases by 1 atm for every 33 feet of saltwater (33 FSW) and for every 34 feet of freshwater (34 FFW). Figure 2.9 shows how **atmospheric pressure** and water pressure are measured.

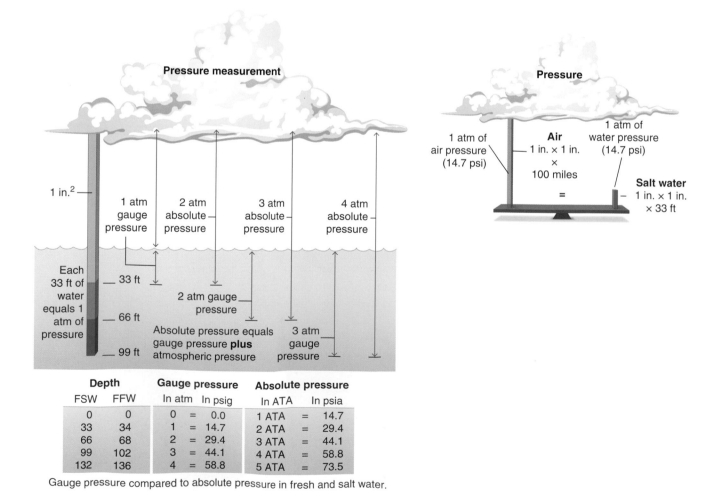

Depth		Gauge pressure			Absolute pressure		
FSW	FFW	In atm		In psig	In ATA		In psia
0	0	0	=	0.0	1 ATA	=	14.7
33	34	1	=	14.7	2 ATA	=	29.4
66	68	2	=	29.4	3 ATA	=	44.1
99	102	3	=	44.1	4 ATA	=	58.8
132	136	4	=	58.8	5 ATA	=	73.5

Gauge pressure compared to absolute pressure in fresh and salt water.

Figure 2.9   Principles of pressure measurement.

The reference for pressure is either the atmospheric pressure at sea level or zero pressure (outer space). A pressure gauge that reads zero at sea level displays only the pressure in excess of one atmosphere. Tire gauges and depth gauges are good examples of instruments that indicate **gauge pressure**, which may be measured in pounds per square inch gauge (psig), feet or meters of seawater, or bars of pressure.

The total pressure exerted is what matters to divers. The pressures of both the atmosphere and the water apply to diving. The reference for the total pressure is zero, as in a vacuum. The total pressure is called **absolute pressure**, which is measured in pounds per square inch absolute (psia). When people express absolute pressure increments in atmospheres, they use atmospheres absolute (ATA).

You obtain absolute pressure by adding atmospheric pressure to gauge pressure. Be sure you understand the concept because we'll use absolute pressure when dealing with the effects of pressure in this and later chapters.

Gas Laws

When you compress a quantity of gas, you reduce its volume and increase its density and temperature. Allowing a quantity of gas to expand increases its volume, decreases its density, and decreases its temperature. Because divers use gases, you need to understand the relationships between these properties (pressure, volume, density, and temperature) of gases.

Boyle's Law

Boyle's law states that for any gas at a constant temperature, the volume varies inversely with the absolute pressure, while the density varies directly with the absolute pressure. If you compress a closed, flexible air space (such as a balloon), you reduce its volume in proportion to the increase in pressure. When you double the pressure, a closed, flexible air space occupies only half the volume that it did originally. No air is lost. The molecules compress into a smaller area. The density of the air is twice as great as it was originally. When you return the compressed air space to its original pressure, the air inside expands until the object reaches its original volume. You compress your lungs during a breath-hold descent, and they return to normal volume when you return to the surface, provided that you do not expel air underwater.

Scuba equipment provides air to you at the exact pressure of the surrounding water. This allows you to expand your lungs to their normal volume regardless of the depth. The density of the air inside the lungs increases in proportion to the water pressure. If the water pressure doubles, the density of the air in your lungs also doubles. Figure 2.10 shows the relationships between pressure, volume, and density for a gas-filled, flexible-walled container.

Boyle's law also applies when you reduce the surrounding pressure. As outside pressure decreases, compressed air in a closed, gas-filled, flexible container expands in proportion to the reduction in pressure; for instance, if the pressure halves, the volume doubles. If a container filled with compressed air at depth is vented correctly during ascent, expanding air escapes through the vent, and the container remains full throughout the ascent. If the container is not vented, pressure inside increases when the container reaches its maximum volume. If the container is weak, the increase in pressure will rupture the container. This concept is important to scuba divers, who have many air spaces filled with

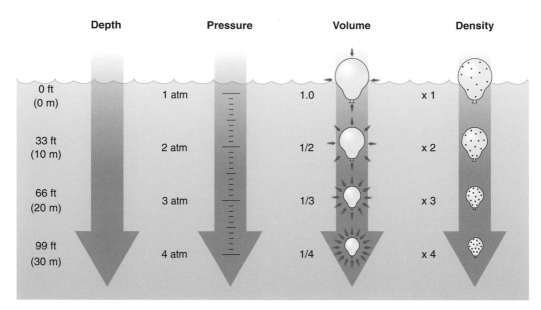

Depth   Pressure   Volume   Density

Figure 2.10   Pressure, volume, and density relationships.

compressed air. Vented air spaces do not pose a hazard. But if your lungs are not vented during ascent, life-threatening injuries will result. If you do not vent air from a flotation jacket during ascent, control of buoyancy will be lost as air expands and the jacket volume increases.

Figure 2.10 shows an interesting point about the rate of change of pressure (and volume) in water. The pressure doubles from 1 atm to 2 atm in 33 feet (10 m) of seawater. Doubling the pressure again requires a depth of 99 FSW (30 m). Note that you must ascend from 99 feet to a depth of 33 feet—a distance of 66 feet (20 m)—to experience the same rate of change of pressure that you experience when you ascend from 33 feet to the surface. In other words, the closer you get to the surface, the greater the rate of change of pressure (and of the volume of an air space). You must be more attentive to compressed air in air spaces the nearer you are to the surface.

The change in pressure that you experience during descents and ascents in water is perhaps the most significant challenge of diving. Changes in pressure have direct, mechanical effects on your body. Pressure imbalance in your body air spaces can cause discomfort. In the air environment, you feel pressure changes as a result of changes in altitude, but pressure changes in water occur at a much greater rate than in air. You can sustain serious injury unless you keep the pressure in air spaces inside and attached to you equalized with the surrounding water pressure. Boyle's law causes **squeezes** and **reverse blocks**, which figure 2.11 illustrates. Knowledgeable and experienced divers routinely equalize pressures to avoid squeezes and blocks. Keeping pressure in air spaces equalized with the surrounding pressure is one of the main subjects of the next chapter.

Gay-Lussac's Law

Boyle's law addresses gas at a constant temperature because the temperature affects the pressure and volume of a gas. Jacques Charles, a French chemist, discovered that the volume of gas at a constant pressure changes with temperature. Joseph-Louis Gay-Lussac, a French scientist, defined the effect of

If the pressure inside an air space is less than the surrounding water pressure, the outside pressure attempts to compress the air space. This condition is a "squeeze."

During descent, squeezes may occur in ears, sinuses, the mask, and other air spaces in or attached to the body.

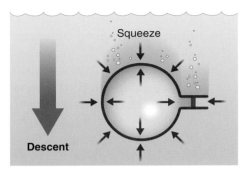

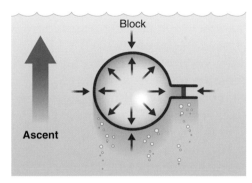

During ascent, the pressure surrounding an air space decreases. If the air inside the space, which was equalized to a higher pressure during descent, cannot escape, a situation that is the reverse of a squeeze occurs. When the pressure inside an air space is greater than the surrounding pressure, the condition is a "reverse block."

A "block" describes a situation where some form of blockage prevents compressed air from entering.

Prevention of both squeezes and blocks involves keeping the pressure within an air space equalized with the surrounding pressure.

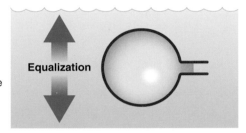

Figure 2.11   An explanation of squeezes and reverse blocks when equalizing pressure.

temperature: For any gas at a constant volume, the pressure of the gas varies directly with the absolute temperature. Just as absolute pressure must be used for pressure calculations, absolute temperature must be used for temperature computations. The absolute temperature scale for Fahrenheit temperatures is Rankine. To convert a Fahrenheit temperature to Rankine, add 460 degrees. The absolute temperature scale for a Celsius temperature is Kelvin. To convert a Celsius temperature to Kelvin, add 273 degrees.

You can observe the effect of **Gay-Lussac's law** with a scuba tank, which has a constant volume. Decreasing the temperature of the air in a tank causes the pressure to decrease. Increasing the temperature of the air in a tank causes the pressure to increase. A scuba tank taken from the trunk of a hot car and cooled in water experiences a drop in pressure, although no air leaves the cylinder. Pressure increases or decreases in a standard 80-cubic-foot (2,265 L) aluminum scuba cylinder at a rate of about 6 psig per degree Fahrenheit temperature change. Pressure increases or decreases in a standard 71.2-cubic-foot (2,016 L) steel scuba cylinder at a rate of about 5 psig per degree Fahrenheit temperature change.

Dalton's and Henry's Laws

A gas can diffuse into or out of a substance. When a gas comes into contact with a liquid, the gas dissolves into the liquid. The amount of gas that diffuses into the liquid depends on the density and temperature of the liquid, the pressure of the gas in contact with the liquid, and the length of time that the gas is in contact with the liquid. Another term for the process of gas diffusion into a liquid is **ingassing**. Because the human body is primarily liquid, the gases you breathe diffuse into your body tissues.

In a mixture of gases, such as air, the percentage of the total pressure exerted by each gas is the **partial pressure** of that gas. **Dalton's law** states that the total pressure exerted by a mixture of gases is the sum of the pressures that would be exerted by each gas if it alone were present and occupied the total volume. The partial pressure of a gas determines the amount of that gas that dissolves into a liquid. **Henry's law** expresses gas absorption: The amount of a gas that dissolves in a liquid at a given temperature is directly proportional to the partial pressure of that gas. Table 2.2 shows the partial pressures of gases in the air at 1 ATA.

The partial pressure of a gas is the percentage of the gas in the mixture times the absolute pressure of the mixture. The partial pressure of a gas at depth has the same effect as a higher percentage of that gas at the surface. If a mixture of gas contains 2 percent carbon dioxide (CO_2) at sea level (14.7 psia, or 1.03 kg per square cm), the partial pressure of the CO_2 is 0.294 psia (0.021 kg per square cm). If the absolute pressure of the same mixture of gases increases to the pressure found at a depth of 99 feet (30 m) in the ocean (58.8 psia, or 4.12 kg per square cm), the partial pressure of the CO_2 is 1.176 psia (0.082 kg per square cm). The amount of CO_2 sensed by the body at 99 feet is four times greater than the amount that is sensed at the surface. Breathing 2 percent CO_2 at a depth of 99 feet is the same as breathing 8 percent CO_2 at the surface! A high level of CO_2 has a profound effect on respiration. The surface-equivalent effect of partial pressures makes minute amounts of contaminants in breathing gases unsafe at depth. Table 2.3 shows the surface-equivalent effect of partial pressures at various depths.

Table 2.2 Partial Pressures of Gases in Air at 1 ATA

	Percentage	Partial pressure at 1 ATA	Partial pressure of gas at 1 ATA (metric)
Nitrogen	78%	11.466 psia	0.803 kg/cm²
Oxygen	21%	3.087 psia	0.2163 kg/cm²
Argon	0.93%	0.137 psia	0.0095 kg/cm²
Trace gases	0.04%	0.006 psia	0.0004 kg/cm²
Carbon dioxide	0.03%	0.004 psia	0.0003 kg/cm²
Totals	100%	14.7 psia	1.03 kg/cm²

Table 2.3 Surface-Equivalent Effect of Partial Pressures

Depth	Pressure	O_2*a	CO*b	CO_2*c
0 ft (0 m)	1 ATA	20%	20 ppm	2%
33 ft (10 m)	2 ATA	40%	40 ppm	4%
66 ft (20 m)	3 ATA	60%	60 ppm	6%
99 ft (30 m)	4 ATA	80%	80 ppm	8%
132 ft (40 m)	5 ATA	100%	100 ppm	10%

*Breathing 20% oxygen at 132 ft (40 m) has the same effect as breathing 100% oxygen at the surface.

*Breathing a mixture containing 40 ppm CO at 66 ft (20 m) is the same as breathing 120 ppm CO at the surface!

*Breathing a mixture containing 2% CO_2 at 99 ft (30 m) is the same as breathing 8% CO_2 at the surface and causes shortness of breath, rapid breathing, and headache.

Additional Information About Gas Laws

The following gas formulas can be used to make precise mathematical calculations of pressure, volume, and temperature.

Boyle's law: $P_1V_1 = P_2V_2$

$$P_1 = \text{Initial pressure (psia or ATA)}$$

$$P_2 = \text{Final pressure (psia or ATA)}$$

$$V_1 = \text{Initial volume}$$

$$V_2 = \text{Final volume}$$

Example: A balloon with 2 pints of air floats from 2 ATA to the surface (1 ATA). What is the volume of the balloon at the surface?

$$P_1 = 2 \text{ ATA}$$

$$P_2 = 1 \text{ ATA}$$

$$V_1 = 2 \text{ pints}$$

$$V_2 = \text{Unknown}$$

Rearranging the formula to solve for V_2, we find that:

$$V_2 = \frac{P_1V_1}{P_2} = \frac{(2 \times 2)}{1} = 4 \text{ pints}$$

Partial pressure = absolute pressure 3 percentage of gas

Example: What is the partial pressure of oxygen if the gas constitutes 20 percent of a gas mixture that has an absolute pressure of 58.8 psi?

$$PP = 58.8 \times 0.2 = 11.76 \text{ psia}$$

Gay-Lussac's law: $\dfrac{P_1}{T_1} = \dfrac{P_2}{T_2}$

$$P_1 = \text{Initial pressure (psia or ATA)}$$

$$P_2 = \text{Final pressure (psia or ATA)}$$

$$T_1 = \text{Initial temperature (°R or °K)}$$

$$T_2 = \text{Final temperature (°R or °K)}$$

Example: A scuba tank with a pressure of 2,250 psig and a temperature of 70 °F is heated to a temperature of 150 °F. What is the pressure of the scuba tank at the higher temperature? First, convert readings for pressure and temperature to absolute measures.

$$P_1 = 2,250 \text{ psig} + 14.7 \text{ psia} = 2,265 \text{ psia}$$

$$P_2 = \text{Unknown}$$

$$T_1 = 70 \text{ °F} + 460 = 530 \text{ °R}$$

$$T_2 = 150 \text{ °F} + 460 = 610 \text{ °R}$$

Rearranging the formula to solve for P_2, we find that

$$P_2 = \frac{P_1T_2}{T_1} = \frac{2,265 \times 610}{530} = 2,607 \text{ psia}$$

$$2,607 \text{ psia} - 14.7 \text{ psia} = 2,592 \text{ psig}$$

When a liquid has absorbed all of a gas that it can hold, the liquid is saturated. When you reduce the partial pressure of the gas in contact with the liquid, gas diffuses out of the liquid. This process is **outgassing**. Ingassing and outgassing provide a foundation for the dive computers and tables used to prevent decompression sickness; these tables are presented in chapter 7.

Air Consumption

The volume of air you breathe per minute during exertion is much more than the volume you breathe at rest—up to 17 times more on land and about 14 times more in the water. In the water, pressure on the torso allows only 85 percent of normal inhalation.

Because the density of the air breathed increases with depth, depth significantly affects the rate at which you consume air. For a given level of exertion, a supply of air lasts only half as long at a pressure of 2 ATA as it does at a pressure of 1 ATA. With heavy exertion at a pressure of 4 ATA (at a depth of 99 feet, or 30 m), you exhaust an air supply over 40 times faster than you would when at rest at the surface! The rapid depletion of your air supply is one reason that you must avoid heavy exertion while diving.

The rate of air consumption is expressed in cubic feet per minute (or liters per minute) or psig (or atmospheres or bars) per minute. By knowing your consumption rate for various levels of activity, you can plan your dives. When you know your consumption rate and the amount of air available, you can calculate air supply duration for future dives.

Heat, Humidity, Light, and Sound

You experience many changes when you enter water. You lose body heat faster, and you lose body moisture when you use scuba equipment. In addition, what you see is deceiving, and what you hear can cause confusion. When you understand what happens to you in water (and why it happens), you can better manage the differences between the water and air environments.

Heat Transfer

The net effect of the various forms of heat transfer is that you can chill quickly while diving. Radiation, convection, and conduction transfer heat from one medium to another (see figure 2.12). Heat waves radiate from exposed surfaces, heat travels upward through fluids by convection, and heat is transferred directly via conduction between substances in contact with each other. Metals are good conductors. Water is a poor conductor compared with metal, but water conducts heat about 25 times faster than air (depending on density). Conduction and convection are the primary means by which heat is transferred from a diver to the surrounding water. Heat rises from the skin, and water carries the heat away. You also lose body heat through the process of evaporation. Moisture evaporates from your lungs when you are breathing underwater and from the surface of your skin when you perspire above water. Scuba equipment expands high-pressure air and cools it. Your body heat warms the air you breathe, and you lose the heat with each exhalation.

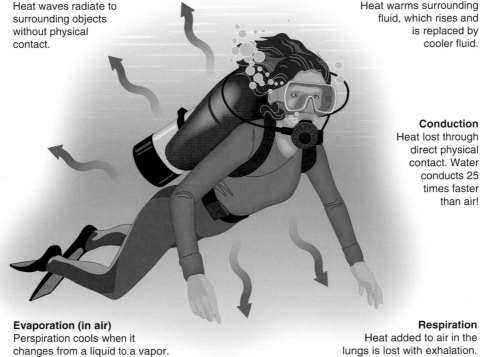

Losing or retaining excessive heat is dangerous!

Radiation
Heat waves radiate to surrounding objects without physical contact.

Convection
Heat warms surrounding fluid, which rises and is replaced by cooler fluid.

Conduction
Heat lost through direct physical contact. Water conducts 25 times faster than air!

Evaporation (in air)
Perspiration cools when it changes from a liquid to a vapor.

Respiration
Heat added to air in the lungs is lost with exhalation.

Figure 2.12   Heat transfer and loss.

You can slow the transfer of heat by insulating yourself with a material that is a poor conductor of heat. Exposure suits help insulate you from the environment, but insulation does not help reduce heat lost through respiration. The next chapter presents ways to manage the problems of heat loss.

Humidity

Scuba divers must be aware of the effects of humidity, or the amount of water vapor present in a gas. The temperature of the gas determines the amount of water vapor a gas can absorb and retain. The warmer the gas, the more humidity the gas can contain.

You humidify inspired air. The process of compressing the air that is put into scuba tanks dehumidifies the air in the cylinder. You lose moisture from body tissues when you breathe dry scuba air. The resulting fluid loss can cause partial dehydration, an undesirable condition, especially for a scuba diver. In the next chapter, you will learn how to avoid the problems of dehydration.

Diving poses other humidity challenges that you must manage. Moisture in the air inside your mask condenses on the faceplate as the air cools. Unless you thoroughly clean your mask lens in advance so that the condensation runs off in a thin sheet, foggy beads of condensation will form and blur your vision. Chapter 6 presents the process for cleaning, or defogging, your mask.

Additional Information About Air Consumption

The following air consumption formulas can be used to calculate consumption rates and air supply duration. To calculate the rate of air consumption, you need three items of information: the depth at which you have remained for a period of time, the length of time you have remained at that depth, and the amount of air you have used during that time.

1. Determine your depth air consumption rate (DACR). This is simply the amount of air used divided by the time at depth. For example, the DACR for a diver who uses 1,000 psi (68 atm) in 10 minutes is 100 psi (6.8 atm) per minute.

$$DACR = \frac{Air\ used}{Time\ at\ depth}$$

2. Convert the DACR to the surface air consumption rate (SACR). You need to express the rate in terms of volume rather than pressure. After you do this, you can apply the air consumption rate to any depth and to a cylinder of a different size from the one used initially to calculate the air consumption rate. Obtain the surface consumption rate by multiplying the DACR by the ratio of the pressure at the surface to the pressure at depth. Because you can express pressure in terms of depth, you can use the following formula:

$$SACR = DACR \times \frac{33\ ft\ (or\ 10\ m)}{Diving\ depth + 33\ ft\ (or\ 10\ m)}$$

If, for example, your depth consumption rate for a depth of 33 feet (10 m) is 30 psi (2 atm) per minute, your SACR is 30 (33/66) = 15 psi per minute, or 2 (10/20) = 1.0 atm per minute.

3. Convert the rate to volume, establish a ratio of the tank volume and pressure (when the tank is full) to the breathing rate volume and pressure, then solve for the breathing rate volume (BRV) as follows:

$$\frac{V_1}{P_1} = \frac{V_2}{P_2}$$

where

$$V_1 = Full\ tank\ volume$$

$$V_2 = Breathing\ rate\ volume\ (BRV)$$

$$P_1 = Full\ tank\ pressure$$

$$P_2 = Breathing\ rate\ pressure$$

so

$$BRV = \frac{V_1 \times P_2}{P_1}$$

For example, the breathing rate volume (BRV) for a diver with an 80-cubic-foot (2,265 L), 3,000 psi (204 atm) tank and an SACR of 30 psig (2.04 atm) per minute is

$$BRV = 80\ ft^3\ 3\ 30\ psi/min/3,000\ psi = 0.8\ ft^3/min$$

$$Metric\ BRV = 2,265\ L\ 3\ 2.04\ atm/min/204\ atm = 22.65\ L/min$$

4. For the same level of activity, you can calculate the approximate duration (in minutes) of any amount of air from a tank of any size used at any depth. Here is an example: How long will 1,750 psi (119 atm) of air from a 71.2-cubic-foot (2,016 L), 2,475 psi (168 atm) tank last at a depth of 70 feet (21.3 m) for a diver with a breathing rate volume (BRV) of 0.8 cubic feet (22.7 L) per minute?

First, determine the volume of air in the tank at a pressure of 1,750 psi (119 atm). The formula for determining the volume of air in the tank is

$$V_2 = \frac{V_1 \times P_2}{P_1}$$

where

$$V_1 = \text{Full tank volume}$$

$$V_2 = \text{Partially filled tank volume}$$

$$P_1 = \text{Full tank pressure}$$

$$P_2 = \text{Partially filled tank pressure}$$

The air supply volume for the partially filled tank is therefore

$$V_2 = \frac{71.2 \times 1,750\,\text{psi}}{2,475\,\text{psi}} = 50.3\,\text{ft}^3,\text{ or}$$

$$V_2 = \frac{2,016\,\text{L} \times 119\,\text{atm}}{168\,\text{atm}} = 1,428\,\text{L}$$

The formula for air supply duration (ASD) is

$$\text{ASD} = \frac{\text{Air supply volume}}{\text{BRV}} \div \frac{\text{Diving depth} + 33\,\text{ft (or 10 m)}}{33\,\text{ft (or 10 m)}}$$

The air supply duration (ASD) for the question posed earlier is

$$\text{ASD} = \frac{50.3\,\text{ft}^3}{0.8\,\text{ft}^3/\text{min}} \div \frac{70\,\text{ft} + 33\,\text{ft}}{33\,\text{ft}} = 20\,\text{min}$$

$$\text{Metric ASD} = \frac{1,428\,\text{L}}{22.7\,\text{L}/\text{min}} \div \frac{21.3\,\text{m} + 10\,\text{m}}{10\,\text{m}} = 20\,\text{min}$$

These calculations may seem complicated at first, but the ideas are simple. The calculations become easy with practice. Let's review the four steps of air consumption calculations: (1) Determine your depth air consumption rate (DACR); (2) determine your surface air consumption rate (SACR); (3) determine your breathing rate volume (BRV); and (4) determine the air supply duration (ASD) for a quantity of air. The abbreviated formulas for the calculations are as follows:

$$\text{DACR} = \frac{\text{Air used}}{\text{Time at depth}}$$

$$\text{SACR} = \text{DACR} = \frac{33\,\text{ft (or 10 m)}}{\text{Diving depth} + 33\,\text{ft (or 10 m)}}$$

$$\text{BRV} = \frac{V_1 \times P_2}{P_1}$$

$$\text{ASD} = \frac{\text{Air supply volume}}{\text{BRV}} \div \frac{\text{Diving depth} + 33\,\text{ft (or 10 m)}}{33\,\text{ft (or 10 m)}}$$

In freezing temperatures, moisture from your exhaled breath can cause a scuba regulator to freeze. Water in other items of diving equipment can also freeze. If you intend to dive in a cold environment, you should complete special training and should know how to prepare and use your equipment in those conditions.

Light and Vision

The density of water makes it challenging for divers to interpret what they see and hear. Light travels faster in air than in water. When rays of light traveling in water pass through the lens of your mask, they accelerate and bend (refract). The effect is that what you see underwater is magnified. Objects appear to be at three-fourths of their actual distance (25 percent closer) and four-thirds of their actual size (33 percent larger). The visual distortion requires adjustments, and you will learn to make these with experience. An object that is 12 feet (3.7 m) away appears to be only 9 feet (2.7 m) away. A fish that appears to be about 2 feet (0.6 m) long is actually only 1.5 feet (0.5 m) in length. Many new divers discover that items they bring back from diving are much smaller than they perceived them to be underwater. Figure 2.13 illustrates how light is perceived differently in water.

One difficulty caused by the refraction of light is that distant objects appear closer than they are. This can create a hazard in clear water when you look downward from a drop-off. You may be tempted to go to a point that appears to be at a safe distance but might actually take you beyond your planned maximum

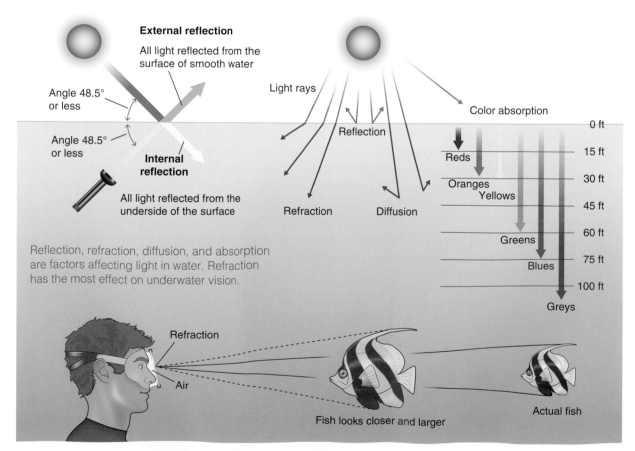

Figure 2.13 Visual perception is distorted underwater.

depth. You must realize that distance perception is inaccurate, and you must rely on your depth gauge instead of your vision.

You have two types of vision: day vision and night vision. You use different parts of your eyes for each type. When you move from a brightly lit area into a dimly lit area, your vision needs 15 to 30 minutes to adapt to the lower level of light. Even after the adaptation, your ability to see fine details is much less than your ability with day vision. In addition, particles in water diffuse, scatter, and attenuate light. The deeper you go, the less light there is. In **turbid** water, the amount of light decreases very quickly with depth. A dive in turbid water involves a change from day vision to night vision.

Water affects light in many ways. The surface of water reflects light. When light strikes the surface of calm water at an angle less than 48 degrees, the water reflects all the light. Early morning and late afternoon sunlight do not penetrate calm water. Light rays going toward the surface from underwater also reflect from the interface, making the underside of the surface appear like a mirror when viewed at the proper angle.

Objects you view underwater often lack their natural colors. White light, such as sunlight, comprises all the colors of the spectrum. Increasing depth absorbs various colors. The water absorbs warm colors, such as red and orange, with only 30 feet (9 m) of depth. Cooler colors, such as blue, penetrate deepest. This is why deep, clear water is blue. The underwater scene appears drab at depths below 100 feet (30 m). Fortunately, you can restore all the colors of the spectrum underwater by using an artificial light at close range.

Another visual challenge is disorientation. When you are weightless in water and do not have a visual reference, **vertigo** can result. Vertigo is the feeling of movement perceived as a spinning sensation. This problem can occur when the water is turbid and visibility is poor, when the water is crystal clear but there are no visual clues for orientation, and when waters of different densities mix together. You will learn how to manage the challenges of disorientation in the next chapter.

A final visual problem is poor visibility in water compared to air. In air environments, visibility is measured in miles, but in water it is measured only in feet. Particles suspended in water cause turbidity, which hampers vision. Reduced visibility makes it difficult to locate objects underwater, to maintain contact with your buddy, and to find your way. You must develop skills to cope with these challenges, including search techniques, buddy system techniques, and underwater navigation skills.

Sound and Hearing

Sound travels well in water. You can hear many sounds while diving. On land you can determine the direction of a sound by the difference in the time it takes the sound to reach one ear and then the other. This interval is brief but sufficient for your brain to discern it. Underwater, you hear sound conducted through water and the bones of your head to your inner ears. Sound travels about four times faster in water than in air. The time delay between a sound reaching one ear and then the other is so small that directional discernment is difficult underwater.

Sound does not transfer well from air to water. Only 0.01 percent of sound can travel directly between air and water. You must use special devices to make voice communications effective underwater.

Summary

The aquatic environment affects your body in several ways. Pressure affects your air spaces: your ears, sinuses, and lungs. The rate of change of pressure in water is many times greater than in air and increases as you approach the surface during ascent. Changing pressures also affect the diffusion of gas into and out of liquids. The level of carbon dioxide in your body controls your respiration, and the partial pressure of the carbon dioxide is affected by depth. Temperature also affects the pressure of a constant volume of gas. Depth and activity have the greatest effect on air consumption. Water absorbs heat from the body, so divers need insulation to help prevent excessive heat loss. Humidity can cause several problems for scuba divers. The difference in density between air and water affects your buoyancy, mobility, heat loss, vision, and hearing. Now that you are aware of the effects of the aquatic environment on your body, you are prepared to learn to adjust to the underwater environment.

Application-of-Knowledge (AOK) Questions

1. If you are exerting underwater and find yourself breathing rapidly and deeply and suddenly feel that you are not receiving enough air, what should you do?

2. A sudden change of conditions while you are diving increases your anxiety, and you notice that your breathing is rapid and shallow. Your anxiety level increases because you feel unable to manage the situation in which you find yourself. What action will help alleviate your anxiety and abnormal breathing?

3. While diving with an experienced diver, you compare tank pressures and discover that you are using twice as much air as your buddy, who is the same size as you. You are using equipment that is identical to your buddy's. What could be causing you to have the high rate of air consumption?

4. Maintained scuba equipment is extremely reliable, but if your regulator started leaking water when you inhaled and you were at a depth of 60 feet (18.3 m), what should you do?

5. While swimming in a pool, you notice a swimmer breathing rapidly and deeply before swimming underwater. You keep an eye on the swimmer because he may lose consciousness without warning while submerged. What is the cause of this problem, and what could you tell the swimmer to help him understand how to prevent an accident?

6. You are diving in water that has a temperature of 60 °F. (15.6 °C) and begin shivering. You decide to increase your activity level to produce more body heat. Is this a good course of action?

Cup corals in the Red Sea

Diving Adjustments

Dive In and Discover

By the end of this chapter, you will be able to do the following:

- Define the terms *hypothermia, hyperthermia, vasoconstriction, heat exhaustion, heatstroke, equalization, Toynbee maneuver, Valsalva maneuver, trapdoor effect, skip breathing, barotrauma, pulmonary barotrauma, arterial gas embolism, mediastinal emphysema, subcutaneous emphysema, pneumothorax, vertigo, perfusion, ambient pressure, half-time, compartment, controlling compartment, decompression illness, dehydration,* and *nitrogen narcosis.*

- State the cause, effect, signs and symptoms, first aid treatment, and prevention of hyperthermia, hypothermia, squeezes, reverse blocks, respiratory distress, pulmonary barotrauma, vertigo, seasickness, decompression illness, and nitrogen narcosis.

- Explain three ways to control buoyancy while scuba diving.

- Explain when to equalize pressure in your ears during descent and what to do if the pressure does not equalize.

- Explain how to minimize resistance to movement for underwater swimming.

To function effectively underwater, you need specific attitudes, equipment, knowledge, and skills. This chapter provides the fundamental knowledge and begins shaping the attitudes required to minimize the risk of injury. You will apply the basic aspects of anatomy, physiology, and physics you have learned to a typical person descending into the depths and ascending back to the surface.

Thermal Adjustments

Maintaining your body's core temperature within a few degrees of normal is challenging in water. When you are immersed in water, you lose body heat rapidly. A water temperature of 50 °F (10 °C) can incapacitate an unprotected diver within 15 minutes. Even water at a temperature of 80 °F (27 °C), which feels relatively warm, can chill a diver within an hour. Wearing only a bathing suit in 80 °F (27 °C) water is the same as being without any clothing in air that is 42 °F (6 °C).

Your brain regulates your body functions to maintain your body temperature. If your core temperature is less than 95 °F (35 °C), you will suffer from **hypothermia**. You need to guard against mild and severe hypothermia, both of which can be dangerous. If your core temperature is higher than normal, you experience the effects of **hyperthermia**. You need to understand the effects of two types of hyperthermia—heat exhaustion and heatstroke—and you must try to prevent them. They both can be dangerous.

Anemone in Bonaire

In chapter 2, you learned about the effects of water on your body. In this chapter, you will learn how to deal with those effects. Most people with average intelligence and normal health can make adjustments to the aquatic environment, such as buoyancy control and the equalization of pressure. You make many adjustments automatically, but some you must make consciously. Learning to make the transition from an air environment to an underwater environment requires professional instruction and guidance. You need to learn what to do, then do what you have learned.

Heat Loss

Your body has a variety of physiological responses to the loss of heat. Respiration increases automatically when you get chilled. This is undesirable because you heat and moisturize inspired air, and you lose the heat and moisture with each exhalation. The more you breathe, the more heat and moisture you lose to the environment (and the shorter your dive time). Water depth compounds the problem because the greater the surrounding pressure, the greater the density of the air that you breathe. Denser air absorbs more heat than air that is less dense. The deeper you dive, the quicker you get cold.

Anything that affects the function of your body—excitement, fear, seasickness, and other forms of illness—can increase heat loss. This is why good health and a confident state of mind are safety recommendations.

One way your body responds to cold is to shunt blood from the extremities through **vasoconstriction**. The circulatory shunting reduces heat loss because it keeps warm blood from passing through areas of your body that have little insulation. Your head, neck, underarms and sides, groin, hands, and feet are the areas of your body most prone to heat loss underwater (see figure 3.1). Fortunately, you can insulate these areas easily. In cold water, you can lose considerable heat from your head and neck because the head receives a large supply of blood and lacks natural insulation. Your body does not shunt blood from your head as it does from other body extremities. In water at a temperature of 70 °F (21 °C) or less, you must be sure to insulate your head and neck.

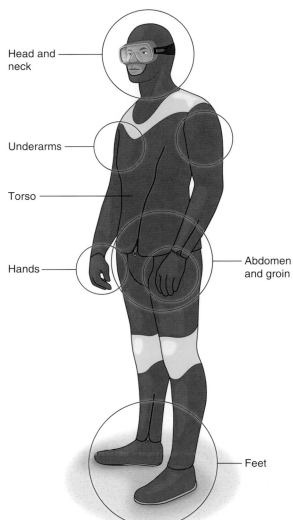

Figure 3.1 **Areas prone to high heat loss.**

Hands have large surface areas relative to their volume. To prevent excessive heat loss from your hands when you get cold, your body shunts blood from them until they reach a temperature of 50 °F (10 °C). At this temperature, your body restores circulation to your hands to partially rewarm them. Hands quickly lose their warmth to the water. If you dive without hand protection in cold water, you lose body heat through your hands. Because your hands may become numb and lack strength when they get cold, you should insulate them to keep them functioning and to conserve body heat.

Small people chill more quickly in water than large people do. Small people have less muscle mass to generate and store heat. Insulation is important for all divers, but protection against heat loss is more critical for those of smaller stature.

Failure to wear adequate insulation leads to hypothermia. Hypothermia also results from repeated or prolonged exposure. Slow chilling of your body is undesirable. You lose muscle strength and feeling, and your muscles may cramp. Severe heat loss also affects your ability to reason. Another body response to heat loss is shivering, which restores heat through muscular activity. Shivering, which generates about five times as much heat as your body produces at rest, is helpful on land, but is not beneficial in water. Water conducts away the heat you produce by shivering, and you get colder. Uncontrollable shivering indicates that you have lost too much heat from the core of your body and that you cannot rewarm yourself without getting out of the water. When you are shivering, you should terminate the dive. Rewarm yourself thoroughly before diving again. To help your body temperature return to normal, you should put on clothes that are warm and dry, stay in warm surroundings, and consume warm nonalcoholic drinks. You can become so cold that shivering ceases. This occurs because severe hypothermia has incapacitated the body's ability to produce heat. A cold person who is not shivering requires medical care.

You must understand that warming the surface of your body is different from warming the core of your body. You may feel warm, but your deep core temperature may remain below normal. If you return to the water in this condition, you will quickly become chilled. The only way to be sure that you are thoroughly warmed is to keep warming yourself until you begin to perspire. Perspiration occurs when the core temperature begins to rise above normal. To warm yourself, get dry, wrap everything except your face in blankets, and stay that way until you perspire. Most people will shed the blanket when their skin is warm, not being aware that the core of their body is still below normal temperature.

Overheating

You can prevent excessive loss of body heat by insulating your body with an exposure suit, but insulation can cause another problem. When you insulate your body to reduce heat loss in water, you reduce your body's ability to rid itself of excess heat above water. The evaporation of perspiration helps cool your body, but if you cover your body, perspiration cannot evaporate. You may become overheated in warm climates when you are preparing to dive. Maintaining your body temperature within acceptable limits before, during, and after dives can be a challenge. Figure 3.2 describes some of the causes and effects of overheating.

When a person is unable to stop the rise of core temperature, **heat exhaustion** occurs. This condition is serious. A person affected by heat exhaustion becomes weak and may collapse. The victim looks pale and feels sweaty. Place a person with this condition in a cool place, remove the exposure suit, and take steps to lower the person's body temperature. If the victim is alert and not nauseous, have him or her drink a diluted electrolyte fluid or water to replace lost body fluids.

A more serious form of hyperthermia is **heatstroke**, which occurs when the body temperature becomes so high that the body's temperature-regulating ability shuts down. A victim of heatstroke looks flushed and has hot, dry skin. The mental status of a heat stroke victim is not normal. The victim may be delirious, or unresponsive, or have seizures. Heat stroke is extremely serious. Cool the patient's body immediately and summon medical assistance.

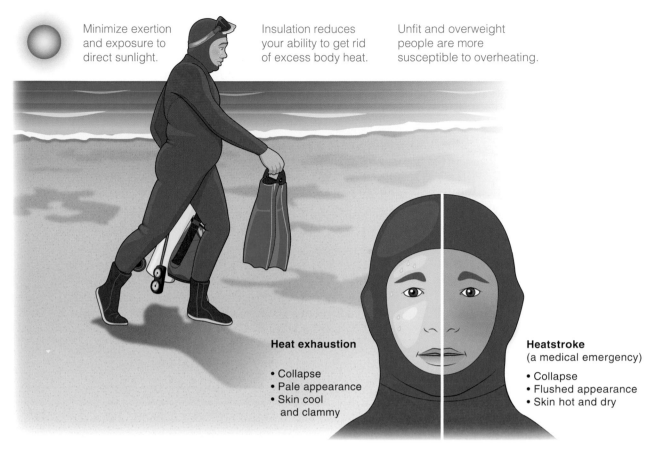

Minimize exertion and exposure to direct sunlight.

Insulation reduces your ability to get rid of excess body heat.

Unfit and overweight people are more susceptible to overheating.

Heat exhaustion

• Collapse
• Pale appearance
• Skin cool
  and clammy

Heatstroke
(a medical emergency)

• Collapse
• Flushed appearance
• Skin hot and dry

Figure 3.2   Take precautions against overheating by learning the symptoms of heat stroke and exhaustion.

Preventing hyperthermia is much better than treating it after it occurs. You should avoid prolonged exposure to warm temperatures when wearing insulation. If the air temperature is warm, douse yourself with water after donning your exposure suit and before donning the remainder of your diving equipment. Stay out of direct sunlight if possible. All thermal considerations for diving are especially important for divers whose physical fitness is marginal.

Buoyancy Adjustments

Exposure suits and other equipment affect your buoyancy. You must adjust the amount of weight you wear to control your depth in the aquatic environment. When you are too buoyant, you must fight to remain submerged; when you carry excess weight, you must work hard to keep from sinking or to stay off the bottom. You need to maintain neutral buoyancy underwater and positive buoyancy at the surface. In chapter 2, you learned the principle of buoyancy and the three states of buoyancy: positive, negative, and neutral. Now you will learn some practical applications of buoyancy.

Your body—which is composed of solids, liquids, and air spaces—has an average density nearly the same as water. A typical human body immersed and relaxed in water has a positive buoyancy of a few pounds when the lungs are filled with air; it has a negative buoyancy of a couple of pounds when the lungs contain the minimum amount of air. Fortunately, the density of water and resistance to movement prevent you from moving up and down rapidly when you breathe.

Factors Affecting Buoyancy

People usually wear some type of exposure suit when diving. Most exposure suits increase buoyancy, so divers wear weights to offset the buoyancy of the suit and achieve neutral buoyancy. These weights are made of lead, which is about 12 times denser than water.

Your initial state of buoyancy in water will depend on the volume of water you and your equipment displace. You can vary your volume—with a negligible increase or decrease in your weight—by adding air to or venting air from your buoyancy compensator (BC). Increasing BC volume increases buoyancy, while decreasing BC volume decreases buoyancy.

Your buoyancy is affected by your physical size and weight, your lung capacity, the equipment you wear, and the items you carry (see table 3.1). Exposure suits use air or small bubbles of gas for insulation. When you descend while wearing an exposure suit, pressure compresses your suit and reduces its volume, so you become less buoyant. You must add air to your BC to compensate for buoyancy lost from suit compression. On the other hand, buoyancy increases as you consume air from your scuba cylinder. Air weighs 0.08 pounds per cubic foot (1.3 g per L). A typical scuba tank contains 80 cubic feet (2,265 L) of air. A full tank weighs 6 pounds (2.7 kg) more than an empty tank. As you consume air from your scuba tank, you must vent some of the air that you added to your BC to compensate for suit compression. The trade-off helps you keep buoyancy constant during a dive.

Inflating your lungs increases your buoyancy, while deflating them reduces buoyancy. A high average lung volume makes you float; a low average volume makes you sink. When you become excited or begin moving quickly, your respiration increases, which affects your buoyancy. For optimal control of buoyancy, you should maintain a calm, relaxed state.

The density of water also affects buoyancy. Saltwater is denser than freshwater, so you are more buoyant in the ocean than in a lake. This means that if you

Table 3.1 Factors Affecting Buoyancy

Factor	Effect
Size and weight of diver	Obese divers are more buoyant.
Type and amount of equipment	Larger equipment is more buoyant (because of increased volume).
Amount of weight worn	Weights decrease buoyancy.
Amount of air in BC	Increasing volume increases buoyancy.
Amount of air in tank	Buoyancy increases as air decreases.
Amount of air in lungs	Exertion or excitement increases volume and buoyancy.
Suit compression	Pressure decreases volume and buoyancy.
Items carried	Added weight decreases buoyancy.
Type of water (salt or fresh)	Denser water increases buoyancy.

At some point, many divers discover a special feeling of becoming part of the underwater world. I remember vividly an overwhelming feeling—a strange combination of peace and exhilaration—that I experienced during a dive in the Red Sea. The goal of training is to help you adjust to a new environment. When you adjust, you can relax, and when you can relax, you can focus more on your exciting new surroundings than on yourself. Meeting the demands of diving is challenging, but when you succeed, the exuberance is worth every adjustment you have to make. People can adjust well to new situations. Training helps people adjust more quickly, easily, and safely than they can by trial and error. Study the remaining chapters carefully to learn how to adjust to the subaquatic environment. I want you to feel what I felt in the Red Sea and have felt many times since while diving. The feeling of being one with the sea is powerful, moving, and unforgettable.

are weighted for neutral buoyancy in the ocean, you must remove some weight to achieve neutral buoyancy for freshwater diving. The amount of weight you remove is about 3 percent of the combined dry weight of you and your equipment. For example, if a neutrally weighted 160-pound (73 kg) diver with 60 pounds (27 kg) of equipment, including 16 pounds (7 kg) of weights, wants to dive in freshwater instead of seawater, the diver must remove about 7 pounds (3 kg) of weight in order to be weighted correctly.

Ways to Control Buoyancy

As a diver, you can control buoyancy in three ways: by the amount of weight you wear and carry, by the amount of air in your BC, and by the amount of air in your lungs. These means of control are coarse, medium, and fine adjustments, respectively. The skills you need to learn in order to adjust to the aquatic environment include determining the correct amount of weight to be worn, regulating the amount of air in your BC, and varying your breathing for minor buoyancy adjustments. Chapter 6 describes these skills.

Pressure Equalization

One of the most important adjustments you must learn is how to handle the effects of pressure changes in water. Pressure changes rapidly as you descend and ascend. To avoid discomfort and injury, you must keep the pressure in the air spaces inside and on your body equalized with the outside pressure. This section identifies the procedures for pressure equalization.

Equalizing Pressure in the Sinuses

Your sinuses equalize pressure automatically as long as they are healthy. But when you have a cold or respiratory illness, the membranes lining your sinuses become swollen. The swelling can close the narrow air passages leading to the sinuses. If you descend with swollen sinus membranes, a sinus squeeze will result. Because the sinuses are formed in bone, they do not compress as a flexible container does. When the pressure inside the sinuses is less than the surrounding pressure, the outside pressure causes the linings of the sinuses to swell and ooze fluids into the cavities. The swelling and fluid reduce the volume and compress the air that is there. Do not attempt this painful method of equalization because your problems are not over after you descend. When you ascend in this condition, the compressed air in the sinuses expands to its original volume. The expansion can force the fluid in your sinuses out through the openings, which are swollen shut. Avoid this painful process; don't dive unless your sinuses are clear and normal. Figure 3.3 shows what happens to both healthy and congested sinuses under pressure.

Do not use medications to relieve stuffiness and congestion caused by an illness before you go diving. Increased pressure can reduce the medica-

Healthy sinus

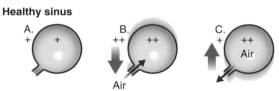

Air can move freely in and out of a healthy sinus (A), so equalization is automatic during descent (B) and ascent (C).

Congested sinus

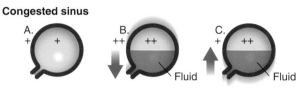

Air cannot get into or out of a congested sinus (A). The body forces fluids into the sinus at depth to equalize the pressure (B). The air in the sinus tries to expand to its original volume during ascent (C).

Figure 3.3 The mechanisms of equalizing pressure in the sinuses.

tion's effects and the duration of its effectiveness. Decongestants do not cure an illness; they simply mask its symptoms. When medication taken to open swollen airways wears off, a rebound effect occurs. The airways become more swollen than they were before you took the medication. If the rebound occurs while you are diving, you can trap high-pressure air in your sinuses. If you are not well enough to dive without medications, you should not dive.

Equalizing Pressure in the Ears

You must equalize the pressure in your ears more often than any other air space. Whereas the air passages to your sinuses are normally open, the **eustachian tubes** from your throat to your ears are normally closed. You must learn how to open the tubes at will to allow air to pass through them and equalize pressure in the air spaces of your middle ears.

You can make several movements to open the ends of the eustachian tubes where they connect with the throat. Swallowing, yawning, lifting the base of your tongue, and jutting the jaw forward (either individually or in combination) should produce a cracking sound in your ears. The opening of the tubes causes the sound. Some divers are fortunate because they can use simple movements to equalize pressure in their ears during descent. Most people require a more forceful means of equalization. Many divers use a technique known as the **Toynbee maneuver**, which you do by blocking your nostrils, closing your mouth, and swallowing. The **Valsalva maneuver** is even more forceful and is done by blocking your nostrils, closing your mouth, and gently attempting to exhale.

You must avoid excessive force when you use the Valsalva method because you could damage your ears permanently by rupturing the round window. When pressure in the outer ear increases, the eardrum bulges inward. The bones of hearing in the middle ear transmit the movement to the oval window in the inner ear. When you attempt to exhale against closed airways, you create an internal pressure on your inner ears. The attempted exhalation pressure in conjunction with the external pressure exerted on the oval window can cause the round window to rupture; this is a serious injury that can result in a permanent high-frequency hearing loss and constant ringing in the ear. Because you control how hard you attempt to exhale in a Valsalva maneuver, you can prevent this injury. Be careful!

You must equalize pressure in the air spaces of your middle ear early (before descent) and frequently. If you delay equalization during descent, increasing pressure will hold your eustachian tubes closed—and if you attempt to force air through them, this will only close them tighter. This is the **trapdoor effect**, a difficulty you can avoid by keeping the pressure in your middle ears and your throat equal. You can then open your eustachian tubes and allow air to pass through them. Figure 3.4 shows the trapdoor effect.

You should equalize pressure in your ears before descending and about every 2 feet (0.6 m) for the first 15 feet (4.6 m) of descent, about every 3 feet (0.9 m) from 15 to 30 feet (4.6 to 9.1 m), and as needed thereafter. You can feel and hear air enter your ears when you eliminate any difference in pressure. If you attempt to equalize pressure but cannot get air into your ears, you should ascend several feet to reduce the pressure on your eustachian tubes and try again. If that works, continue your descent. If that does not work, ascend a few more feet and try again. Your initial descents may be somewhat jerky until you become accustomed to equalization techniques.

Failure to equalize pressure in your middle ears is as bad as trying to equalize forcefully. In an unequalized middle ear, pressure bows the eardrum inward. If the squeeze continues, pressure forces blood and fluid into the middle ear. This

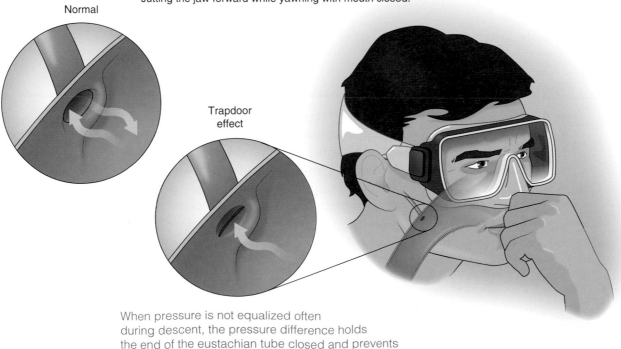

Methods to equalize pressure:
- Blowing gently with mouth closed and nostrils blocked.
- Swallowing with mouth closed and nostrils blocked.
- Jutting the jaw forward while yawning with mouth closed.

Normal

Trapdoor effect

When pressure is not equalized often during descent, the pressure difference holds the end of the eustachian tube closed and prevents any further equalization until the diver ascends enough to relieve the pressure.

Figure 3.4 Helpful techniques for pressure equalization.

process takes time, but it is usually painful. It also damages the ear. If you feel discomfort or pressure in your ears during descent, you should ascend until the pain is gone, and then ascend another couple of feet before trying to equalize.

If you ignore an ear squeeze and continue your descent, the pressure differential can rupture your eardrum. The rupture instantly equalizes the pressure in your middle ear but damages your ear in the process. A rupture of your eardrum causes a temporary loss of hearing and a feeling of fullness in your ear. Cold water rushing into the middle ear can also cause temporary disorientation (see the section on Equilibrium Adjustments and Seasickness later in this chapter). If you suspect an ear injury, see a physician; prompt treatment can minimize the risk of permanent injury.

You can cause an outward rupture of an eardrum if you block the ear canal with a plug or if you cover your ears with a watertight covering. When you obstruct an ear canal, the air in your outer ear remains at surface pressure while the pressure in your middle ear increases with equalization during descent. The difference in pressure between the middle and outer ear pushes the eardrum outward until it breaks. You can prevent such an injury. Do not wear earplugs while diving, and avoid waterproof seals over your ears.

Equalizing is easier when you descend in an upright position as opposed to a head-down position. Membranes line the airways in your head, and gravity affects blood in the vessels within the membranes. When you are upside down in water, the membranes of your air passages swell and narrow.

Difficulties with ear equalization during ascent are uncommon. Air expanding inside the middle ear escapes through the eustachian tube. Air passes out through the tube much more easily than it goes in; you do not have to do maneuvers to open your tubes so the air can escape. But if a plug of mucus happens to block a tube, pressure can build up in the middle ear and cause an uncomfortable reverse block. If you feel pain or pressure in an ear during ascent, stop the ascent. Excess pressure inside the ear usually works its way out if given time. If you are forced to surface, the pain will increase, and an injury can result. Have the ear examined by a physician, especially if you have recurring reverse blocks.

Equalizing Pressure in the Mask

The air space inside the dive mask is affected by changes in pressure. If you descend without increasing the amount of air inside your mask, pressure pulls your face and eyes into the mask slightly. The pulling sensation, if ignored, ruptures capillaries in your eyes and on your face and causes a mask squeeze. After a mask squeeze, the whites of your eyes will be red, and your face will be red and puffy. There is no excuse for a mask squeeze. You can prevent the problem by exhaling through your nose as needed during descent to keep the pressure inside your mask equal to the surrounding pressure.

Breathing Adjustments

Breathing while in water differs from breathing while on land in several ways. You cannot breathe as freely in water as you can on land. Pressure on the lungs from immersion in water prevents you from breathing as fully as you can in air. Also, it is not as easy to get large quantities of air from a scuba system as it is to breathe deeply above water.

When you ascend, compressed air in your lungs expands, which can cause your lungs to rupture unless you allow the excess air to escape. A normal breathing pattern allows expanding air to escape; breath holding does not. A primary rule of scuba diving is to always breathe continuously.

There is a chance that you will inhale some water. This may cause you to choke and gasp when the water strikes your vocal cords. You need to learn the correct methods of breathing while in and under the water.

Lung Overexpansion

The most important aquatic breathing adjustment is overcoming the instinct to hold your breath underwater. When you breathe compressed air at depth, the density of the air in your lungs is greater than it is at the surface. When you ascend, the air in your lungs expands as the surrounding pressure decreases. If you hold your breath, your lungs expand until they reach their maximum volume, then rupture with an ascent of as little as 4 feet (1.2 m). You must avoid breath holding when breathing compressed air underwater. You should breathe continuously or exhale a small amount of air continuously, and you should never hold your breath during ascent after breathing compressed air. Figure 3.5 illustrates why you must breathe continuously, and the section following the figure describes the possible consequences of breath holding while ascending with compressed air in your lungs.

Skip Breathing

Some divers attempt to extend their air supplies by holding each breath for several seconds. This dangerous practice is called **skip breathing**. When you hold your breath, you increase the amount of carbon dioxide in your circulatory system, which increases your urge to breathe and reduces your breath-holding ability. A high level of carbon dioxide in your body will reduce your ability to cope with difficulties that may arise. And if you skip breathe, you may forget to exhale while ascending, or you may have a headache after the dive. You must be sure to breathe continuously when breathing compressed air.

Breathing Problems

Divers can encounter respiratory difficulties if they overexert themselves, breathe contaminated air, inhale water, or run out of air. Fortunately, you can prevent all of these problems.

Overexertion

Scuba equipment allows you to breathe comfortably while underwater. A regulator delivers air with little respiratory effort, but breathing underwater requires more effort than breathing above water. If you do not maintain your scuba equipment properly, the effort required to inhale and exhale can be excessive and can cause respiratory distress.

Scuba regulators have a limited capacity to supply air. Regulators are not designed for activities involving heavy exertion. Commercial divers use helmets with air hoses to supply large amounts of air to meet their requirements while working underwater. You must avoid strenuous activities underwater because

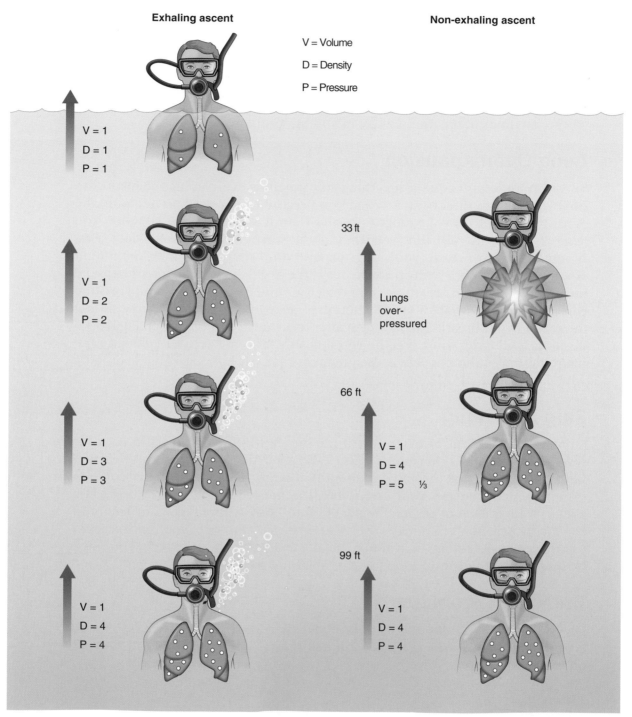

Exhaling ascent   **Non-exhaling ascent**

V = Volume
D = Density
P = Pressure

V = 1
D = 1
P = 1

V = 1
D = 2
P = 2

33 ft

Lungs
over-
pressured

V = 1
D = 3
P = 3

66 ft

V = 1
D = 4
P = 5   ⅓

V = 1
D = 4
P = 4

99 ft

V = 1
D = 4
P = 4

Figure 3.5   A breath-holding ascent after breathing compressed air can cause lung rupture. Breathe continuously while ascending.

you can overbreathe your equipment and experience air starvation, a suffocating feeling of not being able to get enough air.

While diving, you should make your breaths longer and slower than your breaths on land. Pace your activity to keep respiration at a slow, controlled rate. If breathing becomes rapid or labored, cease all activity immediately and focus on exhaling deeply until your respiration returns to a controlled rate.

Contaminated Air

If the compressed air in your tank comes from an air compressor that is not operated or maintained properly, your tank can contain contaminated air. The contamination is likely to be carbon monoxide (CO), a gas produced by incomplete combustion. CO in the body impedes the blood's ability to transport oxygen. Blood hemoglobin's affinity for CO is 210 times greater than its affinity for oxygen. Hemoglobin normally exchanges oxygen for CO_2 about every half minute, but when CO attaches to hemoglobin, the contaminant remains bonded to the hemoglobin for hours. Breathing contaminated air under pressure can make you ill and render you unconscious. Avoid contaminated air by having your tank filled only with pure air. CO is an odorless, tasteless gas, but it is usually accompanied by other gases that have a foul taste and odor. If the air from a scuba tank smells or tastes foul, do not use it. Report the situation immediately to the facility that filled the cylinder. Good air stations have their air tested regularly to ensure purity.

Water Inspiration

If you inhale water, your larynx spasms as a reflex action to keep the liquid out of your lungs. Avoid coughing and choking in water; not only are these reflexes unpleasant, but they can cause you to inspire more water and lose buoyancy. You need to breathe differently underwater than you do on land. Avoid quick inhalations. Begin a breath with a light, slow inhalation to ensure that you are inhaling air and not water. Once air begins flowing, the remainder of your inhalation can be normal.

You can also prevent droplets of water from going down your throat by placing the tip of your tongue on the roof of your mouth behind your upper teeth to act as a splashboard. If, in spite of all you do to avoid it, you inhale some water and start coughing, try swallowing hard three times in rapid succession. The swallowing helps you overcome your coughing reflex.

If water does enter your lungs, it interferes with respiration. If an extensive area of the lungs is irritated by water, you can drown. This is a risk you face in any aquatic pastime. The purpose of your training is to allow you to enjoy the aquatic environment with the minimum risk of injury, especially of drowning. When you follow the rules and practices that you are taught, the risk of injury while diving is negligible.

An automatic response to the inhalation of water is to swallow it in an effort to keep your airways dry. When you swallow saltwater, you can experience illness, nausea, or diarrhea. If you swallow several mouthfuls of saltwater while diving, you should terminate the dive.

Running Out of Air

Some divers do not monitor their air supplies and run out of air at depth. Running out of air underwater is no more excusable than running out of gas on the freeway when you have a working gauge. There are ways to manage an out-of-air situation (which you will learn in chapter 6), but it is much better to avoid the problem by monitoring your instruments and keeping them in working order.

Potential Lung Injuries

Pulmonary Barotrauma

Barotrauma is trauma or injury caused by pressure. **Pulmonary barotrauma** is any lung injury caused by pressure. Failure to allow expanding air to escape from the lungs during ascent can cause several forms of pulmonary barotrauma, either singularly or in combination.

Arterial Gas Embolism

An **embolism** is a blockage of circulation. An embolism resulting from an air bubble blocking the arterial circulation is an **arterial gas embolism** (AGE). This occurs when air expanding in the lungs forces bubbles of air into the circulation. Air bubbles enter the capillary beds of the lungs and pass through the heart, which pumps the bubbles into arteries supplying blood to the body. The diameter of an artery decreases as the distance from the heart increases. At some point, a bubble lodges in an artery and becomes an embolus (plug). It is common for an arterial gas embolism to occur in an artery leading to the brain. The embolus has the effect of a stroke, causes unconsciousness, and is an extremely serious injury. Anytime a diver loses consciousness after a dive, you should suspect AGE. The temporary obstruction of an airway, such as that caused by a cold, increases the risk of AGE. Healthy lungs are a prerequisite for diving.

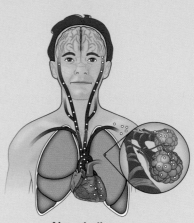

Air embolism

Mediastinal Emphysema

If a rupture of the lung does not force air into the circulation, the air may travel along the bronchi and enter the middle area of the chest (called the mediastinum). This results in a **mediastinal emphysema**, which means that air is in the tissues in the middle of the chest. The injury causes a dull ache or tightness that worsens with coughing, swallowing, or taking a deep breath. Expanding air can interfere with the circulation of the heart and cause loss of consciousness.

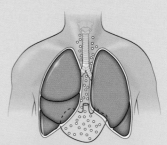

Mediastinal emphysema

Heart and Lungs

Immersion changes your cardiac workload. When you are upright in water, there is greater pressure on your lower limbs than on the upper part of your body. The pressure differential shifts more blood than normal into the upper part of your body. Your heart pumps a greater volume with each beat and works from 1.3 to over 1.5 times harder in this situation than it does on land.

Water temperature alters your heart's rate and rhythm. In addition, physical and emotional stress make your heart work harder. The combined effects of water pressure, exercise, cold, and stress can cause serious problems if your heart is not healthy. If you have heart problems and wish to dive, you should first obtain medical approval from a diving physician. Even minor heart problems can cause you to suddenly lose consciousness in the water, and you could drown. Fitness for diving is an important safety issue.

Subcutaneous Emphysema

Expanding air in the mediastinum can migrate upward along the breastbone. The air then swells the tissues around the neck, producing an injury known as **subcutaneous emphysema**, which means that air is in the tissues under the skin. The injury can cause changes in the voice, crackling of the skin, and a feeling of fullness in the neck.

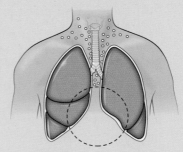

Subcutaneous emphysema

Pneumothorax

If a lung rupture forces air into the space between the lungs and the lining of the chest wall, a condition known as **pneumothorax** occurs. This means that air is trapped in the chest cavity. As the air trapped in the pleural space expands during ascent, it collapses the lung and can affect the action of the heart. Symptoms include severe pain and breathing difficulty.

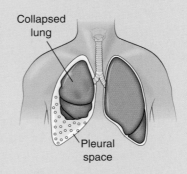

Collapsed lung

Pleural space

Pneumothorax

Lung injuries are serious and can be life threatening. Life support may be required. This is one reason that you should complete a course in cardiopulmonary (heart and lung) resuscitation (CPR). You may have to administer first aid until professional medical treatment (which all lung injuries require) is available.

Failing to allow excess air to escape causes nearly all lung overexpansion injuries. You can prevent injuries by breathing continuously. If you remove the scuba regulator from your mouth for any reason, exhale lightly and continuously to avoid breath holding.

Cold water increases the effort required by your heart because cold causes the body to reduce circulation to the extremities in order to conserve heat. With more blood in the core of the body and an increased workload from pressure, your heart may not be able to pump the increased blood volume. The result can be excess blood in the small blood vessels of the lungs. These small blood vessels will transfer fluid to the air spaces of the lungs to reduce pressure. The accumulation of fluid in the lungs—known as pulmonary edema—causes severe breathing distress and can lead to panic or even loss of consciousness. You should test your circulatory ability gradually. Avoid strenuous dives in cold water until you have gradually adjusted to being underwater.

Your ability to exert effort in water is not as good as it is on land. When under pressure, your heart and lungs do not function as well as they normally do. A situation in which you are trying to work hard underwater can quickly result in a frightening sensation of suffocation when your equipment is unable to deliver the amount of air that your body requires. To stay within your cardiopulmonary limitations, you must learn to limit your activities and to pace yourself.

Equilibrium Adjustments and Seasickness

If you rupture an eardrum, water that is colder than body temperature can come into contact with the semicircular canals of your inner ear. The canals provide information for your brain to maintain equilibrium and are sensitive to temperature and pressure changes. Cold water cooling the semicircular canals can cause vertigo, a subjective feeling of movement perceived as a spinning sensation. This disorientation will pass when the water in the middle ear warms to body temperature. Obviously, it is better to prevent vertigo than to deal with it.

When a sudden change in pressure occurs in the air space of the middle ear of one ear (a change that affects the semicircular canals), this can also produce a disorienting sensation called alternobaric vertigo. The disorientation from alternobaric vertigo passes quickly when the brain recovers from the sudden pressure change.

Vertigo has many causes. Fortunately, instances of severe disorientation are rare in diving. If you experience disorientation while underwater, try to grasp a solid object for a point of reference until the feeling passes. If suspended in the water, close your eyes and hug yourself to reduce the effects of the vertigo. Avoid panic by telling yourself that the sensation will not last long.

Motions detected in your inner ears, visual references, and pressures on the joints of your limbs all affect your equilibrium. When your brain receives mixed signals from your inner ears, eyes, and body, you can experience motion sickness. You must avoid seasickness—motion sickness experienced aboard a vessel—because vomiting in or under the water is hazardous.

Medications can help reduce the tendency to be seasick. The medicine dulls the senses of the organs of balance in your ears. Unfortunately, the medications can have other undesirable effects. If you are prone to seasickness, consult a diving physician about the type of medication you should try. Take some of the medicine several days before you plan to dive, and note the effects, if any. If the medication produces drowsiness or blurred vision, do not use it while diving. Seek an alternative that does not produce side effects. Medications that cause dizziness, drowsiness, changes in heart rhythm, or blurred vision can cause you to lose consciousness under pressure. Many divers do successfully use medications to prevent seasickness; you need to find a type that works for you. Take medication for motion sickness at least 30 minutes before you are exposed to motion.

If you do not want to use medication, you may use other techniques to reduce the likelihood of seasickness. Eat a good, non-spicy meal before diving. An empty, acid-filled stomach becomes upset more easily than a full one. People whose breakfast before diving consists of coffee and orange juice are good candidates for motion sickness. When aboard a vessel, you should position yourself as near the center of the boat as possible. Avoid the front end of the boat. You should also avoid breathing engine fumes and avoid reading. You can reduce your reaction to the boat's motion by lying down for a while with your eyes closed. Being still allows your inner ears to adjust to the motion without visual signals confusing your brain.

You can become disoriented when you are weightless in a dimly lit environment. Under some conditions, it can be difficult to tell which way is up if you rely only on your sense of balance. To prevent disorientation, you must learn to recognize clues about your orientation in the water. Water in your mask settles to the lowest point, bubbles ascend, and heavy objects you hold (such as your weight belt) orient themselves up and down.

Visual Adjustments

Experience will help you adjust to magnified vision underwater. You can adjust so quickly to distance corrections in water that you have to readjust when you surface from a dive. At the end of a dive, the distance to a boat or to the shore can look much greater than it is. You may be surprised to find that you require less time than you think to swim to a destination.

Your vision also compensates for color differences. If you know an object's true color, the object will look more like that color. The use of artificial light at close range makes it easier to view the rich and magnificent colors in the underwater world.

Your vision adjusts to low light levels, but the process takes time. Short, deep dives in turbid water do not allow complete visual adjustment, and details will not be clear. You cannot see well without artificial light. You can improve your ability to see while diving by avoiding bright light and glare before a dive. Wear good, dark sunglasses above water during the day. When you complete training for night diving, you will learn other techniques to help your eyes adjust for diving at night.

Humidity can cause condensation to form on the lens of your mask and obscure your vision. A clean glass surface will not fog, so make sure you clean the lens or lenses of your mask thoroughly before diving.

Ingassing and Outgassing

Your body absorbs nitrogen underwater, and there are limits to the amount of nitrogen that you can safely eliminate at the end of a dive. If you exceed these limits, you can be injured. In this section, you will learn the theory of decompression, which will help you understand how dive tables and dive computers function to help you avoid injuries.

Decompression Theory

Gases diffuse by moving from areas of greater concentration to areas of lesser concentration. When external pressure increases, gases diffuse from your lungs into your blood, and then from your blood into your tissues. When the **ambient (surrounding) pressure** decreases, diffusion occurs in the reverse sequence.

Two factors that affect diffusion of gases in your body are time and **perfusion** (the circulation in a tissue). The greater the circulation in a tissue, the sooner the pressures of the gases in that tissue come into balance with the pressures of the gases you breathe. Reaching this state of equilibrium takes time. The amount of time it takes a tissue to accumulate half of the gas it can hold at a given pressure is a **half-time**. A tissue is saturated (holds all the gas it can at a given pressure) after six half-times. If perfusion permits 50 percent of a gas to diffuse into a tissue in 5 minutes, the tissue saturates in 30 minutes. Outgassing also occurs in six half-times.

Air is primarily nitrogen and oxygen. The oxygen in the air you breathe is of no concern during decompression within the limits of recreational diving (130 feet or 39.6 m maximum) because you use the oxygen. Nitrogen, the primary component of air, is inert. Your body cannot use the nitrogen, so when you ascend, you must eliminate the excess nitrogen that you absorbed at depth. Because nitrogen diffuses from your body, there is no problem unless the reduction in pressure is so great that you cannot eliminate the nitrogen fast enough. When you reduce the pressure on a liquid rapidly and there is sufficient gas dissolved in the liquid, the gas forms bubbles. An excellent example of this is CO_2 dissolved in carbonated beverages (see figure 3.6). The gas remains dissolved in a sealed, pressurized container. When you reduce the pressure suddenly by opening the container, the gas forms bubbles because it cannot diffuse out of solution slowly. If a beverage container has a tiny leak, however, the carbon dioxide comes out of solution slowly without bubbling. There is no bubbling when you open a container that has a slow leak because the gas has already diffused out of solution.

Figure 3.6 Rapid pressure reduction causes dissolved gases to form bubbles within the decompressed liquid.

You must be concerned about the amount of nitrogen in solution in your body and the rate at which you eliminate it. If you absorb too much nitrogen while diving and do not ascend in a manner that allows the excess nitrogen to be eliminated without forming bubbles, the bubbles are likely to cause decompression sickness, a serious diving illness.

Mathematical models provide estimates of the amount of nitrogen in different parts of your body. Because circulation varies in different parts of your body, tissues absorb nitrogen at differing rates. Decompression experts use mathematical models, called **compartments**, to estimate gas absorption and elimination by various areas of the body. A compartment is identified by its half-time. A 5-minute compartment has a half-time of 5 minutes. Experts use compartments ranging from 5 minutes to as long as 960 minutes when calculating gas absorption and elimination.

A compartment that has absorbed gas can withstand some lowering of pressure before bubbling occurs. Originally, scientists believed that a reduction in pressure by a ratio greater than two to one would cause bubbling to occur in divers whose tissues were saturated at a particular depth. This ratio was considered a surfacing limit that could not be exceeded. Then scientists discovered that the surfacing ratios are different for various compartments because of differences in perfusion. For example, brain tissue absorbs and eliminates inert gas faster than bone tissue. Body areas that eliminate gas quickly have a higher surfacing ratio than compartments that eliminate gas slowly. The difference in ratios poses an interesting and complex problem for divers because one tissue controls how long a diver can remain at one depth, while another tissue controls how long the diver can remain at another depth. The **controlling compartment** was used to establish our modern time limits for diving. Do not remain at any depth longer than the time it takes the controlling compartment to exceed its surfacing ratio. If you do, you must prevent bubble formation by stopping during the ascent to allow time to eliminate the excess gas. The time limits for various depths have been conveniently arranged into tables and included in dive computer software. These tools help divers keep the amount of nitrogen in solution in the various tissues of the body within the surfacing ratio of each compartment.

It takes time to eliminate excess gas from tissues. The rate at which you reduce pressure (ascend) is important. The dive tables presented in chapter 7 use an ascent rate, or pressure reduction rate, no greater than 30 feet (9 m) per minute. The mathematical models for some dive computers use rates two or three times slower than the dive tables. You must ascend slowly to prevent the formation of bubbles in your body tissues.

Partial ascents with stops before continuing the ascent can help with outgassing and the prevention of bubble formation. These delays are called safety stops or rest stops, and they are recommended when ascending from any depth in excess of 30 feet. The deeper you dive, the more safety stops you should take when ascending. The recommended practice is to stop for five minutes at half of the deepest depth to which you have been diving and to stop again at a depth of 15 to 20 feet (4.5 to 6.1 m) for five minutes before surfacing.

Decompression Illness

Commonly known as the bends, decompression illness (DCI) is the result of a reduction in pressure (decompression) that is too rapid for the amount of gas in solution in body tissues. The gas forms bubbles in the tissues or in the blood before it can diffuse into the lungs and be eliminated. Scientists do not fully understand what occurs when DCI strikes. The symptoms may appear immediately after surfacing from a dive or days after diving. About half of all DCI cases occur within one hour after diving. The symptoms vary depending on the amount and location of the bubbles. Severe cases of decompression illness can have severe neurological effects and produce permanent paralysis. Common symptoms include the following:

○ A mottled skin rash
○ Joint pain
○ Numbness
○ Tingling
○ Weakness
○ Paralysis

The following factors can increase the chances of DCI:

○ Lack of sleep
○ Tight-fitting apparel

- Alcohol and its aftereffects
- Exercise during and after diving
- Dehydration
- Cramped position
- Illness
- Altitude after diving
- Age
- Scar tissue or injuries
- Cold water
- Medical conditions

Some experts believe that you should avoid postdive activities that stimulate circulation because increased perfusion may contribute to DCI. Specific activities to avoid include physical exercise, drinking alcoholic beverages, and taking hot showers or baths. Reduced pressure at altitude, such as flying in a plane or driving into the mountains too soon after diving, also poses an additional risk factor that can cause DCI. Avoid all activities that increase the likelihood of decompression illness.

A person suffering from DCI requires prompt first aid and medical treatment because it is an extremely serious condition. The illness worsens with time. The best first aid measure is to administer oxygen in the highest concentration possible. Breathing oxygen eliminates nitrogen in inspired air and enhances the diffusion of nitrogen from the body. The patient should remain still and should sip water. Make arrangements to have the patient transported to the nearest medical facility. After initial medical treatment, the medical staff will arrange to transfer the patient to a facility that has a hyperbaric (high-pressure) chamber. The patient is placed inside a large vessel called a recompression chamber (see figure 3.7). Hyperbaric treatment consists of increasing the pressure in the chamber to reduce or eliminate the symptoms, administering medications, and then slowly decompressing the patient. Recompression must be done in a chamber.

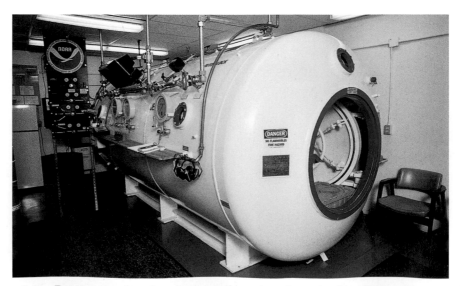

Figure 3.7 Recompression chambers are the only safe method to restore pressure after becoming sick.

Decompression illness is extremely serious because it can cause permanent injury. DCI can cause joint pain and neurological deficits that cannot be cured. To reduce the likelihood of DCI, you should remain well within the established time and depth limits for diving. Surface at a rate no faster than that specified by the dive computer you use. Stop at least twice during ascent (as previously recommended) and eliminate excess nitrogen before surfacing (see figure 3.8). Ascending at the proper rate and stopping are forms of decompression that reduce the likelihood of DCI. (The details about planning your ascent and time delays are provided in chapter 7.) An additional precaution that can help you avoid DCI is to delay excursions to altitude after diving.

Another point to keep in mind is that it is often difficult to distinguish between the symptoms of an arterial gas embolism and DCI. Any diver who has neurological symptoms after a dive should seek medical attention immediately.

Figure 3.8 Divers completing a decompression stop on their ascent to the surface.

Nitrogen Narcosis

The increased partial pressure of nitrogen can cause a condition known as nitrogen narcosis, or rapture of the deep, at depths of about 100 feet (30 m) and deeper. Scientists do not know the exact mechanism of nitrogen narcosis, but its effects are similar to those of anesthetic gases. The feelings associated with narcosis range from euphoria to overconfidence to terror, although some divers do not experience any unusual feelings. Narcosis affects you whether or not you experience abnormal feelings. And it impairs thinking, judgment, reasoning, memory, and the ability to do physical tasks. Narcosis is hazardous; it reduces your awareness and your ability to respond to an emergency. Susceptibility to narcosis varies from person to person and within an individual from day to day.

Narcosis begins suddenly at depth—usually around 100 feet (30m). You can relieve its symptoms rapidly by ascending to a shallower depth to reduce the narcotic effect.

The following factors predispose a person to narcosis:

- A high level of systemic CO_2 caused by exertion
- Alcohol or its aftereffects
- Anxiety
- Cold
- Medications
- Social drugs

Experience, frequent diving, and concentration will reduce susceptibility to narcosis. Preventing narcosis is always better than attempting to cope with it.

Specialty training can qualify you to dive with special gas mixtures that reduce the effects of nitrogen. Diving with mixed gases without completing the required training is dangerous and should never be attempted.

Dehydration Prevention

You need to preserve body fluids to prevent **dehydration**. Getting cold makes you produce more urine than normal. Each breath you take from your scuba cylinder must be humidified as explained in the previous chapter. Breathing dehumidified air causes dehydration. You receive air underwater by creating an inhalation pressure that opens valves in your air delivery system. The inhalation pressure is slight, but it is greater than normal. Inhaling harder than normal is negative-pressure breathing, which also has the physiological effect of increasing urine production. Breathing underwater compounds the problem of dehydration.

Diuretic beverages (such as coffee and alcohol) and some types of medications cause increased urine production. Avoid ingesting anything that makes you urinate more than normal. You must prevent excessive dehydration because the condition predisposes you to diving injuries. To prevent dehydration, you should do the following:

- Insulate yourself to stay as warm as possible.
- Keep your regulator well maintained so you can breathe as easily as possible.
- Avoid diuretic drinks and medications.

○ Replenish body fluids frequently; drink fluids before and between dives.

  Note: If you wait until you are thirsty to drink when diving, you are already dehydrated. Be proactive and drink at least 1 pint (500 ml) of appropriate fluid after every dive. A good after-dive beverage is a sports drink diluted with an equal amount of water. Avoid alcoholic beverages because they increase dehydration.

Mobility Adjustments

The equipment that you wear for diving limits your mobility. It reduces your range of motion and makes it difficult to walk. The colder the water, the thicker your exposure suit, so the less your range of movement.

Diving equipment is fairly heavy, and it is challenging to lift and move. Improper lifting techniques can cause back injuries. Squat down and lift with your legs to pick up a tank or weight belt instead of bending over. The weight of the equipment changes your center of gravity and affects your balance. Keeping your balance during entries and exits can be challenging on a rocking boat or an uneven surface for your feet. Move carefully and hold on to something or someone for support when you move around out of the water.

You wear fins so that you can use the large muscles of your legs for propulsion. When diving, you need to learn to use your legs for swimming and your body angle to control direction. These techniques free your hands for other uses underwater. Minimize the use of your hands for propulsion. Fins make it difficult for you to walk when you're out of the water. Shuffle your feet while moving backward or sideways, keep your knees bent, and be careful not to fall.

Drag slows your movement in the water. One factor affecting drag is the speed of motion. The greater the speed, the greater the resistance to movement. The average diver can sustain a speed of a little more than 1 mile an hour (0.9 knot, or 1.6 km per hour). A knot equals 1.15 miles per hour (1.85 km per hour) and is the method of measuring speed in water. Doubling the speed increases the energy requirement fourfold. Trying to move in water as if it were air causes exhaustion quickly. Use a slow, steady pace and slow, deliberate motions to reduce the effects of drag.

Another factor affecting drag is the size of the object in motion. The larger the surface area exposed, the greater the resistance. A swimming diver is under the influence of four forces: Weight (negative buoyancy) pulls the diver downward, lift (positive buoyancy) pulls the diver upward, thrust moves the diver forward, and drag slows forward progress (see figure 3.9). Divers usually wear weight around the waist, which pulls the lower half of the body downward. Buoyancy from the BC lifts the upper half of the body. The effect of these forces increases the surface area of the diver and therefore the drag. You should adjust the amount of weight you wear so that your body is as horizontal as possible in the water. Correct weighting minimizes drag and the effort required to swim. Also consider placing a small amount of weight near the top of your body to adjust your trim—that is, your position in the water.

Water flows smoothly across a smooth and rounded surface but flows turbulently across an irregular surface. When the surface is irregular, the turbulent flow increases drag. Just as vehicles designed to travel through fluids are streamlined to reduce the drag caused by turbulent flow, you can choose and configure your equipment so that it presents the smoothest surface possible to the flow of water.

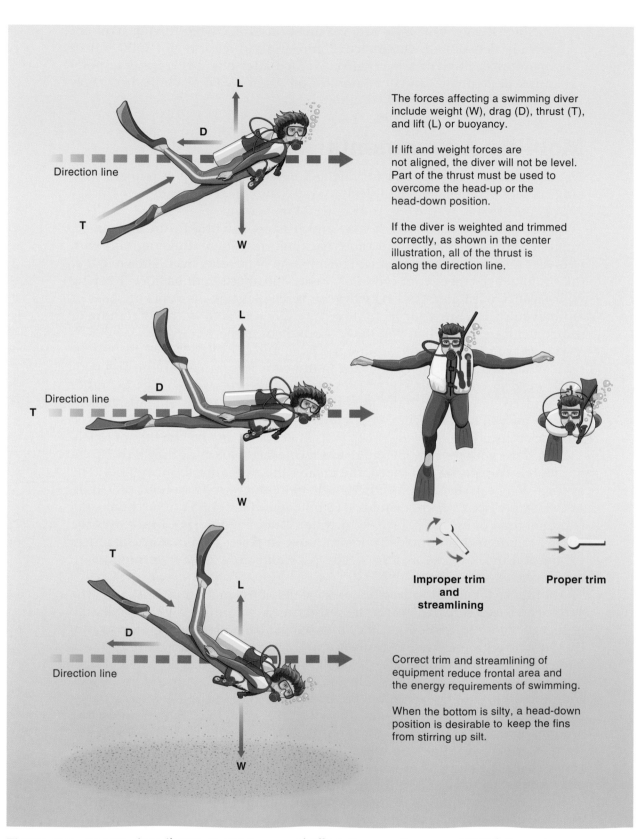

The forces affecting a swimming diver include weight (W), drag (D), thrust (T), and lift (L) or buoyancy.

If lift and weight forces are not aligned, the diver will not be level. Part of the thrust must be used to overcome the head-up or the head-down position.

If the diver is weighted and trimmed correctly, as shown in the center illustration, all of the thrust is along the direction line.

Improper trim and streamlining

Proper trim

Correct trim and streamlining of equipment reduce frontal area and the energy requirements of swimming.

When the bottom is silty, a head-down position is desirable to keep the fins from stirring up silt.

Figure 3.9   Weight, drag, thrust, and lift (buoyancy) affect divers as they move through the water.

Summary

You have to make many changes in your normal behavior to adjust to the underwater environment. The way you breathe is the most important adaptation. You must breathe continuously and avoid breath holding when you use scuba equipment. You must also limit your activity and pace yourself to avoid overexertion. Managing the mechanical and physiological effects of pressure requires major adjustments. You must keep pressure equalized in your air spaces to avoid pressure injuries, and you must limit your depth and time at depth to avoid nitrogen narcosis and decompression illness. Being in the underwater environment seems strange at first, but you can conform to weightlessness and other strange feelings. The sensations of diving become exhilarating as you gain experience in the new world beneath the surface.

Application-of-Knowledge (AOK) Questions

Remember that this is an exercise in thinking, not a quiz. If you carefully consider each situation and how you would respond to it, your time will be well invested even if your thoughts are different from the solution provided. Imagine each situation as vividly as possible.

1. You are wearing a wetsuit and swimming against a current (which is a good idea under most circumstances) in cold water. You are becoming colder with each passing minute. What action, other than ending the dive, can you take to reduce your heat loss?

2. After a dive during which you shivered, you exit the water on a cool, cloudy, windy day. What actions can you take to get warm that are not likely to cause physiological problems? Hint: Rapid rewarming can affect your heart rhythm and may also cause decompression illness.

3. You are wearing 17 pounds of lead weights while diving at a depth of 40 feet (12 m) when your weight belt suddenly slips off. How rapidly do you think you will float upward, and what actions can you take to recover from this situation?

4. You are wearing a wetsuit, a BC, and a weight belt while scuba diving at a depth of 33 feet (10 m). Your buoyancy is adjusted to be perfectly neutral at this depth. You have to ascend 10 feet (3.3 m) to clear a reef. What actions will you need to take to control your buoyancy as you swim over the reef?

5. You are pulling yourself hand over hand down an anchor line to descend to a dive site and are having difficulty equalizing the pressure in your ears. Your normal equalization methods are not working. What should you do to equalize the pressure in your ears?

6. Why do you need to equalize the pressure in your body air spaces and your mask more frequently at the beginning of the descent than when you are approaching your diving depth?

7. You are having trouble keeping up with your buddy, who is swimming ahead. You are breathing heavily and beginning to feel starved for air. What actions should you take?

8. When you switched tanks between dives, you accidently selected one that is almost empty. You were also distracted and failed to check the pressure before you started the dive. You are at a depth of 50 feet (15 m) when it becomes hard to breathe. You look at your pressure gauge and find a reading of zero. Based on what you know at this point in your training, what action do you think is appropriate?

Large, beautiful angelfish at a coral reef in Cozumel, Mexico

Diving Equipment

Dive In and Discover

By the end of this chapter, you will be able to do the following:

- Describe the purpose, types, features, selection criteria, and care and maintenance of skin and scuba diving equipment.

- Contrast steel and aluminum scuba cylinders, wet and dry suits, integrated and nonintegrated weighting systems, and reserve and nonreserve valves.

- Define the terms *buoyancy, compensator, defogging, shorty, jumpsuit, Farmer Johns, K-valve, J-valve, DIN valve, valve seat, burst disk, O-ring, port, stage, octopus, capillary gauge, Bourdon tube, Boyle's law, outgassing, bezel, submersible pressure gauge (SPG), blowout plug, alternate air source (AAS), pony tank, Spare Air unit, lubber line, console,* and *ceiling.*

You will become familiar with the following items in this chapter:

- Masks
- Snorkels
- Fins
- Skin diving vests
- Exposure suits
- Weighting systems
- Buoyancy compensators
- Scuba cylinders
- Cylinder valves
- Scuba regulators
- Alternate air sources
- Instrumentation
- Dive knives and other accessories
- Specialized equipment

You need to be equipped properly to dive in open water. A snorkeler (a diver who remains at the surface) should wear a mask, a snorkel, fins, and a skin diving vest. A skin diver (a breath-holding diver who dives beneath the surface) uses snorkeling equipment and may wear an exposure suit and a weight belt (if the suit requires weights). Scuba equipment includes, at a minimum, a mask, a snorkel, fins, an exposure suit, a weighting system (if needed), a **buoyancy compensator** (BC), a scuba unit (cylinder, valve, regulator, **alternate air source**), instrumentation, and a dive knife. For cold water, a diver also needs a hood, boots, and gloves. Figure 4.1 shows fully equipped divers.

Equipment helps people adapt to the underwater environment. It allows them to see, breathe, move, monitor their position, remain comfortable, have fun, and rest. Diving is an equipment-intensive activity. In this chapter, you will learn what equipment you need, how to select the best equipment for your needs, and how to care for your equipment.

Schooling hatchetfish in the Red Sea

Figure 4.1 **Fully equipped cold-water (left) and warm-water (right) divers.**

Basic Equipment for All Divers

The mask, snorkel, fins, and some flotation device are basic equipment for all types of recreational diving (snorkeling, skin diving, and scuba diving).

Masks

The eyes require an air space in front of them to focus sharply. Your mask provides an air space and a window to another world. Many styles of masks are available, but only two basic types are used for recreational diving: purge and nonpurge. A purge is a one-way valve through which you can expel water that enters the mask. As you will learn in chapter 6, you can remove water from a mask without a valve, so many masks do not feature a purge valve. A third type of mask, a full-face mask, is for commercial and specialty applications only. Figure 4.2 shows the most common types of masks.

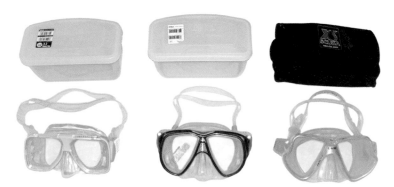

Figure 4.2 **Test dive masks before you buy to ensure a snug and comfortable fit.**

The type of mask you choose is not nearly as important as the fit of the mask on your face. The mask must fit your facial contours perfectly so it will remain comfortable and watertight throughout a dive. Fit and comfort are the most important features to consider when you select a mask. To test the fit of a mask, remove the strap or position it on the front of the mask. Tilt your head back and lay the mask (do not push it) on your face. Make sure your hair is not under the sealing edge of the mask; then inhale gently. If the mask pulls onto your face snugly from the partial vacuum created by your inhalation, the mask fits. If you have to push the mask to get it to seal on your face, the mask will probably leak when you use it underwater.

Factors that affect the fit and comfort of a mask include the style, the type of material, and the type of sealing edge of the mask. The best masks are made from silicone, which is soft, pliable, and nonallergenic and resists deterioration better than rubber compounds (see figure 4.3). The buoyancy of smaller masks poses no problems, but the tug of buoyancy of a larger-volume mask can affect the seal. Low-volume masks are easier to clear of water and provide excellent visibility. A wide, double-edged seal does a better job of keeping out water than a single-edge seal.

A film of oil from production is on the surface of the glass lenses of new masks. You must remove the film completely—a process called **defogging**—or the mask will fog continuously underwater. Clean your mask thoroughly with scouring powder. The glass (which is tempered) is too hard to be scratched by the abrasive, so do not be timid when cleaning your mask. Commercial defogging solutions help keep your mask clear while you dive. If a clean mask fogs slightly during use, you can allow a small amount of water into the mask and wash it across the fogged area to resolve the problem.

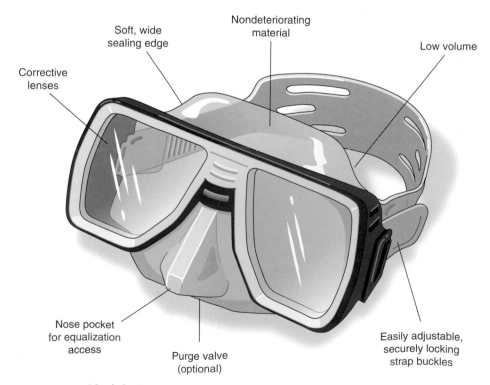

Figure 4.3 **Mask features.**

Several options are available for visual correction if you need it. Hard contact lenses cannot be used, because gases that are released from the body during ascent can be trapped between the lens and the surface of the eye. This can injure the eye. If you wear soft contact lenses, you can use them for diving after you complete your training; however, you should not use them during training because you may lose them when you are learning how to clear water from your mask. Some contact lens wearers prefer a mask with a small purge valve because they can expel water from the mask with little risk of losing a contact lens. Several companies prepare and bond corrective lenses into any diving mask. Interchangeable corrective lenses are available for some masks. If you require only a simple correction, you may be able to obtain corrective lenses for your mask when you purchase it.

Store your mask in a mask box when you are not using it. The box helps keep the mask from getting damaged and helps prevent discoloration of the silicone mask skirt.

Snorkels

A human head weighs about as much as a bowling ball. If you had to swim while holding a bowling ball out of water, you would become exhausted quickly. If you swim while holding your head above water, you will tire rapidly. But if you allow buoyancy to support your head in the water, you can relax and swim for hours. A snorkel allows you to breathe while water supports your head—allowing you to conserve energy and enjoy continuous underwater viewing.

In its simplest form, a snorkel is nothing more than a breathing tube that extends from a diver's mouth to a point above the waterline. A basic diving snorkel is a J-shaped tube with a mouthpiece on one end. Just as with masks, there are two types of snorkels: purge and nonpurge (see figure 4.4). A purge snorkel has a one-way valve through which you can expel water that enters the tube. As you will learn in chapter 6, you can clear water from a snorkel that lacks a purge valve, so some snorkels do not have a valve. Some types of purge snorkels are self-draining; gravity drains water from the tube automatically when you are at the surface of the water.

Additional snorkel options include a swivel mouthpiece and a flexible hose for the lower half of the tube. With the flexible hose, the lower part of the tube—which is usually curved—hangs straight down when you are not using your snorkel (see figure 4.5). The flex-hose snorkel reduces interference between the snorkel and your scuba regulator. Special mouthpieces can be used to maximize comfort, and devices are available to prevent water from entering the top end of the snorkel, although water exclusion devices are not essential.

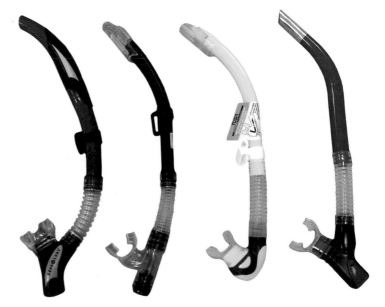

Figure 4.4 Three common types of snorkel are purge (two at left and far right) and nonpurge (center right).

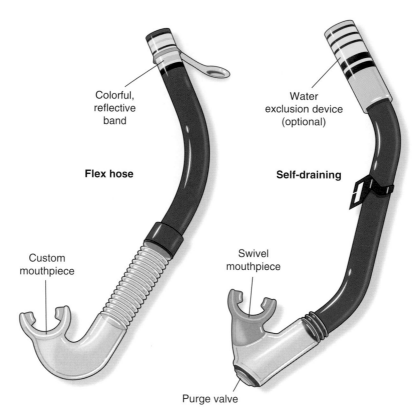

Colorful,
reflective
band

Water
exclusion device
(optional)

Flex hose

Self-draining

Custom
mouthpiece

Swivel
mouthpiece

Purge valve

Figure 4.5   Features of a flex hose and self-draining snorkel.

The fit of your snorkel is the most important consideration, much more important than the type. The mouthpiece must not irritate your mouth, gums, or jaw when in place for extended periods of time. The angle of the mouthpiece in your mouth should not require you to bite hard to hold the mouthpiece in place. A snorkel that fits poorly may cause sore gums or jaws. A snorkel tube should have an inside diameter of approximately 3/4 inch (1.9 cm) so that resistance to airflow through the tube does not make breathing difficult.

Attach the snorkel to your mask strap on the left side using a snorkel keeper because your regulator hose goes over your right shoulder. Several types of snorkel keepers are available. Popular keepers are the simple ones depicted in figure 4.6. The adjustment is correct if the snorkel mouthpiece remains in your mouth when you open your mouth wide.

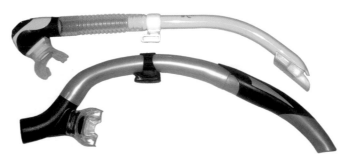

Figure 4.6   Two types of snorkel keepers.

Fins

Diving would be much less enjoyable without fins. Fins increase your ability to move in the water and free your hands for other activities. You move in water by pushing against the water. Fins increase your ability to move by presenting a larger surface area than your hands or feet alone. The muscles of your legs are much larger and stronger than your arm muscles. Your arms would tire quickly if fins were attached to your hands, but your legs are strong enough to handle the load. Fins also help stabilize you in water by providing a large surface to resist movement. The resistance provides leverage for countermovement and directional control.

The two basic types of fins are shoe (full-foot) fins and open-heel fins. Shoe fins slip on to bare feet, so they are good snorkeling fins for tropical climates. You wear open-heel fins with foot coverings called boots. Open-heel fins, generally used for scuba diving, are usually larger and stiffer than shoe fins (see figure 4.7). Small, flexible snorkeling fins may be inadequate for the harder work of scuba diving.

Special materials and designs abound. The fundamental features of a fin are the size and stiffness of the blade (see figure 4.8). The larger and stiffer the blade, the greater the propulsion but also the greater the physical demand when you move the fin through the water. A blade that is too stiff can cause you to cramp and become fatigued. You should begin with fins of a moderate size and stiffness. When you can use those fins for extended periods without difficulty, you may consider fins that can provide greater propulsion.

The most important criteria for the selection of any item of diving equipment are fit and comfort, and this is especially true of fins. To help ensure proper fit, sit down and try on a fin. Wear a boot if you are trying on an open-heel fin. Hold your foot in the air and wiggle it up and down and from side to side. The fin and your foot should move as a single unit. If your foot moves inside the foot pocket, the fin is too large. Diving equipment should fit snugly but not tightly.

Figure 4.7   Three styles of open-heel fins.

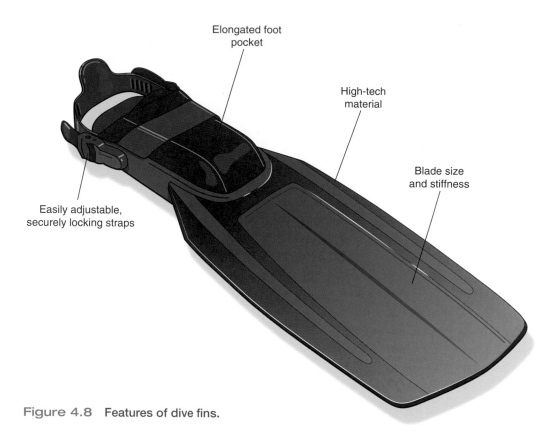

Elongated foot pocket

High-tech material

Blade size and stiffness

Easily adjustable, securely locking straps

Figure 4.8   Features of dive fins.

A fin that is too tight can cause your foot to cramp. The foot pocket of the fin should fit snugly but should not exert pressure on your foot. Select your fins using fit, comfort, and blade size and stiffness as your primary criteria. Features, fashion, and cost should be secondary considerations.

Skin Diving Vests

When you blow air into a skin diving vest (which is smaller and less complex than a buoyancy compensator), you can achieve positive buoyancy (floating). Positive buoyancy is invaluable when you want to rest at the surface or carry items you have collected while diving. Wear a buoyancy device whenever you dive. You can achieve negative buoyancy (sinking) by venting air from the skin diving vest.

Divers use one basic type of skin diving vest; this vest fits around the neck and secures at the waist (see figure 4.9). A standard feature of a skin diving vest is an oral inflation tube, which comes in various sizes. It is easier to use larger tubes with mouthpieces than smaller tubes without mouthpieces.

Figure 4.9   Skin diving vest.

Care and Maintenance of Skin Diving Equipment

Your skin diving equipment will provide years of service if you take care of it properly. Rinse the equipment with clean, freshwater after use; dry it in the shade; and store it in a cool, dark, smog-free location. Prolonged sunlight, smog, salt crystals, and swimming pool chlorine will harm your equipment. Fill a skin diving vest partially with freshwater after use, and swish the water inside. Drain the vest completely, and then inflate it for drying and for storage. Periodically inspect the straps on your mask and fins for drying and cracking, and replace straps when they begin to deteriorate. After your mask has dried, rub a drop of defogging solution on the lens to help keep the lens clean during storage.

Exposure Suits

You should wear some type of exposure protection when diving regardless of the water temperature. An exposure suit provides protection against scrapes and stings in addition to providing insulation.

The two basic types of exposure suits are wet suits and dry suits. Generally speaking, the colder the water, the thicker your suit should be and the more of your body should be covered by the suit. Suits come in many configurations, but most are one piece or a combination of a jacket and pants. Vests are accessories that help conserve heat in vital organs. Hoods, boots, and gloves help reduce heat loss from the head, feet, and hands, respectively.

Wet Suits

A wet suit is a good exposure suit for water temperatures ranging from 60 to 85 °F (15.6 to 29.4 °C). A wet suit allows water inside, but any water that enters can also exit and carry heat with it. The better the fit of the suit, the less water inside and the warmer the suit. Table 4.1 provides a comparison of the various types of wet suits. The following descriptions provide some additional information.

Table 4.1   Wet Suits

Type	Warmth	Features	Temperature range
Spandex	45% more than bare skin	Light, compact; useful as undergarments for thicker suits	78 °F (25.6 °C) +
Thermoplastic	30% warmer than spandex	Neutrally buoyant; no weights required; wicks perspiration; windproof	75 °F (23.9 °C) +
Plush-lined thermoplastic	10% warmer than unlined	Same as thermoplastic	72 °F (22.2 °C) +
Foam neoprene 1/8 in. (2–3 mm) 3/16 in. (4 mm) 1/4 in. (5–6.5 mm)	20-100% warmer than plush-lined thermoplastic	Buoyant; weights required; long drying time; evaporation chills wearer; minor repairs easy to do	Down to 60 °F (15.6 °C)
Hoods, vests, boots, and gloves or mitts	16-66% more warmth	Reduces water circulation; layering allows flexibility for various temperatures	Down to 60 °F (15.6 °C)

Spandex suits are thin, stretchy, attractive, full-body garments that are popular for diving in tropical waters. Spandex garments provide 45 percent more insulation than bare skin and provide protection against stings, scrapes, and sunshine. Spandex suits are light and compact for travel. They are also useful as undergarments for thicker neoprene wet suits, adding an extra layer of insulation and allowing you to slip into the heavier suit more easily. If you live in a temperate climate, you can use a spandex body suit beneath a neoprene wet suit for local diving and use the spandex suit by itself for vacation diving in the tropics (see figure 4.10).

Thermoplastic—sandwiched between two layers of spandex—is another type of wet suit material. A suit made from this three-ply material is about 30 percent warmer than a spandex suit. Thermoplastic suits are thin (1.2 to 1.4 mm) and designed for use in tropical waters (75 to 85 °F [24 to 29 °C]). Some suits feature soft, plush lining for extra warmth. The plush lining increases the warmth of the suit by about 10 percent. You can wear a thermoplastic suit beneath a neoprene wet suit for extra warmth in colder water.

Thermoplastic material offers several advantages: The balance between the weight and volume of this unique material makes it neutrally buoyant, so you may not need a weight belt. The stretchy fabric allows you to move freely. The material draws perspiration away from your body but is windproof.

A third type of wet suit material is foam neoprene, as in the suits shown in figure 4.11. The foam contains tiny bubbles of inert gas, which provide insulation. The thicker the wet suit material, the greater the insulation quality of the suit. A 1/8-inch (about 3 mm) neoprene wet suit is about 20 percent warmer than a plush thermoplastic suit.

The thickness of foam neoprene in wet suits ranges from 1/8 inch for warm-water diving to 3/8 inch (about 9 mm) for extreme cold-water diving. The most common wet suit thicknesses are 1/8 inch, 3/16 inch (about 4 mm), and 1/4 inch (about 6 mm). You can layer wet suit material on critical areas of your body to

Figure 4.10 Common styles of warm-water wet suits: foam neoprene jumpsuit (left), shorty (center), and nylon (right).

Figure 4.11 Common styles of cold-water wet suits: Jackets at left and center (worn with or without an attached hood) are worn over Farmer Johns at right to form layers.

reduce heat loss, but the thicker the insulation you wear, the more difficult it is for you to control buoyancy. Choose the thickness of wet suit material used by experienced divers in the area where you plan to dive.

Nylon usually covers both sides of the neoprene used for wet suits. The nylon increases the strength and durability of the suit, which is glued and sewed together. You can make minor repairs with wet suit cement, but you should have a wet suit manufacturer do extensive repairs.

Neoprene wet suits require weights to achieve neutral buoyancy. The suit provides immediate buoyancy when you release the weights, but the buoyancy of the suit can be either a benefit or a hazard. Neoprene is not windproof, and the evaporation of water from the suit between dives can chill you. You can wear a wet suit overgarment to retain warmth between dives in colder climates. Neoprene suits take longer to dry than other types of exposure suits. Mobility is good with thin neoprene wet suits but decreases as the thickness of the material increases.

Numerous wet suit designs are available, including the **shorty**, the one-piece **jumpsuit**, and **Farmer Johns** (see figures 4.10 and 4.11). You must consider several features when selecting a wet suit design. The more zippers a suit has, the more water circulates inside the suit and the greater the loss of heat. You can get zipperless suits for cold-water diving. Good wet suits feature a spine pad to minimize water circulation along the channel formed by your spine, and some suits for cold-water diving have attached hoods to minimize water circulation at the neck. You may spend time kneeling around and in the water, so knee pads are a desirable feature.

Heat packs are available for wet suits. These packs contain a nontoxic, reusable chemical that heats to about 130 °F (54 °C) for half an hour or more, depending on conditions. The packs fit into special pockets that are an optional suit feature.

You can buy wet suits in standard sizes, or you can have a suit tailored for a custom fit. The fit of a wet suit is its most important feature. The suit must fit snugly all over, but it must not fit so tightly that it hampers your breathing and circulation. A suit that fits well may feel slightly restrictive out of the water. The true test of the fit of a suit is to dive with it. You may be able to rent a wet suit identical to one you would like to purchase.

Wet Suit Accessories

Scuba divers wear footwear for warmth and foot protection. Several types of footwear—called boots or booties—are available for various needs. Boots, usually made from neoprene, may cover only the foot or both the foot and the ankle (see figure 4.12). Boots range from inexpensive neoprene socks to sturdy footwear with durable, molded soles. They may or may not have zippers. Zippered boots are easier to don and remove, but boots without zippers are warmer.

Figure 4.12 Boots are available with or without zippers.

You should wear hand coverings when the water temperature is less than 70 °F (21 °C). Some divers wear gloves for protection, such as when catching lobsters. Types of hand coverings include gloves, mitts, and gauntlets (see figure

4.13). Wear mitts in cold water because they are thicker and have less surface area for heat dissipation than gloves have. Wear gauntlets (neoprene mitts with long cuffs) when the water is extremely cold. Thin neoprene gloves provide sufficient insulation in temperate water. Do not wear gloves in tropical areas. You are more likely to touch things when wearing gloves, and grabbing delicate coral reefs and marine animals while wearing gloves may harm the animals.

Figure 4.13 Gloves and mitts protect divers' hands from cold temperatures and injuries.

A hood is an important warmth accessory that can reduce your heat loss from 20 to 50 percent, depending on the temperature of the water. Two basic types of hoods—attached hoods and separate hoods—are available for wet suits (see figure 4.14). Cold-water divers like attached hoods because they restrict water circulation in a suit more than separate hoods do. Some separate hoods have skirts that end at the base of the neck; other cold-water hoods have large bibs that cover the neck and shoulder area. Thin hoods are used for protection in warm water, and thicker hoods are used for insulation and protection in cold water.

Figure 4.14 Hoods conserve warmth in cold waters.

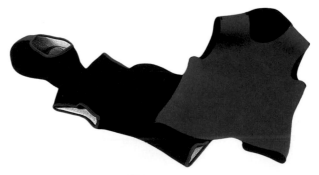

Figure 4.15 The addition of a vest can increase the warmth of your wet suit by as much as 16 percent.

You can increase the warmth of your wet suit by as much as 16 percent by wearing a vest. Wet-suit vests come in all types of material and provide an additional layer of insulation (see figure 4.15). Layering is an effective technique that reduces water circulation while increasing insulation. Some vests have attached hoods.

Wet Suit Care and Maintenance

With proper care, wet suits can provide years of service. Soak your wet suit in clean, warm freshwater after each use. If you can't soak your suit, rinse it. Hang your suit on a wet suit hanger, which is wider than a typical clothes hanger; dry the suit in the shade; and store it on the hanger in a cool, dark, smog-free location. A garage is a poor environment for storing equipment because of emissions from automobile exhaust. Do not fold your wet suit for storage because folds can form permanent creases, which insulate poorly. Inspect your suit regularly for seam integrity and tears. Make repairs or have them made as needed.

Dry Suits

When the water temperature is less than 60 °F (15.6 °C), consider using a dry suit, which is an exposure suit that keeps out water. Dry suits are much warmer than wet suits for three reasons:

1. Air is in contact with your skin instead of water. Because air conducts less heat than water, you lose less heat via conduction.
2. You wear undergarments beneath a dry suit. The undergarments trap a layer of air, which is a good insulator.
3. Suit compression affects two of the three types of dry suits only slightly, so the insulating ability of those types of dry suits remains nearly constant regardless of depth. Constant volume in a dry suit provides an advantage over a wet suit, which compresses with depth and expands during ascent.

Dry suits are identified by the material from which they are made. Table 4.2 compares the three most common types of dry suits. The foam neoprene dry suit is made of the same material as a wet suit, but the dry suit has seals at the wrists and neck, attached dry boots, and a waterproof zipper (see figure 4.16).

A dry suit can cost two to five times as much as a wet suit, but with proper care and maintenance, a good dry suit will last many times longer than a wet suit. If you dive primarily in cold water, a dry suit is a good investment.

A dry suit creates a closed air space that is subject to squeezing. A low-pressure inflator valve, which is a standard feature, allows you to add air to the suit during descent to prevent suit squeeze. Because air expands during ascent, an exhaust valve is another standard feature. Get a dry suit that has a constant-volume exhaust valve that automatically maintains a constant state of buoyancy during ascent.

Diving is a diuretic activity—that is, it increases the amount of urine you produce. Urination in a wet suit is a regular practice by divers in open water, but the problem is more complex when you wear a dry suit. An optional feature for a dry suit is a relief zipper, which is useful only when you are out of the water.

Table 4.2 Dry Suits

Type	Advantages	Disadvantages
Foam neoprene	Form fitting and streamlined	Long drying time; hard to locate and repair leaks; buoyancy control difficult
Crushed neoprene	Durable; easy to repair; long lasting; less buoyant than foam neoprene	Less insulation than foam neoprene; expensive; somewhat bulky
Shell (two kinds) • Coated nylon • Rubberized fabric	Fast drying; easy to repair; nylon suits inexpensive; rubberized suits long lasting	Easily punctured; bulky; nylon suits do not last long; rubberized suits expensive

Divers wearing a dry suit have to exit the water to urinate, and those without a relief zipper must disrobe.

Several types of undergarments for dry suits are available. Some are inexpensive but compress with depth and lose insulating ability when wet. More expensive undergarments are highly resistant to compression and retain most of their insulating quality even if wet. Many divers who wear dry suits prefer to wear two layers of undergarments: a thin garment against the skin to carry perspiration away from the body and a thicker overgarment to provide the bulk of the insulation. Moisture conducts heat, so you are warmer when perspiration is wicked away from your body.

Dry suits have several drawbacks. Controlling buoyancy is more difficult with a dry suit than with a wet suit. Rapid, uncontrolled ascents can occur unless you control the suit. Training is essential before attempting to dive in a dry suit. Dry suits are bulkier than wet suits. It is easier to don and remove a dry suit than a wet suit, but the bulkiness of a dry suit makes surface swimming difficult. A dry suit also restricts your mobility more than a wet suit does. The inconveniences of a dry suit are of little consequence, however, when warmth is your primary concern.

Figure 4.16 Dry suits can be made from foam neoprene, crushed neoprene, or nylon.

Berenika Lychak/iStock/Getty Images

Dry Suit Accessories

Most dry suits have attached boots, a desirable feature. Thin latex booties are found on less expensive suits; more expensive suits have hard-soled boots. You should wear heavy socks for insulation with latex booties, and you must wear wet suit boots over the latex booties to protect them. The end result is that divers who wear dry suits usually need fins with large foot pockets.

You can wear neoprene gloves or mitts with a dry suit. If the water is extremely cold, you can get dry gloves with insulating liners that attach to some dry suits. An attached latex dry hood is an option for some models, but most divers use a separate neoprene dry suit hood. Figure 4.17 shows examples of dry suit accessories.

Dry Suit Care and Maintenance

Dry suits require more care than wet suits. The zipper and the control valves are expensive to replace, so do not allow salt crystals to form in the zipper or in the valves. Soak and rinse the zipper and valves in clean freshwater as soon as possible after a saltwater dive. Wash the neck and wrist seals with soapy water, and then rinse them. Coat latex seals with pure talc after they dry. The talc helps protect the rubber from the elements. Fold dry suits in half over a wide hanger for drying. Lubricate the suit zipper according to the manufacturer's instructions, then store the suit with the zipper open. If the suit needs to be repaired, have an authorized dealer make the repairs. As with wet suits, store your dry

Figure 4.17   Dry-suit boots and gloves help keep divers warm.

suit inside your home. The rubber seals on dry suits are adversely affected by exhaust emissions.

Exposure Suit Selection

You should consider many factors when selecting an exposure suit and accessories: your physical characteristics, where you intend to dive, how you intend to dive, how much diving you intend to do, and what you intend to do while diving. The amount of money you want to invest is also a factor, but keep in mind that buying an inexpensive suit may be false economy. If the suit does not meet your needs, you will have to spend more money for another suit.

The amount of diving you intend to do is an important factor. If you plan to make only one dive per day, your insulation requirements are not as great as they are if you plan to dive several times per day. The more time you plan to spend in the water, the warmer your suit needs to be.

If you are a thin person who gets chilled easily, you need more insulation than the average person for a given water temperature. People with more-than-average body fat may not require as much insulation as those with average body fat; fat is a good, natural insulator. Thermal comfort is essential for diving safety and enjoyment.

If you intend to do most of your diving in one area, the most popular type of suit in the area is probably the best type for you. If the local waters are cold, you have to choose between a wet suit and a dry suit. If you choose to get a wet suit as your first exposure suit for cold-water diving, a layered design with Farmer John pants, a vest, and a step-in jacket with an attached hood retains more warmth than high-waisted pants, a regular jacket, and a separate hood. A custom fit retains more warmth than a suit of a standard size.

Dry suits are not desirable for long surface swims because you can overheat, and the drag caused by the bulkiness of some dry suits may cause you to tire or cramp. On the other hand, dry suits retain much more warmth at depth than wet suits. If most of your diving will be deeper than 40 feet (12 m), if the water is 60 °F (15.6 °C) or colder, and if you can avoid long surface swims, a dry suit is a good choice—as long as you obtain training before using the suit.

If you plan to dive in a variety of climates, a spandex or thermoplastic suit combined with a neoprene wet suit may be a good option. You can wear different parts of the suits to meet different warmth requirements. Your diving activity affects your needs. An underwater hunter looking for game generates more body heat than an underwater photographer whose movements are minimal. The less active you are while diving, the more insulation you need. Your desires, needs, and budget determine the features you select for your exposure suit. When choosing features for your suit, you should consider the features that are popular with local experienced divers and diving leaders.

The accessories you select for your suit depend on the type of suit you choose, the temperature of the water, the activity you intend to pursue, and your budget. A hood may be thin and short for warmer water, thick with a long skirt for colder water, or a dry suit type. Foot coverings may be low cut, ankle high, or attached to the suit. The soles may be soft or hard. Hand coverings range from nothing to thick mitts, gauntlets, or dry gloves.

Local diving professionals can help with your selection of an exposure suit and accessories. No matter what type of exposure suit you choose, keep in mind that it is an investment in your enjoyment of diving. Diving is not fun if you get cold.

Weighting Systems

Exposure suits increase your buoyancy. You need weights for ballast in order to achieve neutral buoyancy. One type of weighting system is a weight belt (see figure 4.18); another type integrates the weights into the scuba unit.

Weights can be attached to or inserted into a belt that you wear around your waist. The belt is heavy nylon webbing two inches (five cm) wide. You can thread the belt through lead weights, wrap pouches of lead shot around the belt, or put weights or pouches of lead shot into pockets on pocket-type belts. A hollow fabric belt that you can fill with lead shot is more comfortable on your hips than hard weights. Lead shot, which comes in different sizes, causes less damage than hard lead weights if you drop the belt accidentally. Smaller-diameter shot weighs more per volume than larger shot, so the more weight you need, the smaller the shot you should use.

Because exposure suits compress with depth, a weight belt around your waist loosens unless it has a means of compensating for the suit compression. An

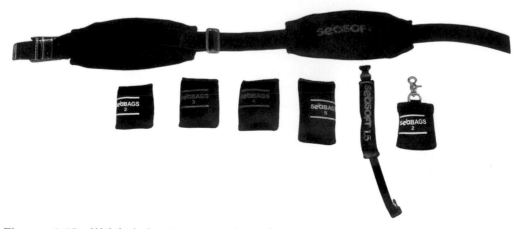

Figure 4.18 Weight belt with various sizes of weights.

elastic compensator is a desirable feature for a weight belt; you can select from a variety of designs.

Secure the weights on your weight belt so that they will not shift position. Pocket-type belts are good in this respect. When you thread separate weights onto a belt, you should secure the first and last weights with retainers, which are available as accessories.

The most important feature of any weighting system is the quick release. In the event of an emergency, you must discard weights quickly to establish positive buoyancy. No matter what type of system you choose, a reliable, easily located, and easily operated quick release is essential.

Several types of weights are available. Large, curved hip weights help offset the buoyancy of cold-water exposure suits. Smaller, rectangular weights find widespread use because they are economical. Coated weights are attractive and practical. Manufacturers mold weights into various shapes and offer a heavy vinyl coating as an option. The coating reduces pollution from lead, improves appearance, makes the weights easier to see in the water, and reduces suit abrasion. Fabric mesh packets filled with lead shot are popular. You can get bulk lead shot for hollow fabric belts. Coated lead shot, although slightly more expensive, is better than uncoated shot. Shot-filled tubular ankle weights are also available, although some diving experts believe ankle weights are unnecessary.

An integrated weighting system eliminates the need for a weight belt by holding lead weight in the **backpack** that holds the scuba cylinder or in the buoyancy compensator. An integrated weighting system makes the scuba unit heavier, but it also allows better distribution of weight than a separate system can provide. Some divers consider an integrated weighting system advantageous because weights are less likely to shift, a suit compression compensator is not needed, and having the weight above the waist improves the diver's trim in the water and reduces strain on the lower back. However, when you raise your center of gravity, you are more likely to lose your balance and fall when you are out of the water. You need strength, good balance, and caution to use an integrated weighting system. Integrated systems usually use lead shot, either in bulk or in pouches.

Weighting System Care and Maintenance

Weighting systems do not require as much care and maintenance as other items of diving equipment. Do not soak or rinse raw lead after use because lead in the runoff pollutes the environment. If gray water seeps from your weight system, replace the lead with new, coated lead. (You can recycle old lead, so do not throw it away.) Pocket-type weighting systems allow you to remove the weights and rinse the remainder of the system.

Regularly inspect the functional aspects, such as the quick release and the compensator. If you use a belt, inspect the weight retainers to make sure they are not broken, and make sure the end of the belt is clean and neat for easy insertion into the buckle. If the end of your belt is frayed, trim and singe it. When you fix a frayed end, be careful that you do not cut or burn yourself.

Weighting System Selection

When selecting a weighting system, you should consider your physical characteristics, the amount of weight you need, and how frequently you will need to change the amount of weight you use.

If you have a large build, your waist is larger than your hips, and your exposure suit is thick, a weight belt may not work well—especially if you need more than 30 pounds (13.6 kg) of weight. In chapter 6, you will learn how to test your buoyancy to determine the amount of weight that you need. Consult with divers whose physical characteristics are similar to yours for advice about weighting systems. If you require more than 30 pounds of weight, you may need weights on a weight belt plus an integrated system. If you require only a small amount of weight, nearly any type of weight system is acceptable.

If the type of diving you do varies, the amount of weight you need also varies. If you dive in freshwater and in saltwater, you need to adjust your weights. When you vary your exposure suit configuration, you also need to vary the amount of weight you wear. The more you need to change weights, the more you need a weighting system that allows changes to be made easily.

Buoyancy Compensators

A buoyancy compensator (BC) helps you control buoyancy. You can inflate your BC at the surface to increase buoyancy, deflate it to reduce buoyancy for descent, and add air to it to achieve neutral buoyancy underwater. Most BCs also contain a backpack to hold your scuba cylinder.

The three types of BCs are jacket style, back mounted, and front mounted (see table 4.3 for style comparison). Most BCs used in diving today have a wraparound jacket design, which provides front and rear buoyancy. There are two basic jacket designs: One style has inflation tubes over the shoulders; a newer style has straps over the shoulders. The straps have convenient, adjustable releases (see figure 4.19).

Figure 4.19 Jacket-style buoyancy compensator with shoulder straps and quick-release clasps.

Table 4.3 Buoyancy Compensators

Type	Location of buoyancy chamber	Advantages	Disadvantages
Jacket style	Front and rear	Even lift; diver can remain upright	Not suitable for skin diving
Back mounted	Rear	Does not interfere with valve operation for dry suits	Pushes diver forward; difficult for diver to remain upright
Front mounted	Front	Suitable for skin diving; allows diver to remain upright	Need separate backpack for cylinders; requires disconnection of inflator hose before removal; does not provide as much lift as jacket

Back-mounted BCs place buoyancy chambers behind you. These systems are useful for underwater modeling and for specialty diving activities. Models look better without bulky BCs covering them, and back-mounted units do not interfere with valve operation on dry suits as much as other types of BCs do.

Front-mounted BCs fit around your neck and cover your chest area. This was the first type of BC, but few divers use front-mounted BCs today. Most divers today believe that BC jackets are superior to front-mounted ones. You can use a front-mounted BC for both skin diving and scuba diving. Jacket-style and back-mounted BCs are not suitable for skin diving.

In its simplest form, a BC is a bladder with attachments (see figure 4.20). The bladder may be coated material that constitutes the BC itself, or a separate bladder may be inside a fabric shell. The seams of a BC bladder are glued or electronically welded, depending on the type of material.

Buoyancy Compensator Selection

When selecting a BC, you should consider your physical characteristics, where you plan to dive, and the type of diving you plan to do. Some BCs provide more buoyancy than others. A cold-water diver wearing a wet suit needs more lift than a warm-water diver wearing a thin exposure suit, although a large amount of lift is not necessarily desirable.

If you are a large, strong individual, the size and bulk of a BC may not be of much concern. But if you are small, you may be wise to choose a small, compact BC. The length of the BC is important. If the BC extends downward too far, this makes donning and removing your weight belt difficult. If you are shortwaisted, consider an integrated weighting system. The fit is important because a BC needs

Figure 4.20   Desirable BC features.

to support you in the water. The BC should fit snugly and not ride up on your body. Models that allow adjustment for a custom fit are desirable.

Another desirable feature is a single-bladder construction, which is less expensive and requires less maintenance than a separate bladder. Renting and using different types of BCs will aid you in making a selection. Talk to experienced divers and diving professionals, and observe BC preferences in the area where you dive.

Buoyancy Compensator Care and Maintenance

Your investment in a BC is large. But, like most diving equipment, your BC will provide years of service if you take care of it. You need to rinse your BC inside and out after use, especially after use in a swimming pool or in the ocean. Chlorine in pool water and salt crystals from seawater are harmful to your BC. Drain the water from your BC after use, fill it about a third full with freshwater, swish the water around, and then drain the bladder. Rinse the inflator assembly thoroughly, and leave the BC fully inflated until it dries. Inflation will test the airtight integrity of the bladder and valves. If the BC does not remain firm for

Diving Equipment Checklist

✓ Mask, snorkel, and snorkel keeper
✓ Fins and boots
✓ Scuba tank (filled)
✓ Buoyancy compensator
✓ Exposure suit, hood, and gloves
✓ Weight system
✓ Regulator with pressure gauge
✓ Alternate air source
✓ Instruments to monitor depth, time, and direction (separate or integrated)

✓ Signaling devices (whistle, mirror, safety tube)
✓ Dive knife
✓ Float, dive flag, and anchor
✓ Dive tables
✓ Dive light
✓ Slate and pencil
✓ Marker buoy
✓ Collecting bag
✓ Gear bag

Spare equipment

✓ Scuba tank(s)
✓ Weights
✓ Straps
✓ O-rings
✓ Snorkel keeper

Secondary equipment

✓ First aid kit
✓ Emergency phone numbers and radio frequencies
✓ Logbook
✓ Swimsuit
✓ Towel

✓ Jacket
✓ Hat or visor
✓ Sunglasses
✓ Dive kit
✓ Save-a-dive kit
✓ Drinking water

at least an hour, take it to a professional repair facility. Anytime your BC fails to function properly, have it professionally repaired. It is hazardous to attempt BC repairs without special training, tools, and parts.

Scuba Cylinders

A scuba cylinder stores compressed air at high pressure. The container must be strong and free of corrosion. Scuba cylinders (also called tanks) are made of either aluminum or steel. Each type has advantages and disadvantages. Figure 4.21 shows examples of various steel and aluminum tanks.

Figure 4.21 Scuba cylinders come in many sizes and are made of steel or aluminum.

Steel Cylinders

Steel scuba cylinders come in various sizes with various pressure ratings. Common sizes are 63, 71.2, 80, and 100 cubic feet (1,784, 2,016, 2,265, and 2,832 L). The pressure to which the cylinders can be filled, called the working pressure, ranges from 1,800 to more than 4,000 pounds per square inch (psi), or 122 to 272 standard atmospheres (atm).

Some compressors pump air only to 2,500 psi (170 atm). When you cannot get air at a pressure higher than 2,500 psi, a steel tank may be more desirable than an aluminum tank. A steel 71.2-cubic foot scuba tank filled to 2,250 psi (153 atm) contains about 5 cubic feet (142 L) more air than an 80-cubic-foot aluminum tank filled to the same pressure. The aluminum tank must be filled to 3,000 psi (204 atm) to obtain 80 cubic feet.

The main disadvantage of a steel cylinder is that it can rust, which can render a tank unsafe and unusable. Do not allow water inside a scuba cylinder. The high-pressure atmosphere has a large amount of oxygen to fuel corrosion. You can keep the inside of a steel scuba tank dry, but the outside is exposed to moisture. Galvanizing inhibits rust on the outside of steel tanks, but the inside may not be galvanized because galvanization affects air purity. Painting a galvanized surface may improve the appearance of a cylinder, but paint alone is an inadequate finish because cracks or chips in the paint allow moisture to reach the steel. The tank will begin to rust unless there is a galvanized coating beneath the paint.

Another disadvantage of a steel scuba tank is that it has a rounded bottom because of the manufacturing process. The tank cannot stand by itself unless you place a rubber or plastic boot, called a tank boot, on the end of the cylinder. The boot makes the base of the tank flat so it will stand. Some boots have flat sides to help keep a tank from rolling when you lay the cylinder on its side. Moisture and salt trapped between the tank boot and the cylinder can cause corrosion. Boots with internal ridges—the preferred type of boot—are self-draining.

Aluminum Cylinders

Aluminum alloy cylinders also come in various sizes with various pressure ratings. Common sizes are 63, 80, and 100 cubic feet (1,784, 2,265, and 2,832 L). The working pressure for aluminum cylinders is 3,300 psi (224 atm).

Aluminum corrodes, but the oxide that forms arrests the corrosive process—this is a significant advantage over the corrosive process of rust in steel tanks. Rust is an accelerating process, but corrosion in an aluminum cylinder is a self-arresting process.

The bottom of an aluminum cylinder is flat. You do not need a tank boot on the cylinder to allow it to stand by itself, but many divers put boots on aluminum tanks to protect the tank and any objects struck by the bottoms of the cylinders.

Aluminum cylinders also have drawbacks. Aluminum is softer than steel, so aluminum tanks can be dented and gouged more easily than steel tanks. On aluminum tanks, brass cylinder valves control the flow of air. Electrolytic action between the dissimilar metals of the cylinder and the valve can cause the valve to seize in the aluminum cylinder threads unless the valve is removed periodically and coated with a special compound. Valve seizing seldom is a problem with steel cylinders.

Aluminum cylinders do not need to be galvanized. You can paint them to improve appearance, but do not bake the paint finish. Temperatures hotter than 180 °F (82.2 °C) reduce the strength of an aluminum cylinder and can cause it to explode when filled. If you would like your cylinder painted, have it done by a professional tank-painting service.

Cylinder Markings

Several rows of markings on the neck of a scuba cylinder provide useful information about the cylinder. You should be able to determine the meaning of several of the marks. Figure 4.22 shows an example of cylinder neck markings.

The first row of marks on tanks manufactured in the United States discloses the government agency that sanctioned the manufacture of the tank, the type of metal from which the tank was made, from, and the working pressure. The first letters in the row identify the government agency, such as DOT (U.S.

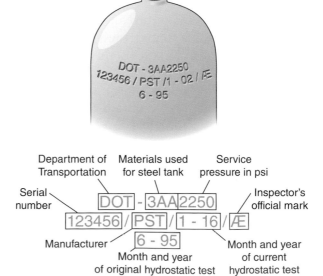

Figure 4.22 Cylinder neck markings.

Department of Transportation), CTC/DOT (Canadian Transportation Commission and the U.S. Department of Transportation), or ICC (the former U.S. Interstate Commerce Commission). The next characters in the first row identify the type of metal that the tank was made from. The marks 3A and 3AA are designations for steel cylinders. The marks 3AL, E 6498, and SP6498 are designations for aluminum cylinders. The final figures in the first row—the important ones for you to remember—are numbers indicating the working pressure of the cylinder in pounds per square inch.

The second row of markings includes the serial number of the tank (which you should record for identification purposes) and letters or numbers identifying the manufacturer of the cylinder. The month and year of the tank's first pressure test are located somewhere below the second row. U.S. regulations require compressed gas cylinders to be pressure-tested before being put into service and every five years thereafter. Subsequent test dates can be stamped anywhere on the neck of the tank. A registered symbol between the month and year of a pressure test identifies the facility that did the testing.

Tanks are filled at an air (or "fill") station (see figure 4.23). When you take your cylinder to an air station for filling, the facility personnel will examine the tank markings to determine whether the cylinder test date is current and to identify the pressure to which the tank can be filled.

Cylinder Selection

The main criteria for the selection of diving equipment—fit and comfort—apply to scuba tanks as well. A small person should use a small tank. Larger divers may require larger tanks because they have larger lungs and use more air.

The material from which a tank is made affects its capacity, size, and working pressure. Although steel is heavier than aluminum, aluminum tanks are larger and heavier than steel tanks with similar capacities. Because aluminum is not as strong as steel, the walls of an aluminum tank are thicker than the walls of a steel tank of approximately the same capacity. The higher the pressure rating, the greater the capacity of a tank of a given size. Modern high-pressure steel scuba tanks are high-capacity cylinders, but they are quite heavy. Good sizes for small divers to consider for an initial scuba tank are 50 and 63 cubic feet (1,416 and 1,784 L). Popular sizes for divers of average size are 71.2 and 80 cubic feet (2,016 and 2,265 L).

Another important factor to consider when selecting a scuba tank is the buoyancy of the cylinder, which is determined by the volume and weight of the tank. Aluminum tanks are more buoyant than steel tanks. High-capacity tanks have a greater change in buoyancy than smaller cylinders as you use air from them. The change in buoyancy between a full and an empty tank can vary by more than 8 pounds (3.6 kg; see table 4.4). Some tanks are negatively buoyant

Figure 4.23 Scuba cylinder filling station.

Table 4.4 Cylinder Size, Working Pressure, and Buoyancy

Capacity (ft³/L)	Working pressure (psi)	Buoyancy (lb) from full to empty
Aluminum 50/1,416	3,000	–2.7 to +1.3
Aluminum 63/1,784	3,000	–2.3 to +2.7
Steel 71.2/2,016	2,250	–2.0 to +3.6
Aluminum 80/2,265	3,000	–2.0 to +4.4
Steel 76/2,152	2,400	–6.5 to –0.1
Steel 80/2,265	3,500	–7.4 to –1.0
Steel 102/2,888	3,500	–7.6 to +0.5

whether full or empty, but most tanks sink when full and float when empty. Buoyancy for tanks varies so much that you should select the tank most often used for diving in your area or try diving with several different tanks to determine which is easiest to manage.

You need to decide whether you are going to dive using compressed air, enriched-air nitrox, or mixed gases. If your breathing gas is anything other than compressed air, your cylinder, cylinder valve, and regulator must be dedicated to the specialized gas. It is unsafe to use a compressed air cylinder and regulator with mixed gases. Regulators, valves, and cylinders must be "oxygen clean" and "oxygen safe" when used with mixed gases.

Multiple-tank scuba units are used for specialty applications. As a beginning diver, you do not need double or triple scuba tanks. A single tank is adequate for most diving activities.

Cylinder Accessories

Fabric or plastic sleeves can help protect the exterior of your scuba cylinder. Some sleeves have places to attach items within easy reach. Tank bands, which secure a cylinder to a buoyancy compensator, vary. Some allow you to attach a small, backup scuba cylinder to your main cylinder. Additional accessories are available to help you carry or transport your scuba cylinders. Tank boots are a desirable cylinder accessory.

Cylinder Care and Maintenance

Scuba tanks are high-pressure vessels. They are strong, but you should handle them with care. Exterior damage can render your scuba tank useless. Avoid throwing scuba tanks or allowing them to roll about on the deck of a boat or in the trunk of your car. Secure cylinders for transportation or storage. Unless you are holding a scuba cylinder, do not leave it standing in an upright position, especially at a dive site. If the cylinder falls, it can injure someone or damage the tank valve or regulator. However, you should store your scuba tanks in an upright position so that any moisture inside will settle to the bottom where inspectors can detect it with relative ease. Rinse the outside of your cylinder with clean, fresh water after use, and pay special attention to the boot area of steel tanks.

Corrosion can ruin a cylinder rapidly, and pieces of corrosion can damage a tank valve or scuba regulator. One way to prevent moisture from entering a tank is to keep air in the tank. Water can get into an empty scuba cylinder while you are diving, so avoid using all the air in your tank. Moisture can enter an empty tank if you store it with the valve open. Store your scuba cylinder with a few hundred pounds (about 20 atm) of pressure inside. A low pressure keeps moisture out but provides little oxygen to aid corrosion if there is moisture in the tank.

The filling process can force water into the tank. A water trap in an air compressor is supposed to remove moisture from air, but if the moisture-removal system does not function properly, water can be pumped into your tank along with air. The filling hose attachments for scuba tanks can get wet, and water inside the filling attachments can be forced into your cylinder. Using a high-quality air station is important.

The diving industry requires an annual visual inspection of scuba cylinders. The examination consists of an external inspection, the removal of the valve from a cylinder, an internal inspection using a special light, special electrical testing for aluminum cylinders, the replacement of the valve, and the attachment of a decal indicating the inspection date. Most air stations require a current inspection sticker on a tank before they will fill it. When you handle your scuba tank, listen for sounds of anything moving inside the cylinder. If you hear anything, have the tank visually inspected.

U.S. government regulations specify that compressed gas cylinders must be pressure-tested every five years. Some countries require pressure testing every year or two. The test is hydrostatic because it takes place in water. An inspector fills a scuba tank with water and submerges it in a closed container that is completely filled with water. The inspector applies pressure to the scuba tank hydraulically, and the tank expands slightly from the pressure. The expansion displaces water from the container holding the scuba tank. The inspector measures the expansion and then releases the pressure. The tank must return to within 10 percent of its original volume within a specified period of time. If the tank is too brittle to expand and contract correctly, the inspector condemns it.

You may transport a scuba tank on an airplane only if the tank is completely empty and the valve is open—a situation that is not good for scuba tanks. Do not transport your cylinder by air. Diving destinations have tanks readily available, so there is no need to take a tank on a dive trip.

Cylinder Valves

Cylinder valves control the flow of a liquid or gas. Four types of valves are available for scuba tanks: the simple valve, the reserve valve, the high-pressure valve, and the multiple-cylinder valve. Because multiple tanks are for advanced specialty diving activities, this section addresses only the simple and high-pressure valves.

Simple Valve

A simple valve is an on-off valve that operates like a faucet. You turn the valve handle counterclockwise to open it and clockwise to close it. The first catalog of diving equipment listed this type of valve as item K, and the valve has been identified as a **K-valve** ever since (see figure 4.24).

The **valve seat** is a soft-sealing surface. It is the portion of the valve that closes and stops the flow of air. You can damage the seat with excessive closing pressure.

Valves for scuba tanks have several features, one of which is a snorkel tube that extends from the bottom of the valve into the scuba cylinder. The valve snorkel prevents moisture or particles from entering the valve when you invert the tank. Another standard feature of tank valves is a thin, metal disk called a **burst disk**. If a tank is overfilled or the heat from a fire causes the tank pressure to increase to a hazardous level, the disk will burst and vent the tank to prevent an explosion. The disks corrode over time, and occasionally a burst disk ruptures. The failure makes a loud noise, and the tank hisses loudly, but the situation is not dangerous (even if it occurs while you are diving, which is unlikely). If the burst disk in your tank valve ruptures, you need to have the valve serviced professionally. Manufacturers rate burst disks for various pressures, and the correct disk must be used. Keep the pressure rating of the burst disk in mind if you want to change a valve from one scuba tank to another. A valve with a low-pressure burst disk will rupture if you use it on a tank with a higher pressure rating.

Figure 4.24　K-valve.

There are two types of outlets for scuba tank valves. The traditional outlet is nearly flush with the surface of the valve and surrounded by a soft, circular ring called an **O-ring**. The ring forms the high-pressure seal between the valve and the scuba regulator, so the ring must be clean and free of nicks or cuts. A newer type of threaded outlet with a recessed O-ring seal is a **DIN valve**, which withstands higher pressures than a traditional O-ring valve (see figure 4.25). Tank pressures in excess of 3,000 psi (204 atm) require a DIN fitting.

Figure 4.25　Close-up of a DIN valve.

Reserve Valve

A **J-valve** (the valve was listed as item J in the first equipment catalog) was designed to maintain a reserve of air to permit a normal ascent. The introduction of **submersible pressure gauges** (SPGs) for scuba tanks has rendered the J-valve obsolete.

The reserve lever on a J-valve created problems. If the lever was in the incorrect position (down), the valve would not maintain a reserve. If the diver failed to put the reserve lever in the up position before a dive or if the lever was bumped during a dive, the diver relied on a reserve of air that was not available. Safety concerns also contributed to the demise of the J-valve.

Valve Care and Maintenance

Cylinder valves are made of soft metal and have thin areas, so physical abuse can ruin them. A protective cap is a good accessory for a tank valve. The cap helps prevent loss of the O-ring, helps keep dirt out of the valve, and helps prevent physical damage to the high-pressure sealing surface around the valve opening. Protection of the valve is one reason that you should secure scuba tanks when you store them and should not leave them standing unattended. If a tank rolls about or falls over, this can damage the valve and render it inoperable.

When you open a tank valve, you should turn it slowly, open it all the way, and then close it one half turn. If something strikes the handle, a valve seat that is fully open will be damaged more than if it were closed slightly. When you close the valve, avoid excessive force, which shortens the life of the valve seat.

Rinsing your tank valve after use is a good idea, but soaking the valve by inverting your scuba tank in a container of warm water is better than rinsing. Water remains in the valve opening after rinsing or soaking. Open the valve momentarily to blow the water from the opening. If you leave the water in the opening and have the tank filled before the water evaporates, moisture will be forced into the tank.

Have your tank valve serviced annually by a professional. Also have your valve professionally serviced anytime it fails to operate easily or when the burst disk needs to be replaced. Valves receive partial servicing (lubrication) during the annual visual inspection of your scuba tank. The large O-ring that seals the valve to the scuba tank can be replaced at the time of the visual inspection. But partial servicing of your valve during a tank inspection is not the annual servicing of the valve. In a complete valve servicing, a qualified repair technician completely disassembles the valve, cleans the parts, replaces various parts, reassembles the valve, and then tests the unit.

Scuba Regulators

The function of a regulator is to reduce high-pressure air to a breathable level. Most scuba regulators use two **stages** of pressure reduction. The first stage of a regulator attaches to the valve of a scuba cylinder and reduces the high pressure to an intermediate pressure of about 140 psi (9.5 atm). The first stage of the regulator connects via a hose to the second stage, which contains the mouthpiece. The second stage reduces the pressure from the intermediate level to the surrounding pressure. A scuba regulator is a demand system; it delivers air only when you demand it by inhaling, unlike a constant-delivery, free-flow system, which commercial divers use. Scuba regulators are highly reliable and have a fail-safe design that turns the demand system into a free-flow system in the event of a component failure. Figure 4.26 provides more information about scuba regulator terms.

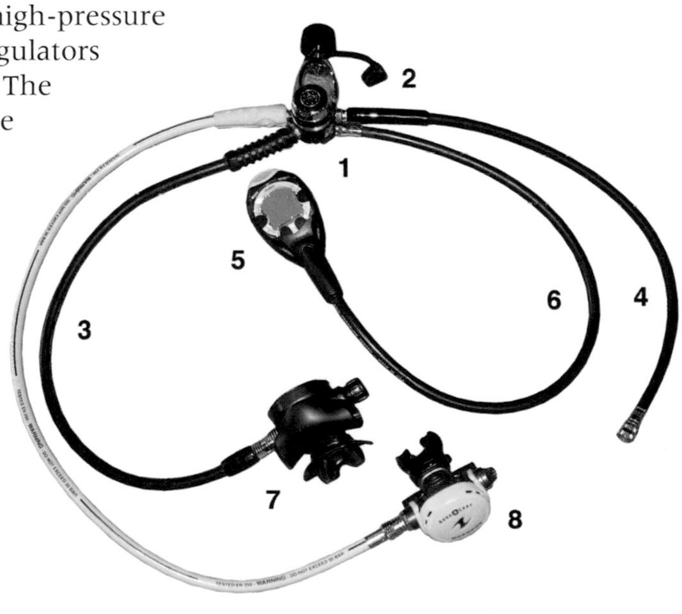

Figure 4.26 Scuba regulator nomenclature: (1) first stage, (2) dust cover, (3) low-pressure hose, (4) low-pressure inflator hose, (5) console, (6) high-pressure hose, (7) primary second stage, (8) extra second stage.

First Stages

The first stages on scuba regulators are either balanced or unbalanced. Changes in tank pressure affect the performance of a balanced first stage only slightly. With an unbalanced first stage, the performance of the regulator changes as tank pressure changes, so a balanced first stage is desirable.

The two main types of valves for the first stages of regulators are diaphragm and piston (see figure 4.27). A diaphragm first stage has a diaphragm that keeps water and dirt from the working parts inside. A bias spring combined with water pressure pushes the valve open. Tank pressure closes the valve when the first-stage pressure equals intermediate pressure plus water pressure. A diaphragm valve has more parts than a piston first stage, so it is more expensive to manufacture and service. The diaphragm valve's exclusion of water and dirt from the mechanics allows high performance for longer periods of time than a piston valve.

Piston first stages have an open, simple design with few moving parts. Water pressure in direct contact with the piston combines with the force of a bias spring to open the piston valve. Tank pressure causes the piston to move and the valve to close when the first-stage pressure equals intermediate pressure plus water pressure. Piston first stages are easier and less expensive to service than diaphragm first stages. But dirt, salt crystals, and mineral deposits that accumulate

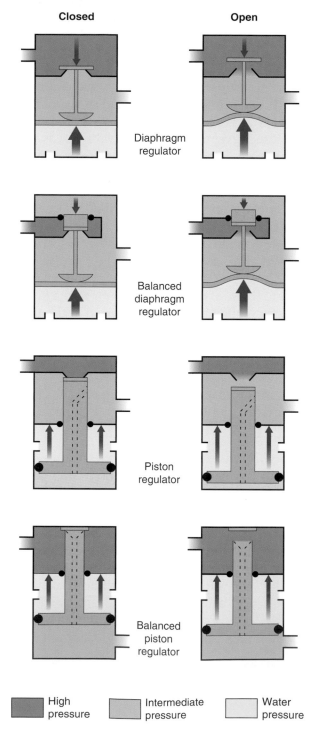

Figure 4.27 Typical regulator first stages. Red arrows represent spring pressure. Black dots represent O-rings.

inside a piston regulator can affect its performance. Each type of first stage has advantages and disadvantages, so either type is acceptable. A diaphragm-piston regulator combines the diaphragm and piston concepts. The diaphragm excludes water and dirt and transfers pressure to a piston.

A first stage must have a means of attachment to the tank valve. A typical regulator has a yoke that surrounds the valve and mates the regulator to the tank valve. The regulator inlet, which has an inlet filter, secures to a tank with a yoke screw. Scuba regulators that operate at above-average pressures use a DIN fitting instead of a yoke screw. A DIN fitting screws directly into a DIN valve and does not have a yoke.

First stages include multiple openings called **ports**. One of the ports is for high-pressure air measurement with an SPG. The remaining ports are for low-pressure air. A regulator should have several low-pressure ports to supply air to the primary second stage, an alternate second stage, a BC inflator, and possibly a dry suit inflator. The sizes of ports vary. The high-pressure port is usually larger than the low-pressure openings. This helps prevent connection errors; a low-pressure hose inadvertently connected to the high-pressure port would rupture.

Some regulators feature environmental shielding by sealing special fluid inside a flexible chamber attached to the first stage. The sealed, flexible chamber transmits water pressure to the regulator, but no water, salt, or dirt can enter the first stage. Extremely cold water can cause an unshielded regulator to freeze, but the fluid in an environmental chamber does not freeze.

Second Stages

The most common second stage is shaped like a cup lying on one side (see figure 4.28). Imagine a pliable diaphragm across the top of the cup, a mouthpiece attached to the bottom of the cup, and an exhaust valve attached to the lower side. A lever that activates a valve inside the container is in contact with a static diaphragm. An inhalation through the mouthpiece creates a partial vacuum inside the second stage. The pressure reduction pulls in the diaphragm, which moves the lever and opens the valve, allowing air to flow from the first stage

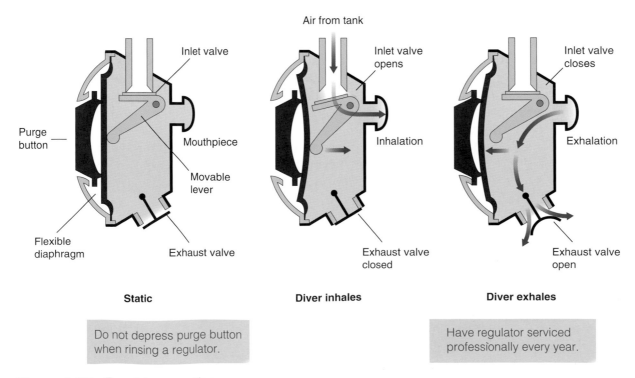

Do not depress purge button when rinsing a regulator.

Have regulator serviced professionally every year.

Figure 4.28 **Regulator operation.**

of the regulator into the second stage. When you stop inhaling, the buildup of pressure returns the diaphragm and lever to their normal positions, closing the valve and stopping the flow of air. When you begin to exhale, increased pressure inside the second stage opens the exhaust valve, allowing air to escape.

The two types of second-stage valves for scuba regulators are the downstream valve and the pilot valve. In a downstream-valve regulator, a small bias spring holds a valve closed. Inhalation moves the diaphragm, which moves a lever. The lever movement overcomes the resistance of the bias spring and opens a valve, allowing intermediate-pressure air to enter the second stage. After inhalation, air flows until the diaphragm moves outward, allowing the bias spring to close the valve. Downstream second-stage valves are simple and inexpensive, and they tolerate more sand and dirt than pilot valves do.

In a pilot-valve regulator, the movement of the diaphragm in the second stage opens a small valve that in turn opens a larger valve. When you stop inhaling from the regulator, the diaphragm returns to its normal position, and the valves close. A pilot valve delivers air up to four times more easily than a downstream valve. But pilot valves are more expensive to manufacture and service than downstream valves, and in shallow water, you may experience the effect of shuddering air movement with a pilot-valve regulator.

All regulators have a purge button or area on the regulator that you depress to manually open the second-stage valve. Use the purge to test the regulator, to expel water and debris from inside the second stage, and to relieve the pressure in the regulator after you close the tank valve.

The location of the exhaust valve varies. The exhaust valve may be at the bottom, the side, or the front of the second stage. The position of the exhaust affects the bubble pattern and the clearing of the regulator when it has water inside and the mouthpiece is in your mouth. Some regulators direct exhaust bubbles by means of an exhaust tee. You will learn more about regulator positioning for clearing in chapter 6.

A regulator is either right-handed, left-handed, or bidirectional, referring to the direction from which the regulator hose must come when the regulator is in your mouth. For example, the hose must come from the right side when you are using a right-handed regulator. The hose may come from either side when you are using a bidirectional regulator. The directional configuration is important only for knowing how to orient the regulator when you place it in your mouth. Figure 4.29 shows the possible directional configurations.

Some second-stage casings feature strong, light, durable materials that do not bend or corrode as metal does. Several types and styles of mouthpieces are available. Use a soft, comfortable mouthpiece that does not cause jaw fatigue. A repair technician can replace mouthpieces quickly and easily.

Figure 4.29 Scuba regulators have different configurations.

Regulator Accessories

A regulator hose is flexible but has rigid metal connectors crimped onto the ends. The points where the hose and the metal meet are stress points because the hose fibers strain against an unyielding surface. To prevent the breakdown of the hose fibers at the stress points, you should use hose protector sleeves. At a minimum, equip all regulator hoses with hose protectors at the first-stage end of each hose.

Padded regulator bags help protect your regulator during transportation or storage. The bag should be large enough to accommodate the regulator and all hoses without bending the hoses sharply.

Adapters allow you to use DIN-fitting regulators on standard cylinder valves. Use protective covers for the threads on DIN fittings.

Purge depressors are a built-in feature on some regulators and an accessory for regulators that do not have them. A purge depressor partially depresses the purge button to remove bias spring pressure from the second-stage valve when you are not using the regulator, thus extending the life of the valve seat.

Colored second-stage covers allow you to color-coordinate your regulator with your other equipment. Other accessories include various mouthpieces and hose adapters (as previously mentioned).

Regulator Selection

It takes effort to inhale and exhale through a scuba regulator. Effort is needed to overcome resistance; good regulators have minimal breathing resistance. Compare the performance data for various regulators, and select one that lets you breathe easily over a wide range of tank pressures, which implies a balanced first stage.

Choose a widely used and easily serviced regulator. You should get a regulator that can be serviced by facilities anywhere you happen to be and that uses readily available parts.

The type of diving you do should affect your selection. If you plan to do most of your diving from shore, you should avoid a pilot-valve second stage, which is adversely affected by sand and dirt. Diaphragm first stages are a better choice if most of your diving is from shore.

If you do not have a scuba tank, consider purchasing the tank and regulator at the same time so that you can match the fittings of the regulator and the cylinder valve. If you will be diving in water that is near freezing, you should select an environmentally shielded regulator. Remember that enriched-air nitrox and mixed gases require specially cleaned and dedicated regulators.

Regulator Care and Maintenance

Your regulator is a precision instrument; it requires care and maintenance to ensure the best possible performance. Keep sand and dirt out of your regulator. Do not allow salt crystals to form inside. Soak your regulator in clean, fresh, warm freshwater as soon as possible after diving in the ocean. You need to remove salt before it dries. If you cannot soak your regulator, you should at least rinse it. A combination of soaking and rinsing is best. Follow these rules when rinsing or soaking a regulator:

○ *Keep the inside of the first stage dry.* The purpose of the dust cover on the first stage is to keep out water and dust. Develop the habit of replacing the dust cover and securing it in place with the yoke screw anytime you do not have the regulator attached to a tank. Make certain the dust cover is in place before you rinse or soak a regulator.

○ *Allow low-pressure water to flow gently through the second stage and also into the openings on the first stage.* High-pressure water can force dirt or grit into crevices, where it causes damage. Gentle pressure washes the dirt away.

○ *Do not press the purge button when you rinse the second stage unless the regulator is pressurized.* If you do not pressurize the regulator and you press the purge button while water is inside the second stage, you open the second-stage valve and allow water to flow through the hose into the first stage.

When the regulator has dried thoroughly, lay it flat for storage. For prolonged storage, place the regulator in a plastic bag to help protect it against the harmful effects of smog. Do not bend the hoses sharply because bending damages hose fibers. Replace hoses that are cut, bulging, or leaking.

You can avoid most problems with your regulator by having it serviced annually. Have your regulator serviced even if it seems to be functioning properly. Failure to invest in regular service can affect your safety and shorten the life of your regulator.

Alternate Air Sources

Several equipment options can help if you run out of air underwater (although running out of air is due only to sheer negligence). Your best option is an alternate air source (AAS), which is a source of compressed air other than your primary scuba regulator. An AAS is valuable if your primary source of air begins free-flowing or leaking during a dive; you can switch to the AAS and make a normal ascent. The two primary types of alternate air sources are extra second stages and backup scuba units. An extra second stage allows two divers to share air without passing a single mouthpiece back and forth. Backup scuba units are fully redundant scuba systems that provide an independent source of air in an emergency. You are not dependent on a buddy to provide air when you are equipped with a backup system. Extra second stages are less expensive than backup scuba units but do not provide the benefits of an independent scuba system.

Extra Second Stages

Two types of extra second stages are available. The first is an extra second stage for your regulator; the second is a BC low-pressure inflator that has an integrated regulator second stage (see figure 4.30). An extra second stage, or **octopus**, should meet the following criteria:

○ The first stage of the regulator should be capable of meeting the airflow demands of two second stages.

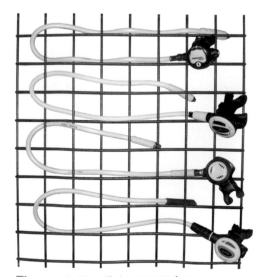

Figure 4.30 **Extra second stages.**

o The hose on the extra second stage should be several inches longer than the hose on the primary second stage.

o The extra second stage should attach to your chest area in such a way that your buddy can remove it quickly and easily. Do not allow the extra second stage to dangle.

o The attachment device should cover the mouthpiece opening of the extra second stage to prevent the regulator from free-flowing and to keep dirt and debris from getting inside.

o The extra second stage should be brightly colored for easy identification.

A regulator second stage may be integrated into a BC low-pressure inflator in one of two ways. The BC inflator can have a built-in regulator second stage, or quick-release hose fittings on the regulator second stage can allow it to be connected in series in the low-pressure hose leading to the inflator assembly. Both types of extra second stages have advantages and disadvantages. An integrated second stage requires one less hose on your regulator because a single hose provides air for both the extra second stage and the BC inflator. When you must share air and you have an integrated second stage, you must breathe from the integrated second stage because the hose is too short for your buddy to use. With an extra second stage, you or your buddy can use either air source. Extra second stages integrated into the BC inflator may leak air. To stop a leak, you must disconnect the low-pressure air, thereby losing the functions of the low-pressure inflator and the extra second stage.

Backup Scuba Units

Two types of backup scuba units are available. A **pony tank** is a small (about 13- to 20-cubic-foot, or 368 to 566 L) scuba cylinder with a separate, standard regulator. You clamp a pony tank to the side of your main scuba cylinder. A **Spare Air unit** is a smaller (2 to 4 cubic foot, or 57 to 113 L) scuba cylinder with a special regulator integrated directly into the valve. A pony tank provides an adequate supply of air for many situations, but a Spare Air unit provides only enough air to permit an ascent from shallow depths. On the other hand, a Spare Air unit is small and light, whereas a pony tank is bulky and heavy (see figure 4.31).

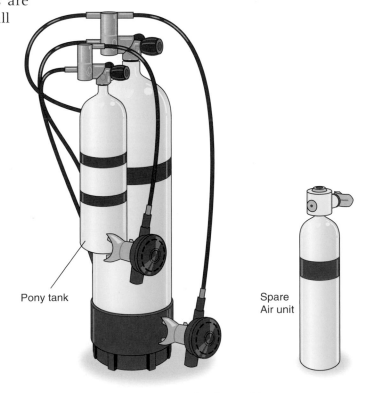

Pony tank

Spare Air unit

Figure 4.31 A pony tank and a Spare Air unit.

Alternate Air Source Care and Maintenance

AAS equipment should receive the same care and maintenance as your primary scuba equipment. Some divers attempt to save money by having only their primary scuba equipment serviced annually. This is false economy. AAS equipment needs servicing just as much as primary scuba equipment does.

Instrumentation

You move in three dimensions in water the way a pilot does in air. Instruments are important safety requirements for flying. A pilot needs information about altitude, direction, time, and amount of fuel remaining. Similarly, you need information about depth, direction, time, and amount of air remaining. The minimum instrumentation you need is a depth gauge, an underwater timer, a submersible pressure gauge (SPG), and a compass. A dive computer is highly recommended. All required instrumentation can be provided by a single integrated device.

Depth Gauges

To tell how deep you have descended, you can use one of four types of depth gauges: a **capillary gauge**, a **Bourdon tube**, a diaphragm gauge, or an electronic gauge. Manufacturers calibrate depth gauges in seawater. Most mechanical gauges do not indicate the correct depth in freshwater, but they indicate the equivalent seawater depth if you use them starting at sea level in freshwater or if they adjust for altitude pressure changes. The reading of gauges in freshwater is acceptable because tables for time limits at various depths are based on sea-level depths. Table 4.5 compares the four types of depth gauges.

A capillary depth gauge is a simple instrument. It is a hollow, air-filled, transparent plastic tube sealed at one end and placed around a circular dial. The open end of the tube aligns with zero on the gauge dial. A capillary gauge uses the principle of **Boyle's law**. Water pressure compresses the air inside the tube during descent. The position of the air–water interface inside the tube relative

Table 4.5 Depth Gauges

Type	Accuracy	Advantages	Disadvantages
Capillary	Accurate only to depth of about 40 ft (12 m)	Rugged, inexpensive	Can clog with debris or air bubbles
Bourdon tube	Reading accurate within 1% to 2%	Accurate	Can be damaged by reduced pressure at altitude
Diaphragm	Very accurate	Can adjust zero setting for pressure changes at altitude	Expensive
Electronic	Reading accurate within 6 in. (15 cm)	Gauge may zero itself to compensate for changes in atmospheric pressure	Must have sufficient battery power; expensive

to markings on the dial indicates the depth. At two atmospheres of pressure, the air column in the tube compresses to one half its original length.

A Bourdon tube is a thin metal tube formed into a spiral. The tube may be open to the water, or it may be closed and placed inside a housing filled with oil. Oil-filled Bourdon gauges are more popular than open-tube gauges. Pressure on an open-tube gauge begins to straighten the tube and increases the coil diameter. The straightening produces a spiral movement of the tube, which is linked mechanically to a needle to indicate the depth. Water pressure causes the coil of a closed-tube gauge to decrease in diameter. The movement of the coil, linked mechanically to a needle, indicates the amount of pressure exerted on the gauge.

The accurate but expensive diaphragm gauge uses elaborate mechanics to connect a thin, movable diaphragm to an indicating needle. Electronic depth gauges, also accurate and expensive, use a pressure sensor (transducer), electrical circuitry, a display, and a battery to indicate depth.

A maximum-depth indicator is a desirable feature for depth gauges. As you will learn in chapter 7, you must know the depth of a dive for planning purposes. A digital depth gauge retains the maximum depth you attain. The instrument displays the information until the next dive or for 12 or more hours after a dive; it then resets automatically. Many modern depth gauges with needle displays have a thin indicating wire that the gauge needle pushes along the dial face. When the needle retreats, the wire remains at the highest point reached on the dial. You can reset the indicating wire by turning a screw on the dial face. When you use this type of gauge, you must remember to reset the maximum-depth indicator before each dive.

Underwater Timers

You can use either an automatic or a manual underwater timer to keep track of time during a dive. Either type may indicate time with hands on a dial or with a digital display. Pressure activates automatic timers, which start timing at a depth of about 3 to 5 feet (1 to 1.5 m) and stop timing when the depth is less than that. Automatic timers are better than watches because you do not have to remember to start or stop the timing of your dive, although you have to reset some watch-type automatic timers before a dive. Waterproof watches that you can use as underwater timers usually feature a rotating **bezel**, a movable ring that you can set to indicate elapsed time. Digital watches are accurate, but their small buttons can make them difficult to operate. The best timers are electronic automatic timers, which can keep track of how long you dive, how long you are at the surface between dives, and how many dives you make. You do not have to remember to reset or activate anything when you use an automatic electronic timer. Dive computers track underwater time precisely. Some computers can display a timed profile of the dives that you make.

Dive Compasses

Rarely can you see more than 100 feet (30 m) underwater, so a navigational aid can be valuable. If you dive without a directional reference, you can end a dive a long distance from your planned exit point. A dive compass can help you avoid long surface swims or swims through thick surface canopies of water plants. You can use a compass to navigate beneath the canopies, where there are passages through the plants. A compass is also useful for relocating a precise area underwater and as a surface navigation device if fog arises.

Three types of compasses are card types, needle types, and electronic. Card and needle compasses are mechanical. Magnetic deposits in the earth near the North Pole attract either a magnetized disk or a magnetized needle to provide a directional reference. The compass card or needle can deviate from its correct alignment if it is in close proximity to ferrous metal or a source of magnetic forces such as a magnet or electrical motor.

The earth's magnetic field varies in different locations, and the variations affect the balance of the compass card or needle. Some manufacturers offer compasses balanced for different zones of the earth. A good compass has a good tilt potential of plus or minus 30 degrees. Be sure to ask about balancing when selecting a compass.

Diving compasses have liquid inside to dampen the swinging of the needle or disk. To be useful for diving, a compass needs a reference line, called a **lubber line**, to indicate the direction of travel relative to the needle reference. Another desirable feature is a rotating bezel with bracketing index marks that allows you to mark the needle position for a specific direction.

You view some compasses from the top and some from the side. Side-reading compasses display the course in a window on the side of the instrument. You look across a top-reading compass. You will learn how to read and use a compass in chapter 6.

Digital compasses are usually an integrated component of a dive computer (see figure 4.32). The direction of travel is displayed both graphically and numerically. A heading (desired direction) can be set and the device will indicate any correction needed to remain on course. Bearings can be stored in a memory device.

Figure 4.32 Console with computer and SPG (left) and electronic dive compass (right).

Submersible Pressure Gauges

An SPG is analogous to the gas gauge of a car and is just as essential. The SPG measures scuba cylinder pressure. You can use either a mechanical or an electronic SPG. A mechanical SPG is a high-pressure Bourdon tube. High-pressure air from the cylinder passes through the regulator first stage, through a high-pressure hose, and into a Bourdon tube inside a housing at the end of the high-pressure hose. The pressure tries to straighten the spiral tube, which moves a needle on a dial to indicate the tank pressure. Physical shock can damage a mechanical SPG.

An electronic SPG has a pressure sensor (transducer), circuitry, a battery, and a display. It is a form of a high-pressure depth gauge. The display may be digital or graphic. Either a symbol or numbers (in pounds per square inch, atmospheres, or bars) indicate the amount of air in your tank. If the electronics get wet or if the battery dies, an electronic SPG will not function. Some electronic SPGs are hoseless—they do not require an air hose between the cylinder and the gauge, which usually serves multiple functions (dive computer, compass, and SPG). You should retain at least 300 to 500 psi (20 to 34 atm) in your tank at the end of a dive. Mechanical SPGs typically have a red area on the dial for the last 500 psi. When you dive, you should monitor your air supply and make sure that you surface before the needle gets into the red area. Electronic depth gauges usually warn of a low supply of air by blinking the display.

An SPG has a **blowout plug** to relieve pressure in the housing in the event of a high-pressure leak. Identify the blowout plug on your SPG, and do not place anything over the plug that will prevent it from functioning. If the plug cannot come out to release high pressure inside the SPG housing, the face of the instrument can explode.

Instrument Consoles

You can purchase diving instruments individually or in combination. It is convenient to combine several gauges into a display unit called a **console**. An instrument console attaches to the high-pressure hose coming from your regulator first stage. When your instruments are in a console, your arms are free of gauges, and dive preparations are quicker.

The two types of instrument consoles are mechanical and electronic. A mechanical console contains an SPG and a depth gauge. Some also contain an underwater timer, a compass, and a thermometer. The instruments usually feature luminous displays, which are easy to read in low light.

With an electronic console, all instrument information is in a single display (see figure 4.32). If one gauge fails in a mechanical console, the remainder can still function; but when an electronic console fails, all the information provided by the unit is lost. Electronic displays are difficult to read in the dark unless they feature some type of illumination.

Dive Computers

A dive computer is an electronic instrument with a pressure sensor, electronic circuitry, a battery, and a display. A programmed computer inside the instrument uses pressure and time information to continuously calculate the uptake of nitrogen by various compartments that have different half-times. A half-time is the length of time required for a mathematical model (compartment) to increase or decrease its gas absorption or elimination by one-half. A compartment—which resembles, but does not duplicate body tissues—is completely saturated or desaturated in six half-times. When the absorption by any one of a computer's compartments reaches a predetermined level, the device indicates that you are approaching the time limit after which a direct ascent to the surface will no longer be possible. On reaching that time limit, the computer indicates a minimum depth—a **ceiling**—that you cannot exceed during ascent. You risk decompression sickness unless you wait until the computer indicates that sufficient outgassing has occurred to allow you to continue your ascent. A dive computer provides extremely accurate time and depth information. Other common features are a low-battery warning, a rapid-ascent warning, a dive log mode, a dive-planning mode, and information about flying after diving. Additional information about dive computers is provided in chapter 7.

Instrument Care and Maintenance

Physical abuse can damage instruments, so protect your instruments from shock. Secure your console instead of allowing it to swing freely.

Heat or prolonged exposure to hot sunlight can cause oil in a liquid-filled gauge to expand and break the seal on the housing encasing the instrument. If you break the seal, you must have the gauge repaired. Hot water in a whirlpool or a shower can cause an underwater timer to expand, break a seal, and allow water inside. Do not subject diving instruments to high temperatures.

Have air leaks in SPGs repaired at the first opportunity. Have your depth gauge tested for accuracy from time to time by a professional repair facility, or compare your gauge with an extremely accurate instrument, such as a digital depth gauge. Follow all the manufacturer's recommendations. Reduced pressure at elevations above sea level can damage some instruments. Unless an instrument is designed for use at altitude, pack it in an airtight container for flying. Soak and rinse instruments with clean, fresh water after use. Give special attention to pressure-sensing areas to prevent them from becoming clogged with dirt or salt crystals.

Electronic gauges require batteries. Some gauges must be returned to the manufacturer for battery replacement. Gauges that permit the consumer to replace batteries will flood if the batteries are not replaced properly.

Dive Knives and Accessories

This section addresses some additional required and optional equipment. Figure 4.33 shows examples of a dive knife and other dive accessories.

Dive Knives

A dive knife is a required equipment item. Lines and cords in water can cause entanglements, so you must have a knife to cut yourself or your buddy free if necessary.

The many designs of dive knives include large knives and small knives. A small knife positioned

Figure 4.33 Dive knives and accessories.

where you can reach it easily is better than a large knife that you cannot reach. The most important feature of a dive knife is an effective cutting edge. Good blades are corrosion resistant and hold a sharp edge; serrated blades cut lines more effectively than straight blades.

Some knives are multipurpose tools designed for prying, digging, pounding, and measuring in addition to cutting. If you have a multipurpose knife as a diving tool, you should also have a small, separate dive knife.

A dive knife comes with a sheath, which has some means to lock the knife in place. Make sure the sheath lock is reliable to prevent losing a knife. You can attach a small knife to your leg, your arm, your console, or your BC. Wear a large knife on the inside of your leg and secure it with straps that stretch to compensate for exposure suit compression.

To prevent corrosion, rinse your dive knife after diving. Inspect the edge for sharpness, remove any rust, and coat the blade with grease.

Accessories

You are likely to need several small, but important, accessory items. These items include a gear bag, a dive flag and float, dive lights, dive kits, signaling devices, dive slates, and a diver's first aid kit.

Gear Bags

You need so much equipment for diving that you also need a means to carry it. Gear bags can be simple or complex. They can feature multiple compartments, padding, novel ways for carrying or moving, sealed fabric edges, and various fabrics. The best type for you depends on your needs and how much you want to invest. Be sure to get a bag with webbing handles that completely surround the bag to provide full, durable support. No matter what your budget, you need a gear bag for your equipment.

Dive Flags and Floats

In many areas, local law requires the use of a dive flag while diving. In the United States, the traditional dive flag is a red flag with a white diagonal stripe (see figure 4.34). The flag is usually vinyl, mounted on a fiberglass staff, and stiffened with

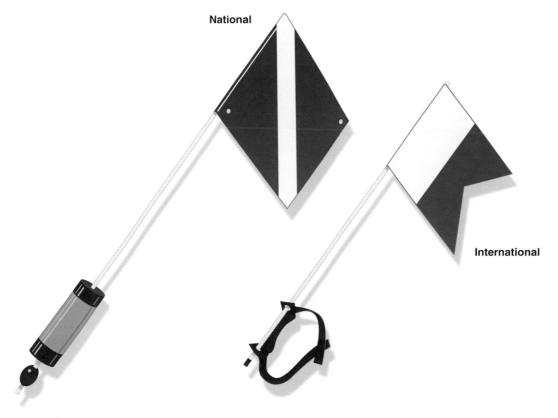

Figure 4.34 Dive flags.

a wire so that it stands out from the staff at all times. In addition to the red and white flag, you should use the international Alpha flag—a swallow-tailed blue and white flag—when diving from a vessel. The Alpha flag is a general dive flag in countries other than the United States.

Unless you are diving from a boat, you need a float to support your dive flag. Some flagstaffs have a float attached. You can also get attachments to secure a dive flag to an inner tube. Another option is a flag-holding canvas covering for an inner tube.

Dive Lights

A dive light can increase your diving enjoyment. Light levels are low underwater, and a light restores color to objects at depth and allows you to peer under ledges and into holes. You can see and enjoy much more when you use a dive light.

The many types of dive lights available include large, powerful, rechargeable lights and small lights that use disposable batteries. Consider a small dive light initially. A large light is for night diving, which is an advanced activity. A small light is easy to carry and is useful both for day dives and as a backup light for night diving. Many of today's small dive lights are bright and compact (see figure 4.35). Maintain your dive light according to the manufacturer's instructions.

Figure 4.35 Dive lights are useful during the day or night to restore color visibility and illuminate dark places.

Kits

Two equipment kits are recommended: a dive kit and a save-a-dive kit. The dive kit contains items you use frequently for diving. The save-a-dive kit contains items you may need to salvage a dive. See the Equipment Kits sidebar for items that you might include in each kit. Because the items in your dive kit are small and get wet, you may want to keep them in a container by themselves so you can find them easily.

Once you get yourself and your equipment to a dive site, you don't want a minor equipment problem to keep you from diving. A broken strap, a missing O-ring, and a torn mouthpiece are examples of problems that can stop you from diving unless you have spare parts. Keep save-a-dive items in a waterproof box. Do not mix wet items from your dive kit with dry items in your save-a-dive kit.

Dive Slates

You need to record and refer to information around and in the water when you dive. Plastic slates are better than paper because water does not affect the slates. You can write on dive slates with a standard lead pencil or a grease pen.

Equipment Kits

Dive Kit

- Defogging solution for your mask
- Lip balm
- Wet suit shampoo
- Seasickness medication
- Sunscreen

Save-a-Dive Kit

- Mask strap
- Regulator mouthpiece
- Fin strap
- Crescent wrench
- Snorkel keeper
- Screwdrivers
- Tank valve O-rings
- Cable ties
- Quick-release buckle
- Twine
- Weight keepers
- Duct tape
- Superglue
- Extra batteries
- Heavy nylon thread and heavy-duty needles
- Neoprene cement
- Fiberglass cast tape for temporary repairs

Dive slates include checklist slates, reference slates, logbook information transfer slates, and writing slates. All types have value. You will probably have several slates when you become an experienced diver. Initially, you should have an equipment checklist, a dive-planning slate, and an underwater writing slate.

Signaling Devices

Long-range signaling devices are invaluable if you become adrift, especially in areas where currents are strong. You should have a whistle readily available. A whistle is more effective than shouting to gain attention. The sound from a whistle does not require much energy to produce, and it travels well over water.

A diver's air horn, powered by low-pressure air, works with as little as 50 psi (3.4 atm) of tank pressure and produces a sound that can be heard up to a mile away. Although this device is small, it is so loud that you must point the horn away from yourself to avoid hearing damage.

You can get long, bright, thin, inflatable safety tubes that fit easily into your BC pocket. Inflate a safety tube at the surface to make yourself easier to spot in the water.

You can use a signal mirror to flash sunlight long distances over water. Other forms of signaling devices for divers are flashlights, strobe lights, and waterproof flares. The greater the chance of being caught in a current, the greater your need for signaling devices.

Diver's First Aid Kit

Diving takes place in remote areas, and because it is a physical activity, someone may be injured. You need to be prepared for an emergency. You should have a first aid kit at the dive site. See the First Aid Kit sidebar for items that should be included in a standard first aid kit. Pack the items in a waterproof container. Chapter 6 addresses the use of the first aid items.

First Aid Kit

Rescue breathing mask

Tweezers

Seasickness medication

Bandage scissors

Isopropyl alcohol

Penlight

Hydrogen peroxide

Coins for emergency phone calls

White vinegar

Emergency contact information
  for diving accidents

Baking soda

Diving first aid book

Analgesic and antiseptic ointment

Space blanket

Hot packs

Pen and small notebook

Eyewash

Rubber band tourniquet

Triangular bandages

Specialized Equipment

Other specialized equipment for scuba diving includes nitrox (oxygen-enriched air) equipment, mixed-gas equipment, and rebreathers. This equipment permits divers with specialty training to obtain longer dive times. The risks associated with the use of specialized equipment make training and adherence to the rules pertaining to its use absolutely essential.

Enriched-Air Nitrox (EANx)

Breathing gas that contains levels of oxygen greater than the 21 percent found in air provides benefits for divers. Higher oxygen levels reduce the amount of nitrogen absorbed, thereby reducing the problems posed by decompression illness. However, divers must know the technical requirements and dangers associated with the use of EANx. Dedicated equipment and specialty training are essential.

Filling standard cylinders with EANx is not permitted. Nitrox equipment is clearly marked to differentiate it from standard scuba equipment (see figure 4.36). Nitrox blending stations are available at many modern dive facilities. Standard blends of nitrox are EAN32 and EAN36, which contain 32 and 36 percent oxygen respectively (also called Nitrox32 and Nitrox36). Nitrogen and oxygen are blended together during the filling process, but the final mixture may not be exact. Divers need to test the oxygen percentage of the gas in their cylinder before diving. The divers use a handheld oxygen analyzer to ensure that the oxygen level is acceptable.

If you breathe oxygen at a partial pressure that is too high,

Figure 4.36 Nitrox tanks have explicit markings to differentiate them from standard cylinders.

convulsions can occur. Partial pressures of oxygen must be kept within safe limits (1.4 to 1.6 atm or bars). For this reason, there are maximum operating depths (MODs) for nitrox diving. The MODs for EAN32 and EAN36 are 110 feet (33.5 m) and 95 feet (29 m) respectively. These are absolute depths and must not be exceeded. Additionally, divers must determine equivalent air depths (EADs) for decompression. Modern dive computers allow divers to select the type of breathing gas being used. The computers automatically calculate EADs and are recommended for mixed-gas diving.

Dive operators and gas blending facilities require proof of specialty training for the use of EANx. Training is widely available.

Technical Diving

This form of diving is even more specialized than the use of enriched-air nitrox because it involves the use of mixed gases and highly technical equipment. Breathing gases include helium, neon, nitrogen, and oxygen; these gases are mixed in various quantities depending on the depth. Obviously, divers need substantial training before they attempt this method of diving. Some gas mixtures will not sustain life until the partial pressure of the oxygen in the mix increases with depth. In this instance, technical divers must use travel tanks to reach a safe depth before switching to the low-oxygen mixture in the primary unit. The principal goal of technical diving is to allow divers to exceed recreational depth and time limits. Technical diving has greater risks than recreational diving, but many consider the rewards worth the risk.

Some technical divers use multiple large-capacity cylinders for open-circuit scuba diving. Others use complex and expensive closed-circuit rebreathers (CCRs) to obtain greatly extended dive times. Rebreathers, which use a mixture of oxygen and inert gas, allow exhaled oxygen to be breathed repeatedly until it is metabolized. Additional oxygen is added as needed to the inert gas in the system to maintain required levels. Exhaled carbon dioxide is absorbed by a canister called a scrubber. Oxygen replacement may be controlled automatically by a central processing unit or may be controlled manually by a valve. The result, which is not affected by depth, allows a diver to remain submerged for hours at a time or to make multiple dives with a single fill of breathing gas. Figure 4.37 illustrates a modern CCR.

Dive preparation and predive procedures vary greatly from open-circuit scuba diving. For example, a diver needs to prebreathe a CCR to activate the absorption process of the carbon dioxide scrubber. This procedure can take several minutes and is affected by the temperature of the absorbent. The diver also needs to check the unit's calibration at a depth of 20 feet (6 m) during descent. Changes in the gas mixture that are made during ascent must be managed by a central processing unit or managed manually by the diver. This truly is technical diving.

Figure 4.37 CCR 2000 rebreather.

Courtesy of Dan Wible.

SCUBA WISE

If you want to avoid diving accidents, you should use familiar, correctly fitting, well-maintained dive equipment the way that it is intended. As I look back over several decades of dive experience, I can recall many instances when divers got into trouble because they did not follow the essential equipment safety procedures summarized in the previous sentence. Diving allows us to explore an alien environment using life-support equipment. Modern scuba equipment is manufactured well, but you must take care of it and have it serviced periodically to keep it functioning properly. Would you even consider going into outer space with life-support equipment that was not carefully maintained and serviced? We go into inner space when we dive. Our life-support equipment is just as vital to us as an astronaut's.

Equipment problems while diving do arise, but equipment failure is rarely the cause of an accident. Problems cause anxiety and stress. A diver experiencing stress from environmental factors and fear may panic from the added stress that a minor equipment problem might pose. Learning to manage yourself and your equipment helps you reduce stress, avoid panic, and prevent an accident. One of the most important rules of accident-free diving is to have good, familiar equipment that is in good condition and to use it properly.

Oxygen levels are managed by employing multiple sensors, which are accurate devices when maintained and calibrated. Current CCRs lack reliable carbon dioxide sensing devices. Carbon dioxide toxicity can be fatal, and a diver's symptoms are not a reliable indicator. This problem requires the usage time of the carbon dioxide absorbent to be monitored and the absorbent must be discarded when time limits (based on statistical tests) have been attained.

Because CCRs are expensive, must be used frequently, and require extensive maintenance, they are used by relatively few divers. But the advantage of greatly extended dive times appeals to many divers, so the popularity of rebreathers is increasing.

Summary

Diving involves a great deal of equipment. You are beginning to understand the equipment you need to have, how to select it, and how to care for it. You will learn more about equipment from your instructor, from retailers, from magazines, and from other divers. Get good equipment, and give it the best care possible. Diving is not enjoyable if you have constant equipment problems.

Application-of-Knowledge (AOK) Questions

1. Diving equipment is expensive. What are the best procedures to follow that will increase the life of your equipment?

2. What two concerns are most important when selecting diving equipment?

3. You were unaware that your regulator was free-flowing behind you at the surface at the end of a dive, and your tank lost all of its air. When you move your tank after the dive, you feel water sloshing inside. How was the water able to get into your cylinder?

4. You have weighted yourself to be weightless in water and are able to sink with your BC deflated just by exhaling. At the end of the dive you are unable to stop your ascent as you near the surface, even when you exhale completely. What is causing this undesirable change in buoyancy?

5. You are diving in a dry suit. You have added air to the suit to maintain a constant volume as you descend. You find a small anchor on the bottom and decide to salvage it. You pick up the anchor and carry it with you. To offset the weight of the anchor, you add more air to your dry suit. Why is this action a dangerous practice?

6. You and your buddy are practicing compass navigation by swimming a compass course. You place your compass next to your buddy's to compare headings and proceed along your planned course, but you missed your mark and had to surface. You find that you swam in the wrong direction. What caused this error?

7. What is the best way to remove salt, debris, or chlorine from you diving equipment?

8. A scuba regulator can have four or five hoses attached to the first stage. Can you think of the purposes of these hoses?

9. What are the best reasons for having good dive equipment and maintaining it properly?

School of barracuda in the Florida Keys

Diving Environment

Aquatic Biology

The plants and animals of the underwater world are wondrous and diverse. The millions of animals in the aquatic realm range from those that are microscopic to those weighing tons. To appreciate, respect, and enjoy aquatic life, you need to learn a bit about biology. This section familiarizes you with the flora and fauna of the aquatic realm. Aquatic life fits into three categories: life-forms that drift with the currents, those that swim freely and are able to move against the currents, and those that dwell on the bottom.

Drifters

The drifters are called **plankton**. Animals that drift are called zooplankton. Drifting plants are called phytoplankton. Plankton begins the food cycle in the waters (see figure 5.1). Small animals eat plankton, and larger animals eat the smaller animals. When the large animals die, their remains sink to the bottom and decompose. The decomposed material rises to the surface, where it becomes food for the plankton. Warm water and nutrients cause some plankton to multiply. Overpopulations of plankton, called **blooms**, can color the water, destroy underwater visibility, and form toxins in animals that feed by filtering water. Toxin from blooms makes clams and mussels unsafe for consumption during summer months in some areas. One type of red phytoplankton often creates blooms, known as **red tide**, in the seas. Diving conditions are poor in areas affected by plankton blooms.

Another type of aquatic plant, called algae, is an important part of the aquatic world. Plants use light to produce their own food and become food for animals. They convert water and carbon dioxide to oxygen and carbohydrates through the process of photosynthesis. Various types of algae are found in underwater areas where light is available. Most algae grow in shallow water where light is most abundant. Thick moss drapes objects in some freshwater areas. Turtle grass is a grasslike, green, tropical saltwater plant that provides a habitat for many forms of life. Some types of long, flowing algae in cold and shallow water, such as surf grass or eel grass, can cause you to trip if you try to walk in them. Slippery plants cover rocks and can cause you to slip and fall unless you move cautiously.

Giant algae, called **kelp**, produce long strands, called **stipes**, in which you can become entangled. You can learn how to avoid and how to deal with this problem. A rootlike structure, called a holdfast, anchors kelp to the bottom; numerous gas bladders, called floats, lift

Learning to dive gives you an opportunity to become more familiar with the aquatic environment, which covers over 70 percent of the surface of the earth. The underwater world is fascinating. This chapter introduces you to biological and physical conditions of the diving environment. You will learn the effect of people on the environment and the effect of the environment on people. You affect the underwater world more than you might imagine.

A juvenile octopus in California

the top parts toward the surface. What appear to be the leaves of kelp are **fronds**. Large areas of kelp are known as kelp beds, which have thick canopies that blanket the surface of the water (see figure 5.2). It is difficult to swim through a kelp canopy at the surface, but it is easy to swim between the clumps of stipes beneath the surface. Underwater navigational skills are important when diving in areas where kelp is dense. Kelp forests are popular diving areas because they contain great quantities of life.

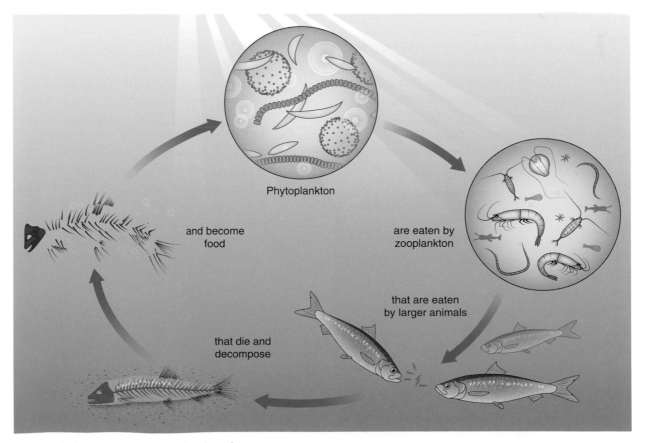

Phytoplankton

and become food

are eaten by zooplankton

that are eaten by larger animals

that die and decompose

Figure 5.1 **The underwater food cycle.**

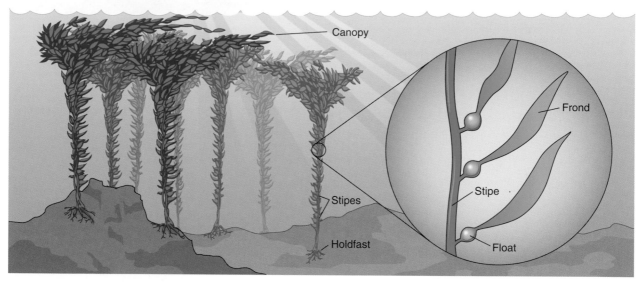

Figure 5.2   A typical kelp bed.

Swimmers

One of the rewards of diving is seeing fish. Fish can be found in nearly all the waters of the world. You cannot outswim even the slowest fish, so do not chase them. If you want to observe fish closely, you must blend into the environment. Fish will get closer to you than you could ever get to them.

Collecting for aquariums requires specialized knowledge and procedures. Most fish have an internal air bladder for buoyancy control. If a fish is taken to the surface too quickly, the air bladder expands and kills the animal. Avoid handling fish because the experience can be traumatic as well as physically damaging to the animal. And the fish's spine could injure you.

Eating some types of fish can harm you, as some fish are poisonous. Types of fish poisoning include **ciguatera**, **scombroid**, and **tetrodotoxin**. Ciguatera results from eating fish that consume a certain species of algae. Ciguatera poisoning causes gastrointestinal problems within 6 to 12 hours. Scombroid poisoning, which produces nausea and vomiting within an hour, can result if you eat fish that have not been kept chilled. Tetrodotoxin, the most serious fish poisoning, results from eating exotic fish such as blowfish or puffer fish (figure 5.3). Tetrodotoxin poisoning can cause death within minutes. Avoid eating large and unusual-looking fish. Check with local fishermen to determine which fish are safe for consumption.

Many large mammals—sea lions, seals, dolphins, whales, and manatees—inhabit the water. They are graceful, beautiful, and sometimes awesome in

Figure 5.3   Eating improperly prepared puffer fish can result in potentially fatal poisoning.

appearance. Viewing them is an exciting experience. Some are curious and may approach you. Aquatic mammals will usually not harm you in the water if you leave them alone. But sea lions and seals are defensive on land and might bite if you get too close.

Bottom Dwellers

Bottom dwellers include animals that are stationary, such as coral and sea fans, as well as animals that move about, such as crabs and lobsters. Living, stationary bottom dwellers are usually not included in fish and game regulations, and you should not take them. Do not take coral, sea fans, and animals that appear stationary, such as starfish. If you hunt crabs and lobsters for food, you should know how to determine the gender of the animals, how to catch them without harming them, and how to measure them for minimum size. Do not take females, particularly those bearing eggs. Some divers take only one claw from a crab to conserve the species. A crab can feed and defend itself with one claw and can regenerate a new claw to replace the one taken.

Hydroids

If you dive in saltwater, you should know about hydroids, a category of animal that includes bottom dwellers, such as coral, and swimmers, such as jellyfish (see figure 5.4). Some hydroids, such as the beautiful sea anemone, have a round, columnlike body with a mouth surrounded by tentacles. This is a polyp form of hydroid. Another type, called the colonial form, can assume many different

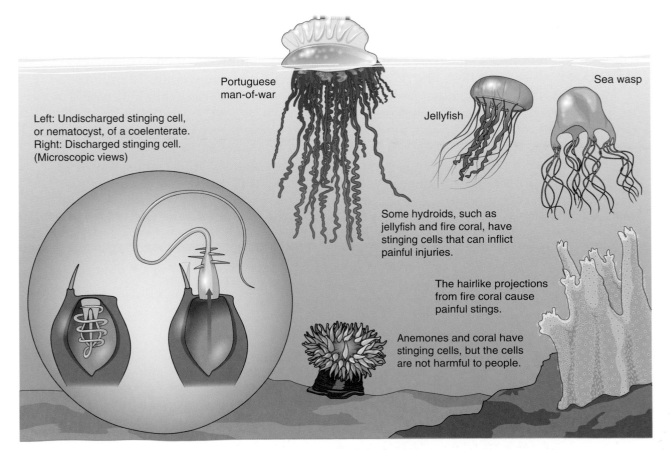

Portuguese man-of-war

Sea wasp

Jellyfish

Left: Undischarged stinging cell, or nematocyst, of a coelenterate. Right: Discharged stinging cell. (Microscopic views)

Some hydroids, such as jellyfish and fire coral, have stinging cells that can inflict painful injuries.

The hairlike projections from fire coral cause painful stings.

Anemones and coral have stinging cells, but the cells are not harmful to people.

Figure 5.4 Several types of hydroids have stinging cells.

shapes. Colonies of hydroids can encrust a surface, and groups of colonies form jellyfish. Learn to recognize and avoid hydroids that can injure you.

Potentially Dangerous Aquatic Animals

Aquatic animals use a variety of mechanisms to obtain food and to defend themselves from attack. You can minimize your chances of injury by being familiar with the ways in which animals can inflict injury. Aquatic animals are rarely aggressive toward humans; they flee, hide, or stand still as you approach. If you do not touch, threaten, or provoke an animal, the animal is unlikely to injure you intentionally. But remember, aquatic animals are wild animals (figure 5.5). If you feed them, and they bite you in the process, you should not blame the animals. Table 5.1 lists types of injuries that you could sustain from aquatic animals and recommended first aid.

Animals That Cause Abrasions or Cuts

Many animals, such as some types of coral and barnacles, have sharp, hard structures that easily cut flesh. Such cuts can be painful, are slow to heal, and can get infected. Avoid contact with reefs and rocks covered with sharp animals. Some fish have knifelike protrusions on their gill plates or at the base of their tails. They defend themselves by flailing rapidly back and forth and slashing anything near them.

Animals That Puncture or Lacerate

Sea urchins are the porcupines of the seas. Cold-water urchins have short, thick spines, while warm-water urchins have spines that are long and thin. The spines of all urchins can penetrate an exposure suit if you bump into them. The spines break off in your flesh and produce a painful, red, swollen wound. The spines can be difficult to remove, so if you are unable to avoid a sea urchin injury, see a physician to have the spines removed.

Some fish have a row of long, sharp spines along their back. The scorpionfish has hollow dorsal spines that have venom-filled sacs at the base. If you are punctured by the spines and compress the venom sacs, you inject yourself with a toxin. The toxin of some species, such as the stonefish, can cause serious symp-

Figure 5.5 Potentially dangerous aquatic animals: (a) White tip shark; (b) cone snail; (c) sea snake; and (d) jellyfish with jacks.
Scott Frier: www.wildlifephotoworkshops.com

toms. Some fish, such as the lionfish (also called the turkey fish or zebra fish), have spines in other fins. The toxin of a lionfish produces serious symptoms in humans. Freshwater catfish also have venomous spines.

A shellfish called the cone shell uses venom to kill animals for food. The venom is highly toxic, and these animals can inject their venom into humans. Do not handle conical shells in tropical waters.

Rays are bottom dwellers that are round and flat. Some rays have a sharp, serrated barb at the base of the tail. The rays blend into the bottom. When someone disturbs a ray, it defends itself by arching its back and thrusting its barb into the attacker. A sheath, which often remains in the laceration wound, covers the barb and contains a toxin. Stingray wounds in the ankles of divers, waders, and swimmers are common in some areas. Avoid stingray wounds by shuffling your feet along the bottom as you walk. The torpedo ray, an animal found on the West Coast of the United States, can generate electricity. This ray can stun a diver, so you need to be able to recognize it. Avoid contact if you encounter one.

Animals That Bite

Use discretion to avoid being bitten by aquatic animals. One large freshwater fish that can bite is the gar. Turtles can inflict serious wounds. Muskrats may attack in defense, and moray eels in the ocean can deliver a serious bite. Alligators also have the potential to inflict an injury but have not been known to hurt divers.

Sharks can bite, but attacks on scuba divers are nearly nonexistent. Hollywood has exaggerated the danger of sharks; only a few species of sharks are aggressive, and it is rare to encounter these types in the waters visited by divers. Most divers would be delighted to see a shark because these animals usually retreat from an area frequented by scuba divers.

Retreat from snakes if you encounter them. Do not handle snakes; they can be extremely venomous. A sea snake's bite can produce a life-threatening emergency. Some freshwater snakes, such as the cottonmouth, are also venomous. The blue-ringed octopus, while only the size of a golf ball, is one of the most toxic creatures on earth. Don't allow curiosity to endanger your life.

Animals That Sting

Many aquatic animals can sting. Learn to identify and avoid contact with jellyfish, featherlike or whiplike hydroids, certain worms, and even some sponges.

Table 5.1 Potentially Dangerous Aquatic Animals

Injury	First aid
Abrasions or cuts	
Barnacle	Scrub and disinfect the wound.
Coral	
Punctures or Lacerations	
Cone shell	Soak the injured area in hot water. For a cone shell sting, apply a venous tourniquet and immobilize the injured area. It is advisable to seek medical attention for injuries caused by the spines of the scorpionfish family.
Sea urchin	
Venomous fish (e.g., scorpionfish, lionfish)	
Stingray	
Bites	
Barracuda	Stop the bleeding; clean and disinfect the wound. For a blue-ringed octopus bite, apply pressure to the wound and seek immediate medical attention—it may be necessary to administer rescue breathing. For a sea snake bite, apply pressure, immobilize the area, and get prompt medical attention.
Blue-ringed octopus	
Moray eel	
Sea snake	
Shark	
Turtle, muskrat, alligator	
Stings	
Bristle worm	Soak the injured area in vinegar.
Fire coral	
Fire sponge	
Jellyfish	

Seek medical attention as needed for any injury.

Hydroids have tiny stinging cells, called nematocysts, that they use to kill food. The sting of some animals, such as encrusting fire coral, is merely annoying; but the sting of others, such as the Portuguese man-of-war or the box jellyfish, can cause a medical emergency. A tropical marine worm, called a bristle worm, has tufted, silky bristles along the sides of its body. The bristles, which are fine and brittle, penetrate the skin easily, are difficult to remove, and cause a burning sensation. Do not touch or handle these worms. You should wear an exposure suit at all times while diving in the ocean. The suit provides protection from stings, but be careful when you remove it. The stinging cells of marine animals remain active even if they are not on the animal. Parts of jellyfish and other animals that are on your equipment can sting if they come into contact with your skin when you remove the equipment. Avoid contact with any unusual debris clinging to your equipment after diving in salt water because it could be part of a jellyfish. Some jellyfish come to the surface at night in tropical waters. Dangerous stinging animals are seasonal in some regions. Check with local divers to find out what to avoid and when to be on the alert.

Avoiding Danger

Many aquatic animals are potentially dangerous. Tropical waters have the most dangerous animals. Serious injuries to divers are not common because divers avoid animals that can hurt them. You should respect animals, but do not be overly concerned about them. Do not panic or flee just because you see a potentially dangerous animal; simply avoid contact with it. Learn to recognize the dangerous animals in an area, know where to look for them, be alert for them, and keep clear of them. Move slowly and look carefully. Shuffle your feet when wading. Don't touch anything unless you know it is safe to touch it. Neutral buoyancy—the ability to hover—is an excellent defense against aquatic injuries.

The biology of the underwater world is so interesting that many divers study it as a hobby. It is fun to learn about animals and plants and then observe them in their natural habitats. Some divers, fascinated with aquatic life, pursue biology as a career.

Conservation and Preservation

Life in the waters is beautiful and precious, but pollution from people jeopardizes life in the lakes and seas. Divers are physically ruining beautiful reefs. Unless we take action immediately, there is a real danger that many areas of the underwater world will become barren and lifeless. We must preserve and conserve the resources of our waters.

Because the waters are so vast, people often take them for granted. Lakes and seas seem too big to be harmed, but that is not the case. The underwater environment is fragile, the balance of nature can be upset more easily than many people realize. We think of the seas as being great and powerful because we see big waves and pounding surf. People who do not see beneath the surface may not realize the delicate nature of the animals that inhabit the waters. Some living things in the seas grow slowly, only a fraction of an inch (or centimeter) per year.

As a diver, you can help reduce damage to the underwater world. Every diver should take two actions: (1) Do everything possible personally to preserve the diving environment, and (2) do everything possible to educate others and help them learn to preserve the aquatic environment. You will get closer to the aquatic environment than most of your friends. You will see firsthand the effects of pollution, litter, and exploitation. You will also see the beauty and abundance that are possible when the environment is clean and unmolested. Your influence in society can make a difference. If you do not become part of the solution to problems in the aquatic environment, you are part of the problem.

Pollution

Stemming pollution is one of the greatest challenges facing the world. Humans are incredible polluters of the environment; we have polluted the air, the land, and the waters. People dump billions of gallons and pounds of waste into water every day. People seem to think that when something is out of sight, it is no longer a problem. This is not true of pollutants. Sewage, industrial waste, garbage, and sediment have killed and are continuing to kill many underwater environments.

If we stopped all pollution today, the aquatic environment would continue to suffer for decades from the waste materials that are already in the water.

Runoff from land that enters rivers and streams and flows into the ocean also causes pollution. Chemicals used in agriculture, on lawns, and in gardens cause death and destruction in the aquatic environment. Sediment from construction and drilling finds its way into water. The sediment blocks out life-giving sunlight and smothers bottom-dwelling creatures.

Lakes and oceans have been viewed as bottomless toilets for waste disposal. There are two problems with this narrow view: (1) Animals and plants live in the water and are killed by the pollution; (2) the water cannot be replaced because large bodies of water cannot be flushed.

Diver Impact

As a diver, you can harm the environment in several ways. You can remove living things from the environment, you can smash and kill living things while moving about underwater, and you can stir up clouds of silt on the bottom. The silt can choke and kill some organisms. Good intentions can also cause problems; handling and feeding animals can kill them.

You can be an effective predator underwater. Many animals are available for you to hunt and take. A few callous individuals kill things for sport, but responsible people take only what they will eat. Although the impact of divers is of little significance compared with commercial fishing, you should keep in mind that you do have an effect. If you spearfish on a reef, the fish in the area will soon be unapproachable by divers. If you want to be a predator, you must do so in a responsible manner. Conservation and preservation of aquatic resources are important topics that are discussed later in this section.

It is difficult to resist touching animals underwater, but you should refrain until you know what animals may be touched and how to touch them without harming them. Many animals are delicate; rough handling will kill them. Predators will eat animals that a diver removes from a protected area for viewing. Some animals, including fish, have a protective coating of mucus. If the coating is removed by handling, the animal can develop an infection and die. The stress of being handled by a gigantic, bubble-blowing monster may be more than some aquatic animals can take. Sea turtles may abort their eggs after being harassed by a playful diver. Do not be guilty of killing things for your amusement. After

SCUBA WISE

There are similarities between the environments above and below water. Temperature, weather, plants, and animals change when you travel from region to region on land. We enjoy the variety of mountain, plain, forest, and desert regions. Similarly, the world beneath the water varies from region to region. The enjoyment that the various underwater environments provide is a major reason why dive travel is so popular.

When you go to places on land that are rugged, remote, and hazardous, you need special training and equipment. There are dangers everywhere you go. Careful planning and preparation help minimize risks and are essential. A guide makes exploration safer and more enjoyable. When you go diving in places that are rugged, remote, and hazardous, the same requirements apply. Enjoy the wonderful differences beneath the waters—coral reefs, vertical walls, wrecks, and so forth—but always be properly prepared and equipped and always obtain an orientation to a new area.

you learn how, you can get extremely close to animals underwater. You can interact with them and enjoy them without handling them.

Feeding animals underwater was a popular activity until environmentalists showed that this is harmful (not to mention dangerous). Several potential problems are associated with feeding aquatic animals. Unnatural food given to animals can interfere with their digestion. The animals may become dependent on the food fed to them by divers and may not be able to forage if the food supply is discontinued. Food can make animals overcome their natural fear of divers. When an animal that would normally take cover at the sight of a diver becomes accustomed to divers providing food, the animal will readily approach a diver who is a hunter.

A diver underwater has the potential to be a bull in a china shop. Overweighted divers plow along the bottom with their fins pointed downward, stirring up great clouds of silt. Buoyancy difficulties cause divers to hold on to and crash into reefs and other living things. Divers who rest on the bottom crush plants and animals without realizing the damage. Divers who swim too close to a reef often kick animals to death.

Prevention of Diver Impact

One of the most important reasons for developing good buoyancy control skills is to prevent damage to the underwater environment. An environmentally responsible diver is properly weighted and in control of buoyancy at all times. Make your diving no-contact diving. You should be able to hover above a reef, move your mask within inches of an animal, and view it without touching anything but water and without stirring up silt. Learn to use your hands to scull into position while your fins remain still. Sculling is positioning achieved with short movements of the hands (not the arms). Buoyancy control and sculling are excellent skills for reducing diver impact. Figure 5.6 shows a diver sculling.

Another way to protect the environment is to keep your equipment secured close to you so that it does not dangle and drag. Equipment that drags along the bottom for an entire dive can do a lot of damage. Streamline your equipment. Moving slowly underwater conserves energy and air and makes you less likely to come into contact with animals. This helps you avoid injuring both yourself and animals.

If you must hold on to something underwater or push yourself away from something, you should look before you touch, and you should avoid touching anything that is living. If you must settle onto the bottom for some reason, select an area where there is no visible life. If you are weightless, keep in mind that one finger may be all you need to provide the leverage to move. Leave no evidence that you ever visited an underwater area.

Figure 5.6 Sculling helps minimize the diver's impact on the aquatic environment.

Conservation

Many animals that were once plentiful are nearly extinct because of a lack of conservation. Buffalo and passenger pigeons are good examples of this happening on land. In some areas, this is happening to aquatic animals. Bait fish that once swarmed in enormous schools in some areas no longer exist. With no food to eat, larger predatory fish no longer frequent the areas.

Fish and game regulations are designed to conserve natural resources. Rules regarding sizes, seasons, limits, and the means by which game may be taken have been established to help ensure an ongoing supply of a resource. Obey fish and game regulations, and encourage others to abide by them as well. In most areas you need a license to harvest fish and seafood. There are written regulations you need to be familiar with. Size, sex, limit, and season laws can impose a stiff fine if you fail to adhere to the regulations. Check with your local Department of Fish and Game. The rules can benefit everyone in the long run.

If you take living things from the water, do it in a responsible manner. Avoid taking animals from areas that are popular dive sites. Limit hunting and collecting to remote areas where the impact of divers is much less. Take only what you need, not what you can get or what you are allowed. The two types of hunters most harmful to the environment are the quantity hunter and the trophy hunter. The quantity hunter seeks to take as much and as many of everything as possible to build an image as a mighty hunter. The trophy hunter seeks the largest animals, which destroys the fittest of the breeding stock. If you kill an animal, you have a duty to know how large one must be to breed and what the maximum size of the animal is. You should take animals that have had the opportunity to reproduce, but do not take the largest ones. It is difficult at times to be selective, but you should attempt to conserve life.

Nature left undisturbed maintains a balance of life. Animals are both predator and prey. An animal eats another animal and is in turn eaten by others. If there are too many predators, their population diminishes because of an inadequate food supply. If there is a temporary overpopulation of prey, the number of predators increases. People upset nature's balance. We are the most reckless predators of all. We disturb the food cycle with pollution, hunting, fishing, boating, and every other way that we affect the aquatic environment. It takes nature longer to recover from our impact than from any natural disaster. People must lessen their effect on the environment to reduce interference with the natural management of the life within the waters.

Preservation

Preservation is everyone's business, but it is more your business now than it was before you became a diver. You probably know more than your friends and neighbors about the aquatic environment. You must be an ambassador for preservation. You must educate and motivate people to help preserve the diving environment.

What people do above water affects life beneath the surface. What people put down their drains and toilets winds up in the aquatic environment, as do the chemicals they use on their lawns and gardens. Litter in and around the water kills animals, birds, fish, and shellfish Think twice about the products you buy, how you use what you purchase, and how you dispose of your wastes. Where will the toxic chemicals and waste you use end up? Be environmentally conscientious; then teach others to be so, too. A simple act, such as the use of detergents without phosphates, can make a difference. Phosphates are powerful nutrients that upset the balance of nature when dumped into the aquatic environment.

Be involved in your community. Be concerned about issues such as sewage treatment, toxic wastes, and construction, which can be extremely harmful. Waste products from manufacturing are also harmful. Help others understand the seriousness of pollution.

Become more informed and keep informed. Join groups that are working to preserve the environment. Organizations such as the Ocean Conservancy, the Reef Environmental Education Foundation (REEF), and the Oceanic Society merit your membership. These groups provide up-to-date information and details on how you can help. Various organizations sponsor underwater cleanups from time to time; these are enjoyable and worthwhile. (For a list of environmental organizations you can join, see Appendix A.)

There are actions you can and should take when you go diving. Dispose of trash properly, and encourage others to do the same. If you have a boat for diving, anchor it away from reefs to avoid reef damage caused by the anchor and chain. Retrieve trash you find in the environment, especially plastic. Collect plastic, monofilament, lead, and stainless steel leaders. Not all trash is bad. Bottles and cans provide homes for animals. Report unlawful dumping and lost or discarded fishing nets and traps, which continue to catch and kill after abandonment.

Aquatic Conditions

The particular state of the environment and the physical situations in which divers find themselves are referred to as the aquatic conditions. The conditions of concern include the temperature, visibility, and the degree of movement of the water. You need to be familiar with aquatic conditions in general and local aquatic conditions specifically.

The Big Picture

Many factors affect the seas. The sun bears down on the earth at the equator more directly than on other parts of the earth. The climate and waters near the equator are warm; the greater the distance from the equator, the colder the water. The difference in water temperatures in different parts of the world causes the movement of air and water by convection currents. Winds move from areas of high pressure to areas of low pressure. Winds and the turning of the earth move water. On a global scale, water currents move in a clockwise direction in the northern hemisphere of the earth and in a counterclockwise direction in the southern hemisphere. Weather generally moves from west to east. The gravitational attraction between the earth and other planetary bodies produces changes in the water level called tides. Storms at sea produce energy in the form of waves that travel thousands of miles before giving up their energy in the form of surf.

Seasonal changes, winds, and storms affect inland bodies of water. Water from snow and rain in the mountains and hills flows into streams, rivers, and lakes. Water seeping into the ground resurfaces in quarries and springs.

Weather, seasons, geography, and other factors affect both surface and underwater diving conditions. The water can be rough at the surface but calm at depth. There may be a current at the surface but none on the bottom. The visibility may be good at the surface but poor on the bottom, or vice-versa. The temperature is usually warmer at the surface than it is at depth. You should become familiar with both surface and underwater conditions and their effect on your diving.

Perhaps the most important fact to remember about diving conditions is that they vary. Thus, an environmental orientation is important when you dive in a new region. The diving conditions usually dictate the way you dive. What works well in one area may be totally ineffective for another. An understanding of the effects of diving conditions in an area is important. You should know what conditions to expect, how the conditions affect your approach to diving, and how to manage the effects of the conditions. For example, in one area, it may be safe to wade into the water and put on your fins; however, in another area, you may need to put your fins on before you wade in.

General Freshwater Diving Conditions

Freshwater is 2.5 percent less dense than saltwater, so you are less buoyant in freshwater than in saltwater. The density of water varies with temperature. Freshwater is most dense at a temperature of 39.2 °F (4 °C)—the usual temperature and density of the water at depths greater than 60 feet (18 m) in freshwater lakes and quarries. The water becomes lighter when it is either warmer or cooler than this. Freshwater often forms layers: a layer of warmer, lighter water on top of a layer of colder, denser water. The change from the warm water to the colder water, called a **thermocline**, is abrupt. When the water is calm, the thermocline appears to have wisps of smoke on top of it when viewed from above. The refraction of light is different when the density of the water is different, so there is a slight visual blurring at the interface of a thermocline. When you dive in freshwater, you must insulate yourself for the water temperature below the thermocline. Although the surface of a lake may be warm and sunny, the water at the bottom may be close to freezing.

The best season for diving in a freshwater lake or quarry depends on the body of water. Spring and fall are often good times because the water temperature is the same from surface to bottom, there is oxygen for fish at all depths, populations of plankton are low, and visibility is usually good.

In later spring, the sun warms the surface water, and the lack of wind keeps the surface water from mixing with the colder water at depth. The water stratifies, and a thermocline forms that remains until fall. The layer of water below the thermocline stagnates in most lakes during the summer. Decaying matter depletes oxygen and creates toxins. Fish seek refuge above the thermocline. Sunlight and warm water often lead to plankton blooms, which are aggravated by pollution.

In the fall, the surface water in lakes and quarries cools until it equals the temperature of the water at depth. Colder water and reduced sunlight stifle plankton growth, and visibility improves. Winds cause water circulation. The movement of water from the top to a depth of about 60 feet, called an **overturn**, carries oxygenated water to the bottom and leads to what is called spring diving conditions. Visibility tends to be poor during an overturn.

In the winter, the surface water in a lake or quarry is colder than the water at the bottom. A **reverse thermocline** exists and remains until the temperature of the surface water warms to that of the water at the bottom. This allows the spring overturn to begin. Water becomes 10 percent lighter when it freezes. If ice sank when it froze, bodies of water could become solid ice from top to bottom.

Ice that forms over water insulates the water beneath it. Figure 5.7 shows the annual cycle of freshwater lakes and the concept of thermoclines.

When a strong wind blows along a shore for a sustained period over a body of water, the surface water is pushed away from shore. This water is replaced by colder water flowing up from the depths. This is called an **upwelling**, which can also occur in the ocean. If the wind conditions persist, the water temperature can become constant throughout the water column, even in the summer. An upwelling carries nutrients from the depths into shallow water and brings animals into the area. After an upwelling, a bloom can occur because of the increase in nutrients in warm, shallow water.

Specific Freshwater Diving Conditions

People can have good diving experiences in many kinds of freshwater environments. Springs, low-altitude lakes, and quarries are good sites for divers who do

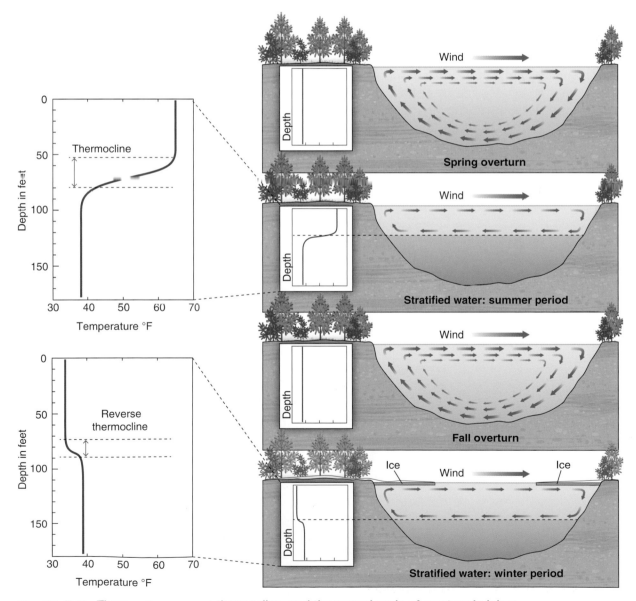

Figure 5.7   Thermocline, reverse thermocline, and the annual cycle of overturn in lakes.

not live near a coast. Other freshwater environments—such as rivers, caverns and caves, high-altitude and frozen lakes, and areas with submerged wreckage—can be dangerous. You should complete specialty training courses before diving in any hazardous area.

You may encounter strong currents in rivers (see figure 5.8). The currents are strongest at the surface and on the outside of bends. Countercurrents and swirling currents, called **eddies**, are common, and entanglements are likely in many rivers. Water flowing through a porous obstruction, such as a pile of logs, can pin a diver against the debris. Currents can undercut the bank of a river, so direct access to the surface can be impossible at times. Rivers are especially prone to seasonal changes and are often unpredictable.

Freshwater springs can provide beautiful diving environments. The flow of clean, calm water, which is usually at a moderate temperature (65 to 78 °F, or 18 to 26 °C), provides excellent visibility. The water often flows through underground limestone cave systems that extend for thousands of feet. Diving in open-water basins in a spring is appropriate for certified divers, but a diver should not enter any overhead area where a direct, vertical ascent to the surface is not possible. A large, roomlike opening where light from the surface can be seen is called a **cavern**. Areas that extend farther than a cavern where no surface light can be seen are called **caves** (see figure 5.9). Divers must complete specialty courses and must meet several requirements to dive in caverns and caves. Entering such an environment—even for a short distance—without the required training and equipment can be fatal. No amount of diving experience without cave diving training qualifies a diver to enter a cave. It is easy to

Figure 5.8 Because many rivers have strong currents and pose other unique diving challenges, specialty training is advised.
Berenika/iStock/Getty Images

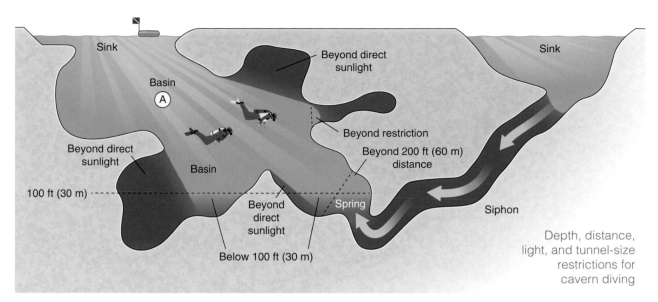

Depth, distance, light, and tunnel-size restrictions for cavern diving

Figure 5.9   Dark blue areas are caves; light blue areas are caverns.

become disoriented, to stir up thick clouds of silt that instantly reduce visibility to nothing, and to panic and drown. You may dive in spring basins, but stay out of caverns and caves unless you meet the requirements to dive in them. Appendix A contains contact information for organizations that offer training in cavern and cave diving.

Sometimes the earth collapses into an underground cave system and forms a **sink**. The water flowing into the sink forms a basin. An opening called a **siphon** channels water from a sink back into the system. Diving in siphons can be dangerous. The amount of water moving through a system depends on the amount of rainfall in the area. Under extreme conditions, the normal flow of water can reverse.

People dig pits to excavate sand, gravel, and stone. At some depth, they encounter the water table, and the pit floods, forming a quarry or sand pit. At some of these sites, you can see submerged construction equipment that was abandoned when the pit flooded. Sand pits and quarries tend to have fair to good visibility, although the disturbance of silt that has settled to the bottom can ruin the visibility quickly. Gravel quarries usually have more silt than other types of quarries, so the water may be turbid.

Lakes can be excellent dive sites. There are freshwater lakes at altitudes above 10,000 feet (3,048 m). Diving at altitudes above 1,000 feet (305 m) is a specialty called altitude diving. This type of diving presents many hazards because the rate of pressure change is greater when you descend into water at an atmospheric pressure that is less than the pressure at sea level. You must follow special procedures to avoid decompression sickness. Problems can also result from the thinner air, which provides less oxygen with each breath taken above water.

When ice forms over water in the winter, diving becomes hazardous. Perils of ice diving include hypothermia, the freezing of regulator and buoyancy control valves, and getting lost beneath the ice. Ice diving can be beautiful and adventurous, but it is dangerous when attempted without the proper training, equipment, and procedures.

Potential hazards when diving in freshwater include body heat loss, submerged trees, wire, fishing line, hooks and lures, log jams, debris, currents, rapids, whirlpools, poor visibility, silt, and overhead restrictions. You can minimize these hazards with training, experience, equipment, correct diving techniques, area orientations, and good judgment.

General Saltwater Diving Conditions

The earth contains five oceans. Seas, gulfs, and bays are smaller sections of the oceans. The land beneath the oceans is not flat. The **continental shelf** is an underwater area that extends from land and slopes gradually to a depth of about 600 feet (183 m). Beyond the continental shelf are great underwater canyons and mountains, as well as hills, valleys, and great plains. In some areas, the tips of mountains and volcanoes extend above the surface of the ocean from great depths, forming islands. In other areas, deep canyons sever the continental slope, creating deep-water conditions close to shore.

The saltwater environment varies greatly from one part of the earth to another. The clear waters of the Caribbean, with temperatures that can exceed 85 °F (29 °C), feature coral reefs covered with beautiful, lush animals that look like plants. Schools of colorful tropical fish abound. Temperate waters, with temperatures ranging from 55 to 70 °F (13 to 21 °C), may have great forests of kelp, which contain more life per volume than a tropical rain forest. Cold ocean waters in northern latitudes are nutrient rich and teeming with life. Beautiful sights and wonders can be experienced in all the oceans of our planet.

Oceans are always in motion. Tides, winds, and currents cause water movement. An underwater earthquake can move water by creating gigantic seismic waves known as a **tsunami**. Although these giant waves are also called tidal waves, the tide has nothing to do with them. Tsunamis can cause great destruction, but they are rare and can be forecasted.

The energy source for movement of ocean water may be local or may originate thousands of miles away. You need to understand what causes water to move, how it moves, and how to dive in ocean water that is in motion.

Tides

The gravitational attraction between the sun, the moon and the earth pulls water toward these heavenly bodies. The resulting increase in water depth is a high tide. Water pulled away from the sides of the earth in the process produces a decrease in water depth called low tide. A high tide forms on the side of the earth opposite the moon because the attraction of the moon is least at that point and because of the centrifugal effect created by the rotation of the earth. At any given time, two areas on the earth are experiencing high tides and two areas are experiencing low tides. During a brief period of time called a **stand**, the tide neither rises nor falls; four tidal stands can occur per day—two high and two low. Geographical formations interfere with or enhance the rising and falling of the water in some areas.

The sun also affects the tides, but only about half as much as the moon because the moon is much closer to the earth. When the moon and the sun are aligned with the earth, which occurs twice monthly (during the new and full moons), tides are highest and are called **spring tides** (see figure 5.10). When the moon and sun are at right angles to each other in relation to the earth, tides are lowest and are called **neap tides**.

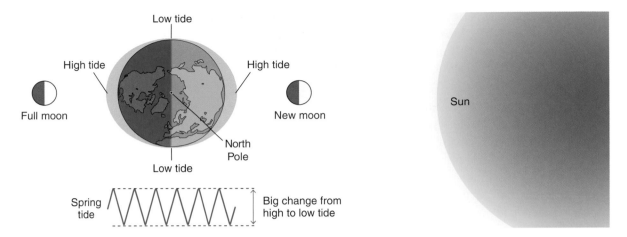

Figure 5.10   The effect of the sun and moon on tidal patterns.

The moon rotates around the earth in the same direction that the earth spins; therefore, the duration of a lunar day (moonrise to moonrise) is nearly 25 hours. This causes tides to occur at different times each day and explains why the heights of subsequent tides vary.

During a tidal change, water flows from one area to another. The water movements caused by the tides are called tidal currents, and they vary in velocity between tides. The flow of water into an area because of high tide is called a **flood**. The flow of water away from an area because of low tide is called an **ebb**. Between flood and ebb, a period of time occurs when the water has minimal movement. The term for this period is **slack water**. Because of geographical features of the earth, water cannot move instantly in many areas. There is usually a delay between the predicted time of a tide and the time when the water is slack.

Tidal changes affect diving activities and operations. Large differences in the water level between tides affect visibility and other conditions. Water height also affects entries and exits, shoal areas when boating, the mooring of boats, and the loading and unloading of vessels. Divers should know how high the tide will be. Tidal changes are small (less than 2 feet, or 0.6 m) in some areas or on some days, but they are large (more than 6 feet, or 1.8 m) in other areas or on other days. The greater the difference between high and low tide, the greater the effect of the tides.

Because the earth, moon, and sun follow set courses, the tides are predictable. Tides vary because the distance between planetary bodies and their positions relative to one another change constantly. Despite all the variables, scientists can predict with accuracy when the tides will occur and the heights of the tides. The U.S. government publishes tide tables, and national weather channels broadcast tidal information continuously. Local correction tables and current tables can provide more precise information. Tide tables refer to the height of the tide in relation to an average of the low tides in an area (see figure 5.11). Wind and barometric pressure affect the height of tides, aiding or opposing the movement of tidal waters.

November 2015							
	Low tide				**High tide**		
	a.m.	ht.	p.m.	ht.	a.m.	ht.	p.m.	ht.
	Sunrise 6:19		-PST-		Sunset 5:08			
1 Su	1:35	1.0	2:35	0.5	7:49	6.4	8:46	4.7
2 M	2:06	1.3	3:17	0.9	8:21	6.7	9:36	4.4
3 Tu	2:38	1.7	4:06	1.0	8:56	8.8	10:35	4.0
4 W	3:14	2.1	5:02	0.9	9:33	6.7	11:44	3.7
5 Th	3:50	2.6	6:03	0.7	10:19	6.5	—	—
	Sunrise 6:24		-PST-		Sunset 5:03			
6 F	4:42	3.0	7:17	0.4	1:14	3.5	(11:15 | 6.0)
7 Sa	6:00	3.3	8:36	0.2	2:57	3.8	12:28	5.4
8 Su	8:23	3.3	9:43	0.1	4:15	4.0	2:03	
9 M	10:12	2.8	10:42	0.1	5:01	4.4	3:39	
10 Tu	11:22	2.1	11:27	0.3	5:37	4.9	4:55	
	Sunrise 6:28		-PST-		Sunset 5:00			
11 W	—	—	12:14	1.4	6:09	5.3	5:	
12 Th	12:06	0.6	12:59	0.8	6:34	5.6	6	
13 F	12:38	0.9	1:38	0.3	6:59	5.9		
14 Sa	1:07	1.3	2:13	0.1	7:24	8.1		
15 Su	1:31	1.6	2:45	0.3	7:47	6.2		
	Sunrise 6:33		-PST-		Sunset			
16 M	1:56	2.0	3:21	0.4	8:1			
17 Tu	2:21	2.2	3:53	0.3				
18 W	2:40	2.5	4:33	0.				
19 Th	3:03	2.7	5:1					
20 F	3:21	3.0						

Figure 5.11   Tide table.

Generally, it is best to dive at high tide, but you may need to time your diving to coincide with slack water in areas with strong tidal currents. The timing may not be important in areas where tidal changes are small. Consider local knowledge about the effects of tides when planning your dives.

Waves and Surf

Ripples form when wind blows across water. You can see this in a puddle on a windy day. When ripples form on a large body of water and the wind continues to blow, the sides of the ripples form a surface against which the wind can push to set the water in motion. The longer and harder the wind blows in a constant direction, the larger the waves that form. As waves move away from the area in which they were created—an area called the **fetch**—the tops of the waves become rounded, undulating forms called **swells**. The water within a swell moves in a circular motion but has little forward motion. The effect is similar to the transmission of a waveform along a rope that is tossed up and down at one end. Waves of energy travel along the rope, but the rope itself does not move forward.

Swells are energy forms that can travel thousands of miles through water and still contain a great deal of energy. The top of a wave is called the **crest**. The bottom is called the **trough**. The distance from the crest to the trough is the **wave height**. The distance between waves is a **wavelength**. The time it takes two waves to pass a given point is a **wave period**. A long series of waves is a **wave train**. The greater the height of a wave and the greater the wavelength of a train of waves, the greater the energy contained in the waves. Two trains of waves can have phases during which the waves of each train reinforce one another and produce larger waves, called wave sets. The formation of larger and smaller waves can occur in phases. By timing the rhythm of the surf, you can make entries and exits easier by moving through the surf zone when the wave sets are small. Figure 5.12 illustrates fundamental concepts of waves and surf.

The water within a passing wave moves in a circular motion (this motion is called an orb). The diameter of the motion equals the height of the wave at the surface and diminishes with depth. Motion from a passing wave can be felt to a depth equal to half the wavelength for a series of waves. If there is 100 feet (30 m) between waves, you can feel the effect of a passing wave to a depth of 50 feet (15 m).

When waves enter shallow water, contact with the bottom interrupts the circular motion of the water within the waves. The circular movements flatten and eventually become a back-and-forth subsurface motion called **surge**. Wave contact with the bottom causes waves to slow and to become steeper. The wave height increases as the depth of the water decreases. When the depth of the water is about the same as the wave height, the wave becomes unstable and tumbles forward. At this point, the water within the wave moves forward and gives up its energy in breaking waves known as **surf**. In areas with offshore reefs, sand bars, and underwater obstructions, waves can break in shallow water, pass over the obstruction, reform, and break again in shallow water near the shore. Waves that break offshore indicate the presence of shallow water in the area where the waves are breaking.

Waves can break and release their energy all at once, or they can spill forward and expend their energy over a wide area. Waves that build quickly and break suddenly form plunging breakers. Waves that spill forward over some distance to shore are spilling breakers. Plunging breakers occur on steeply sloping shores,

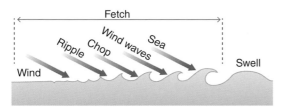

Wind over water causes waves—undulating forms of energy that can travel thousands of miles.

Wave movement is a flow of energy similar to that caused by vertically shaking one end of a rope.

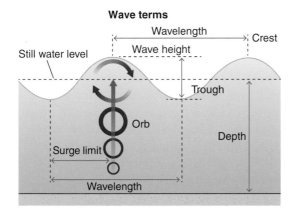

As a wave passes, water particles (represented by the circles) do not move with the wave; rather, they complete their orbit by returning to their starting point.

Wave sets resulting from two wave trains

Types of breakers

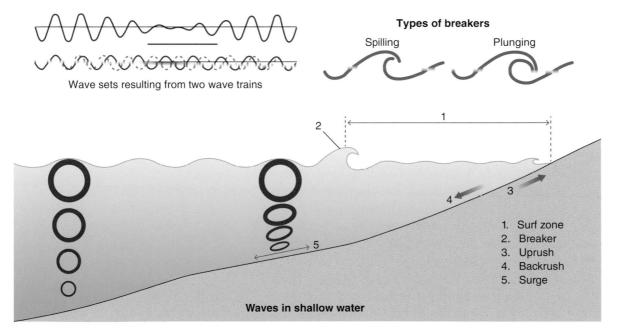

Figure 5.12   Wind speed, the absence or presence of obstacles, and the shape and depth of the ocean floor influence the formation of waves and surf.

while spilling breakers occur on bottoms with shallow slopes. Spilling breakers tend to reduce visibility more than plunging breakers.

The crashing water of surf contains air. The white water and foam in the surf zone do not provide as much buoyancy as water that does not contain air. It can be difficult to remain above water in the foam of surf, but you should not attempt to rise above the breakers because you can be picked up and tossed forward by the moving water. You should remain low in the wave and breathe from your scuba regulator.

Surf rushes up the face of a beach and then flows back again to the still water level. The return flow of water is called the backrush. This countercurrent, sometimes called an undertow, does not extend beyond a depth of three feet (about a meter). Although backrush can be strong when surf is large on a steep beach, the belief that an undertow can carry a swimmer out to sea is a misconception.

The surf's crashing onto the shore moves sand. Gentle summer waves carry sand onto the beach. Large, rough winter waves carry the sand offshore, where it forms sand bars. This action explains why some beaches are rocky in the winter and smooth in the summer.

Currents

Currents are to water what wind is to air—fluid in motion. Because water is 800 times denser than air, water poses much more resistance to movement than air. You need to know how and why water moves and how to move with it. The force of water in motion is too great to resist. You must learn to use the flow of water to your advantage.

Wind, gravity, tides, and convection cause currents; the most common currents are wind-generated surface currents. Because of the rotation of the earth, currents flow at an angle to the wind that generates them. When the wind pushes water away from an area, a compensating current replaces the water displaced. Overall, the effect on the earth is to produce large circulating currents, called **gyres**, that move clockwise in the northern hemisphere and counterclockwise in the southern hemisphere.

When wind blows along a coast, a vertical compensating current—an upwelling—occurs. Another vertical current, the opposite of an upwelling, is a **downwelling**. A strong downwelling current is rare, but it can occur under the right conditions where there is a steep drop-off near shore. It is frightening to be pulled downward in water. You should find out if and where a downwelling occurs in an area, and you should avoid that location. If you get caught in a downwelling, swim horizontally until you are clear of the current. Trying to swim up against the current can lead to exhaustion and panic.

Water flows in layers (see figure 5.13). The water at the surface moves quickly with the wind, whereas the water a few feet beneath the surface moves slower. The greater the depth, the less the effect of a surface current. After 12 hours of a sustained wind in a given direction, the speed of a surface current is approximately 2 percent of the wind that drives it. Because water flows in layers, it is possible for a surface current to flow in one direction and for a subsurface current to flow in the opposite direction only a few feet beneath the surface.

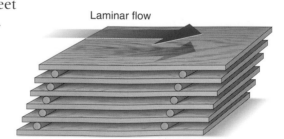

Figure 5.13 The laminar flow of water is similar to a stack of boards with rollers between them. When the stack is tipped, the top board moves much farther than the bottom board. Surface water moves more than water at depth.

Surface water at the equator expands as it is warmed and flows slowly toward the poles of the earth. At the same time, water cooled near the poles increases in density and sinks. Slow-moving convection currents result. These currents do not affect diving procedures, but they greatly affect the oceans by moving nutrients and pollution.

Water can move swiftly, and water movement intensifies whenever an amount of water passes through a restriction. When water moves past irregular formations, turbulence produces dangerous eddies and whirlpools. Swift-water diving is a specialty that is considered hazardous even with experience and training.

Incoming waves can pass over an underwater obstruction, such as a sand bar, and trap water on a shore. If the backrush of water flows back to sea through a narrow opening in the obstruction, a **rip current** exists. The current is narrow and strong and moves away from shore. The current dissipates shortly after passing through the restricted area. You can identify rips by a fan-shaped area of water on the shore, by muddy and foamy water in the rip area, and by a section of waves that breaks before the other waves (see figure 5.14). Rip currents can be stationary or moving. You must learn to recognize and avoid rip currents. If you are unable to swim toward shore, you are probably in a rip current. Swim parallel to the shore for about 60 feet (18 m) to get clear of the rip; then turn and proceed toward shore.

Waves breaking on a shore at a slight angle move water along the shore. The current is called a longshore current, and it affects diving. On steep beaches, the current can cut a shallow trough in the bottom close to shore. The trough, called a longshore trench, is a sudden drop-off and can cause an unsuspecting wading diver to fall. Items dropped into the surf zone move along the shoreline in the direction of the longshore current. The movement of sand on beaches occurs because of wave action combined with longshore currents.

Two types of currents result from all the forces of nature: standing currents, which are constant, and transitory currents, which occur briefly. The Gulf Stream that flows around Florida and up the eastern coast of the United States and the Antilles Current that flows through the Caribbean are examples of standing

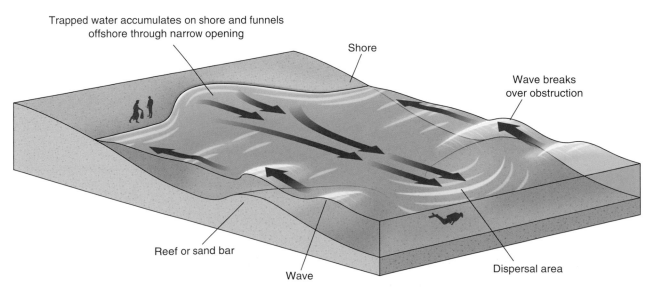

Figure 5.14   A classic rip current.

currents. A longshore current is a transitory current. A rip current can be either type. You should be familiar with the currents you will encounter or may encounter in an area.

Currents can flow at a rate of hundreds of feet per minute. The speed of a current is its **drift**, and the direction assumed by a current is its **set**. A fully equipped diver can swim at a rate of 60 to 100 feet (18 to 30 m) per minute (0.6 to 1.0 knots). Attempting to fight even a mild current is a futile waste of energy. Strong water movement can dislodge equipment, cause regulators to free-flow, and cause rapid heat loss. You must learn to recognize and estimate currents. If the currents are strong, you must avoid them. Even if they are mild, you should avoid struggling against them. The primary rule for diving in currents—when you begin and end your dive at the same point—is to dive in a direction opposite the flow at the surface; then use the surface current to aid you when you return at the end of the dive. (See chapter 7 for techniques to estimate currents.)

You also need to know some other general rules for diving in currents. Water movement is minimal at the bottom. Whenever possible, descend along a line from the surface to the bottom. If the current is still strong when you reach the bottom, ascend on the line and abort the dive. When you are unsure of your location during a dive, it may help to surface, determine the direction to the exit point, redescend, and move along the bottom toward your destination.

When there is a surface current, you should minimize the time spent at the surface. Whenever possible, hold on to a fixed object at the surface to keep from drifting downcurrent at a dive site. When a surface current is mild, swim against it to maintain your position at the surface. Develop the habit of noting your surface position in relation to a fixed reference. If you are caught in a sudden, strong current, swim across it to escape from it.

A dive in which the diver moves with the flow of a current is a **drift dive**. Simple drift dives along a coast are acceptable when planned. You enter the water at one point, move along the shore with the current, and exit at another point downstream. Another type of drift diving, which is a specialty activity, involves diving in currents from a boat. This type of diving is hazardous because the boat must be operated while divers are in the water. Do not attempt drift diving from boats unless you have completed specialty training and have a trained, experienced captain for the vessel.

Potential saltwater diving hazards include body heat loss, currents, surf, marine life, poor visibility, and fishing nets and equipment. You can minimize the hazards of ocean diving by following the recommendations that were described in this section.

Boat Diving

All divers eventually dive from boats, either small private boats or large charter vessels. Space is limited aboard boats, so you should organize your equipment compactly and pack it in the order in which you will need it. You may need to carry equipment for some distance to a boat, so plan to wear your scuba tank and weight belt and carry a bag in each hand. One bag should contain your dive gear, and the other bag should hold your lunch, camera, and any items that you want to keep dry.

Charter Boat Diving

You need to be well rested, so you should avoid partying the night before boat diving. Eat a meal that is free of acid and fat before you depart. Arrive at least 30 minutes before the scheduled departure time. Check in with a crew member. Usually, you must sign a roster and complete some forms. Ask where to stow your gear, and pick out a suitable space to store your dry items. If you are prone to seasickness, take preventive medication before the boat gets underway.

Tour the vessel. Locate the head (bathroom) and the emergency equipment. Stay out of the engine room and the wheelhouse (see example in figure 5.15). If you did not come with a buddy, you should find one before reaching the dive site. Listen carefully to the orientation provided by the captain or crewmember.

If you begin to feel queasy after the boat gets underway, you should go outside to the center of the boat and concentrate on the horizon. Sleep may help you acclimate to the boat's motion. If you are nauseated or vomiting when it is time to dive, avoid scuba diving. Vomiting underwater is hazardous. Mildly seasick divers may recover by snorkeling or by swimming to a nearby shore and waiting until they feel better.

Diving operations begin only when indicated by the captain. When you are ready to enter the water, check out with the divemaster. Typically, you will enter the water by stepping off the side of the boat, and you will exit the water by boarding a swim step at the stern (rear) of the vessel. Using the anchor line for your descent is a good practice.

Begin your dive against any current so that the water movement can assist you back to the boat at the end of the dive. Crew members often deploy a **trail line**—a long line with a float attached—to the stern for you to use in pulling yourself to the boat against the current (see figure 5.16). You should dive upcurrent; however, if you end up downcurrent from the boat and are unable to reach the trail line, you should make yourself buoyant, signal the boat, remain calm, and wait to be picked up after all the other divers have boarded the vessel.

If you hear a yelping, sirenlike sound while underwater, you should surface. The sound is from an electronic diver recall system. Remain where you are, and

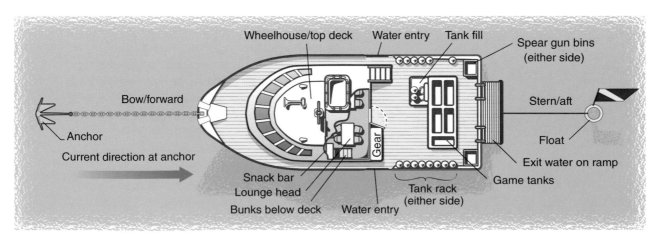

Figure 5.15   Typical charter boat configuration.

Figure 5.16 Divers can use a trail line to pull themselves to the boat if they surface downcurrent.

look to the boat for instructions. Learn the vessel's recall procedures in advance.

At the end of the dive, return to the boat by swimming along the bottom or at the surface. You should avoid skimming (swimming just beneath the surface), because you cannot be seen and you could be struck by a passing boat. Also avoid crowding the exit area. Divers should exit one or two at a time and remain clear of divers climbing the boarding ladder. Retain your equipment until immediately before exiting the water. If you do not know what equipment to remove, ask for instructions. Immediately after exiting, pick up any equipment that you handed to someone during your exit, and clear the exit area to make room for others.

After your last dive, pack your equipment before the boat gets underway. Be available for a visual roll call, which is required. Watch and learn from experienced divers.

Charter boat dives provide memorable diving experiences. Learn the proper techniques for diving from charter boats and then do what you have learned.

Small-Boat Diving

When you plan to dive from a small boat, make sure the boat is equipped for safety and has all the equipment required by the Coast Guard. The boat should also have a first aid kit. Leave a float plan—information about where you are going and when you plan to return—with someone who can summon assistance if you are delayed. Have a radio or cell phone aboard for emergency communications. Check the weather and water conditions in advance, and reschedule the dive if conditions will be unfavorable or are marginal on the planned dive day. Diving is not good when the weather is bad.

Small boats pitch, roll, and pound, so stow your equipment securely and expect it to get wet. If the trip to the dive site is short, you should suit up on shore. Doing so is easier and safer. If you must suit up in a small boat, remain seated and help one another. Before you enter the water, make sure that there is a means to get back into the boat. More than one diver has been stranded alongside a boat, unable to exit the water. Display the dive flag, but only while diving. Deploy a trail line and float.

The usual entry from a small boat is a seated back roll made by two divers at the same time. This method enables the divers to avoid rocking the boat and causing one diver to lose balance and fall in when unprepared. The descent should be down the anchor line to ensure that the anchor is set and clear. If possible, you should leave an operator in the boat. A sudden weather change, a slipping anchor, or a change of water movement could pose serious problems at the end of a dive if the boat is unattended.

At the end of the dive, remove your weights and scuba unit before exiting. If you cannot hand them to someone in the boat, clip them to gear lines that have been hung over the side. Exit the water and pull in your equipment.

Boat diving is good diving. Be prepared, conserve space, plan ahead, learn the rules, and follow those rules. Learn more about boating to make boat diving more enjoyable. Complete a course in seamanship and small-boat handling.

Summary

The aquatic environment is vast and wonderful. We depend on it for our existence. We need to learn about it, care for it, and respect it. We must protect the environment and encourage everyone we know to assist in that effort. Because the environment varies greatly from place to place, you need an area orientation before diving. There are hazards in the underwater world, just as there are hazards on land. You can minimize aquatic hazards with training, experience, planning, proper procedures, and common sense.

Application-of-Knowledge (AOK) Questions

This chapter provides knowledge but does not explain how to apply it. In the remaining chapters you will learn the skills for diving in various environments. Right now you need to digest what you know about the diving environment and consider how it might affect your diving.

1. In what ways will the temperature of the water affect your diving?
2. In what ways will the visibility under water be affected by the environment and by you?
3. What ways can you recall that can help you manage currents while diving?
4. When you encounter strange animals while diving, how should you respond?
5. How much training and experience are required until you are able to dive anywhere at any time?
6. When you are an experienced scuba diver, where is the safest and most comfortable place to be when diving?
7. If you were equipped for diving in the ocean and wanted to dive in fresh water, what equipment changes would you need to make?
8. What do you think you need to know about diving conditions when you intend to go diving?

Beautiful coral reefs in the Red Sea

Diving Skills

Dive In and Discover

By the end of this chapter, you will be able to do the following:

- Prepare, assemble, don, adjust, inspect, and disassemble your equipment for skin and scuba diving.
- Demonstrate 16 skin and scuba diving hand signals.
- Explain how to test and control buoyancy.
- Explain how to clear water from a mask, a snorkel, and a scuba regulator.
- Explain how to descend, swim with fins, and ascend when skin and scuba diving.
- Explain how to handle, remove, and replace skin and scuba diving equipment.
- Describe various entry and exit techniques for skin and scuba diving.
- Explain how to use dive flags.
- Explain the buddy system and lost buddy procedures.
- Explain how to use a compass for underwater navigation.
- Explain how to prevent and manage seasickness, dizziness, stress and panic, overexertion, coughing, cramps, entanglement, loss of buoyancy control, loss of air supply, and dive emergencies.
- Explain how to rescue a diver who is not breathing and the first aid procedures for an injured scuba diver.
- Define the terms *buddy system, flutter kick, scissors kick, modified frog kick, dolphin kick, surf, neutral buoyancy, diver's push-ups, open-valve ascent, reference descent, nonreference descent, buddy line, compass heading, compass course, reciprocal compass course, flaring,* and *buddy breathing.*

You will learn most of the diving skills in controlled conditions; when you have developed the basic skills, you will apply them in open water. (Open water is any body of water representative of dive sites in the local area.) When you can demonstrate the skills of diving in open water, you are ready to receive your diving certification.

Preparing to Skin Dive

This section covers the skills of skin diving, many of which apply to scuba diving. When you swim at the surface and breathe through a snorkel, you are snorkeling. Scuba divers snorkel to conserve the air in their cylinder for underwater activities. When you breathe through a snorkel at the surface, hold your breath, and dive beneath the surface, you are skin diving. As a diver, you need to master the skills of snorkeling, skin diving, and scuba diving in order to enjoy all that the underwater world has to offer.

Preparing Equipment

Be ready to start your lesson when you come to your first water session. Prepare your mask, snorkel, and fins in advance. Clean your mask lens thoroughly so it will not fog (a description of the cleaning procedure is provided in chapter 4). Adjust the mask strap so it is snug but not tight. Attach the snorkel to the mask strap on the left side, and adjust the snorkel so it is comfortable in your mouth. If your fins have heel straps, adjust them so they are snug but not tight. Complete all adjustments before your first water session.

Inspect your skin diving vest or buoyancy compensator by inflating it, making sure it does not leak, and then deflating it. Put it on, reinflate it, and adjust the strap or straps so it will stay in position in the water. You may need to use a strap that runs between your legs and attaches to the front and back of the flotation device to keep it from riding up when you are in the water.

If you wear an exposure suit, your instructor will suggest an initial amount of weight for your weight belt. Adjust the length of the belt at the buckle end so the excess strap at the opposite end does not exceed 6 inches (15 cm). Allow 2 inches (5 cm) for each two-slot weight that you thread onto the belt. Distribute the weight on both sides of the belt so that you will be balanced in the water. Lock the weights in place with weight retainers.

Mark your personal equipment with your initials so that you can identify it. You can use special paint or markers (available at dive stores) or colored tape. Pack

Diving requires many skills, and you must repeat these skills correctly until you can execute them automatically. When you have mastered the skills of diving, your enjoyment can begin because you will be able to devote more attention to things of interest. The basic skills of skin diving and scuba diving are introduced in this chapter.

Anemones and clownfish in the Red Sea

your equipment—with the exception of your weight belt—in a gear bag. Place the items you will don last, such as your fins, on the bottom. Place the items you will don first, such as your exposure suit, on the top.

Donning and Inspecting Skin Diving Equipment

Don the pants or legs of your exposure suit first, then your boots, and then the top part of your suit. Donning a snug-fitting wet suit is easier if you wet the inside of your suit with water (to which you have added some mild shampoo) or if you wear a spandex suit as an undergarment. Place the ends of the legs of your wet suit over the tops of your boots so that water can drain from your suit when you exit from a dive. If the boots are outside the legs of your wet suit, water from the suit will balloon your boots when you get out of the water. If you become warm while donning the exposure suit, cool yourself before proceeding with your preparations. For open-water diving, don a cold-water hood before donning your wet suit jacket so that the skirt of the hood is underneath your jacket.

After you put on your exposure suit, you should clean and defog your dive mask and then set it aside until you are ready to don it (see the description of the cleaning procedure in chapter 4). Leave about 1/2 inch (1.27 cm) of water inside the mask so it will not dry before you put it on, and place the mask where it will not get damaged.

Don your skin diving vest or BC next. Place the skin diving vest over your head, and then secure the straps. Inflate the vest fully to make sure it will not be too tight. The straps should be as snug as possible without being uncomfortable or interfering with breathing.

Don your weight belt after the skin diving vest so the belt will be clear of the vest straps. Grasp the free end of the weight belt (the end without the buckle) in your right hand, and grasp the buckle end in your left hand. Pick up the belt, step through it, pull it into position across your back, and bend forward so that gravity supports the weight of the belt. Then tighten the belt and secure the quick release. Always wear the weight belt with a right-hand release, even if you are left-handed, so that a rescuer will know how to release your belt in an emergency. If you always hold the free end of the belt in your right hand when donning it, you will always have a right-hand quick release.

Don the remainder of your skin diving equipment—mask, snorkel, and fins—at the water's edge or, if it is calm, in the water. Place the mask on your forehead and pull the mask strap over the back of your head using both hands to position the strap. Position the mask on your face, clearing any hair from beneath the sealing edge of the mask. Reposition the mask strap so it lies flat. If the mask has a split strap, position the split above and below the crown of your head. Don your snorkel when you don your mask. Check the adjustment of the snorkel when your mask is in place.

Stabilize yourself when putting on fins so that you don't lose your balance and fall. Hold on to your buddy (see "The Buddy Diving" section later in this chapter) or an object for support, or sit at the water's edge. Hold one side of a fin, bend one leg into a figure-four position, push the fin onto your foot, and pull the strap or heel pocket into place (see figure 6.1). Repeat the process for the other fin. Avoid walking with fins. If you must walk a few steps while wearing fins, shuffle your feet and walk backward. If you try to walk forward, you can lose your balance or damage your fins.

After you have donned your equipment, you should inspect it for completeness, correct positioning, and adjustment. When you are satisfied with your

Figure 6.1   Donning fins.

equipment, inspect your buddy's equipment while he inspects yours. Inspect from head to toe. You may be able to see something that your buddy could not see, or vice versa. Develop the habit of inspecting each other's equipment before every dive.

Skin Diving Skills

Diving skills can be divided into three categories: skin diving skills, scuba diving skills, and problem management skills. This section introduces skin diving skills.

Using Skin Diving Hand Signals

You cannot talk with a snorkel in your mouth and your face in the water, so you must use hand signals as a primary means of communication. You need to learn and use the standard hand signals shown in figure 6.2. You will learn additional hand signals for scuba diving. Display hand signals clearly and deliberately when you send them, and acknowledge all hand signals you receive.

Figure 6.2   Skin diving hand signals.

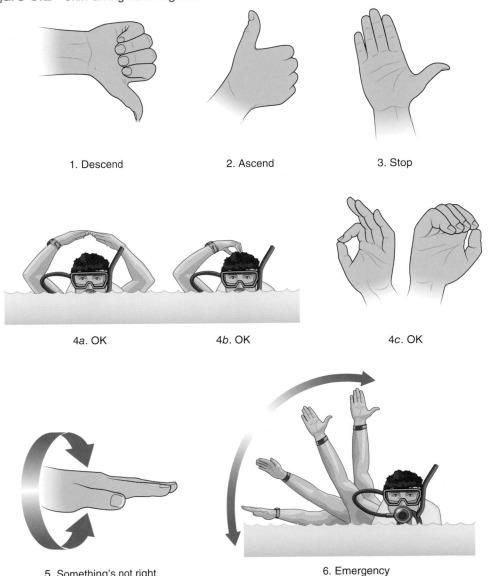

1. Descend   2. Ascend   3. Stop

4a. OK   4b. OK   4c. OK

5. Something's not right   6. Emergency

Using a Skin Diving Vest

You inflated and deflated your skin diving vest as part of your diving preparations. You also need to learn how to deflate and inflate the vest in the water. To deflate the vest, position your body so the vest's exhaust port is the highest point. Hold the deflation valve open while you sink lower in the water. The water pressure helps force the air from the vest. You may have to hold the collar of the vest down with one hand to remove the air from that area. When you have vented all of the air from the vest, close the valve to prevent water from entering. Get your buddy to confirm that all the air is out of your vest.

Inflating the vest in the water is easier with your head underwater instead of above water. Take a breath of air, duck your face beneath the surface, insert the oral inflator into your mouth, open the valve, exhale into the vest, and close the valve. Repeat this process until you have the desired buoyancy.

Testing Buoyancy

Your buoyancy should be neutral at the surface. If you are too buoyant, you will have to struggle to descend and remain underwater. If you are not buoyant enough, you will tire quickly at the surface and sink while swimming underwater. You must be able to adjust your buoyancy correctly.

If you are wearing an exposure suit, you need weights to offset the buoyancy of the suit. With all equipment in place, position yourself in chest-deep water. Exhaust all air from your skin diving vest. Take a full breath, hold it, lift your feet from the bottom, and remain motionless while you slowly count to 10. If you sink, remove some weight and try again. If you exhale half of the air in your fully inflated lungs and still can't submerge, you need to add weight until you can. When your weighting is correct, you remain at the surface while holding a full breath and sink when exhaling. Adjust your weighting until you achieve neutral buoyancy, which means that you neither sink nor float when holding an average breath. Have your buddy watch while you make the final test. With your lungs about half full of air, the top of your head should remain even with the surface of the water when you are motionless in a vertical position.

Clearing the Mask

When your head is above the surface, water inside a mask will run out if you pull the bottom of the mask away from your face. Water inside a mask underwater also flows out the bottom of the mask if you displace the water with air. Putting air inside the mask is easy: Just exhale lightly through your nose. A long, light exhalation is better than a short, forceful one because a strong exhalation blows air past the seal of the mask and does not displace water effectively.

To clear a mask that has a purge valve, seal the mask against your face, tilt your head downward to make the purge the lowest point in the mask, and exhale through your nose until the mask is clear of water. To clear a mask without a purge, hold the top of the mask against your forehead, take a breath, and start exhaling slowly (see figure 6.3). When the level of the water is below your eyes, tilt your head back while continuing to exhale, and the remainder of the water will flow out the bottom of the mask. You must be exhaling when you tilt your head back or water will run up your nose. Bubbles from the bottom of the mask indicate when you have cleared all the water from your mask. It may

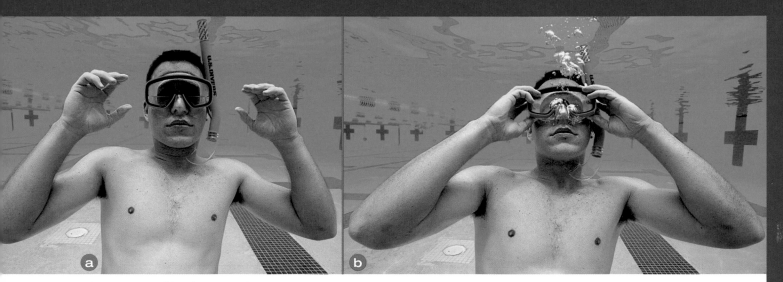

Figure 6.3 Clearing a mask.

sound as though it takes a long time and a lot of air to clear a mask, but with practice you will be able to flood and clear your mask several times after a single inhalation. Clearing requires only a few seconds.

Using the Snorkel

Stand in the water and lean forward with the snorkel in your mouth. Place your face in the water and inhale gently. If you inhale forcefully at first, you might inhale water. When you are sure the tube is clear, you may breathe more forcefully through your snorkel. When you descend beneath the surface, the snorkel tube can fill with water. Self-draining snorkels drain nearly all the water from the tube when you surface.

If your snorkel is not the self-draining or water exclusion type, you have to blast the water from the tube with a strong, sharp exhalation. To do this, blow hard into the snorkel to force the water out. Inhale cautiously after exhaling. If a little water remains in the tube, you can breathe past it if you inhale gently. After you fill your lungs again, expel the remaining water with another forceful exhalation.

If you have a simple snorkel without valves, you can clear the tube while ascending by using the displacement method. Begin by looking up to invert the snorkel; then exhale a small amount of air into the tube. As you ascend, the air expands according to Boyle's law and displaces the water in the tube, which will be clear of water when you reach the surface. The tube is inverted at this point, however, so when you turn it to the upright position, water will flow into the tube unless you exhale while rolling your head forward at the surface. Continuous exhalation prevents water from entering the tube. When you use the displacement method, which is easier than the blast method, you can take a breath the moment you reach the surface. Figure 6.4 shows the displacement method.

Figure 6.4 Displacement method of clearing a snorkel.

Learn to keep the snorkel in your mouth when you are in the water. Avoid the temptation to remove the mouthpiece and shake the water from your snorkel. You do not have to remove the mouthpiece when you can clear your snorkel proficiently. When your hands are occupied, you will not be able to remove and replace the snorkel to clear it.

Using Fins

Fins provide large surfaces that you can push—using the strong muscles of your legs—against the water for propulsion. The blades of the fins need to push the water the way a broom sweeps a floor. A broom cannot sweep if you move it up and down, and your fins will not provide propulsion if you move them length-wise in the water. You must kick them back and forth in wide, sweeping kicks. Small fins allow short, quick kicks, but larger fins require wider, slower kicks. Moving efficiently, not speedily, is your objective when wearing fins.

The most common fin kick is the **flutter kick**, which is an up-and-down kick that you can do facing down, up, or to the side. Your fins need to be underwater to provide propulsion. It is easier to keep your fins submerged at the surface when you are on your back or on your side instead of your belly. Move your legs up and down from the hip while bending your knees only slightly. Extend your legs almost fully throughout each stroke, and use wide, slow kicks. Keep your hands at your sides or extend them in front. Do not use your hands and arms to swim. Figure 6.5 shows the flutter kick.

The **scissors kick**, shown in figure 6.6, is a resting kick. The scissors kick is similar to a flutter kick, but it requires less energy. While lying on your side, slowly extend one leg backward while you extend the other leg forward, and then pull your legs together quickly. Hold a streamlined position with your toes pointed while you glide through the water. When you come to a stop, repeat the stroke. Extend your legs almost fully throughout the stroke.

A **modified frog kick** is useful because it uses different muscles than the flutter and scissors kicks. Changing kicks is helpful if you become tired or develop leg cramps. The modified frog kick is different from a swimmer's frog kick. Assume a facedown position with your fins perpendicular to the bottom. Rotate your ankles so that the tips of the fins point outward, slide the fins tip first in an outward direction, then pull the bottoms of the fins together quickly in a wide, sweeping arc. Extend your legs almost fully throughout the stroke, and then hold the final position with your feet together and your toes pointed while you glide (see figure 6.7). When you come to a stop, repeat the stroke.

Figure 6.5 Flutter kick.

Figure 6.6 Scissors kick.

The **dolphin kick** is also useful for a change of pace or if you lose a fin. Hold both feet together continuously. Exert force against the water with a wavelike up-and-down motion of your body. To begin, straighten your body, extend your feet together, bend your shoulders forward, and pull your feet slightly backward. Next, lift your shoulders, thrust forward forcefully with your hips, and then pull down with your fins. When you see this kick demonstrated, you will be able to learn it by imitation. If you lose a fin, you can use the dolphin kick to propel yourself. Cross your legs and put the leg without a fin behind the one that has a fin. Figure 6.8 shows the dolphin kick.

Performing Surface Dives

You need to be able to dive down to see the beautiful world beneath the surface. The initial dive beneath the surface of the water is a surface dive. The principle of a surface dive is simple: You raise part of your body above the water and point yourself straight down; the part of your weight above the water drives you downward. Once you are submerged, you start swimming to continue your descent.

You should learn three types of surface dives: the pike, the tuck, and the feet-first dive (see figure 6.9). You do the pike dive while moving forward at the surface. Bend forward at the waist to make your trunk vertical in the water. Next, quickly lift your legs out of the water to a vertical position. The more of your legs you can lift out of the water, the farther your surface dive will push you under the water. For shallow dives, you can do the pike dive by lifting only one leg.

When you have learned the pike dive, you are ready for the tuck dive, which is similar. Do the tuck dive from a stationary position. Begin in an upright position in the water, pull your knees to your chest, and sweep backward with your arms to roll yourself forward in the water. When you are inverted, extend yourself fully into a vertical position. The procedure is a coordinated movement that you must do quickly to get your legs above water. After you extend your legs, the remainder of the dive is the same as the pike dive.

Use a feet-first dive in areas where surface plant growth is dense because you are less likely to get entangled. Begin in a stationary, upright position, and use a strong scissors kick to propel yourself up and out of the water as far as possible. Pull your arms downward to your sides for added lift. When you reach the highest point, point your toes downward, and hold your arms to your sides. The weight of your body will push you below the surface. Raise your arms upward when you are below the surface to push yourself even lower. When your downward momentum ends, do a tuck dive to invert yourself, then continue your descent.

Figure 6.7   Modified frog kick.

Figure 6.8   Dolphin kick.

Pike

Tuck

Feet-first

Figure 6.9 Surface dives.

Performing Descents, Underwater Swimming, and Ascents

To prepare to descend, vent all air from your flotation device. Use an ear-clearing maneuver (described in chapter 3) at the surface so that it will be easy to equalize pressure in your ears while you descend. Hyperventilate three times, inhale as fully as possible, and don't exhale until you return to the surface.

Initiate your descent with a good surface dive. Equalize the pressure in your ears and mask every couple of feet during your descent. Use wide, slow, powerful kicks to propel yourself to your desired depth, and then relax as much as possible.

Swimming underwater sounds simple, but some people have trouble controlling direction. Your head is your rudder. Pull your head backward while swimming facedown to go up. Bend your head forward to go down. Bend your trunk to the left or right to turn. With practice, you can go in any direction you choose without using your hands.

Follow these four rules for ascents:

1. Reach up; extend one arm over your head for protection (see figure 6.10).

2. Look up to avoid obstructions and to determine when the surface is near.

3. Come up slowly. A slow ascent is better than a rapid ascent because swimming rapidly uses more oxygen.

4. Revolve once or twice during your ascent to check your surroundings.

Alternate breath-hold dives with your buddy. One diver should remain at the surface, watching, while the other diver is underwater. Make sure your buddy knows where you are at all times.

Handling Equipment

Occasionally you may need to remove, adjust, and replace skin diving equipment while you are in the water. You should be able to handle your equipment easily with training and practice.

Figure 6.10 Extend your arm for protection during a skin diving ascent.

To remove, adjust, and replace your mask, begin by inflating your skin diving vest. Because you will make the adjustment above water, you should use buoyancy to reduce the effort. After you make the adjustment, replace your mask using the procedure for donning the mask described earlier in this chapter.

You may need to adjust a fin strap or remove sand or gravel from your fins while diving. The fins are easier to remove, adjust, and replace than the mask is. You do not need as much buoyancy to work with your fins because you can look into the water and make the adjustment underwater. In fact, too much air in your skin diving vest can be a nuisance. Keep your face in the water, breathe through your snorkel, and work with one fin at a time.

You may need to tighten, adjust, or replace your weight belt. The weights may slip, or the belt may fall off. To tighten or replace your weight belt, you need to get the belt across the small of your back while you are in a facedown position breathing through your snorkel. If you try to replace or tighten the belt in an upright position, you will have a constant fight with gravity. When you are in the correct, facedown position, gravity becomes your ally while you secure the buckle. To get the belt into position across your back, begin in an upright position, holding the free end of the weight belt against the outside of your right thigh. Lean back into a horizontal, faceup position momentarily, and then roll to your left to a facedown position while continuing to hold the free end of the belt against your right thigh. At this point, the belt will be draped across the backs of your thighs. Clear your snorkel so that you can breathe. While holding the free end of the belt in your right hand, reach down with your left hand, grab the buckle end, pull the belt into position across your back, and secure the buckle.

Removing Equipment

Your equipment helps you adapt to the underwater environment. Develop the habit of keeping your equipment in place while you are in the water. You may need to defog your mask or make an adjustment, but other than that you should wear your equipment continuously. Avoid the tendency to prop your mask on your forehead when you are at the surface. Mask propping is a sign of distress and a good way to lose your mask and snorkel. If you must remove your mask while in the water, pull it down around your neck where it will be secure.

Bottom conditions at the dive site determine whether you should remove your fins when leaving the water. In some areas, you can remove your fins in waist-deep water and wade out of the water. In other areas, you need to wear your fins until you are clear of the water. Fins can be removed in several ways. When you prepare to climb a boat ladder, hold the ladder continuously while crossing your legs in a figure-four position to remove each fin. If the boat has a platform at the rear, swim onto the swim step and remove your fins in a kneeling position. When you remove fins in waist-deep water or on land, you should use your buddy for support. On steep beaches, you may choose to crawl from the water. Your buddy can remove your fins while you are on your hands and knees. Your buddy then crawls ahead of you, and you remove your buddy's fins. When you stand up, you exchange fins.

Weight belt removal also varies. When you can walk or climb out of the water, keep your belt on while doing so. When you remove a weight belt, lower it gently instead of dropping it. You can cause damage or injury if you develop the habit of dropping your weight belt. If you must pull yourself onto a dock or into a small boat, remove your belt first and hand it up.

Keep your skin diving vest in place until you are clear of the water. Remove your skin diving vest, and then your wet suit. Remove your wet suit by turning it inside out. Be sure to remove your boots before your wet suit pants. You will need assistance from your buddy to remove a pullover jacket or a jumpsuit.

Preparing to Scuba Dive

Nearly all of the skills of skin diving are used in scuba diving, but you need to learn many additional skills for scuba diving. This section introduces the preparatory skills of scuba diving; the next section covers basic and postdive skills. The more familiar you become with the skills by studying them, the better you will be able to perform them. You must learn the skills correctly from the outset in order to develop good habits for diving safety.

Packing Equipment

Nothing is more inconvenient than getting ready to dive and discovering that something is missing or not right. You should take steps to prevent equipment inconveniences. Begin by using a checklist when you pack your diving equipment to ensure that you have everything you need (see the diving equipment checklist). After taking inventory, inspect your equipment as you pack it. If you have not used your equipment for a while, assemble it and test it first. Make sure everything works properly.

Pack your equipment in your gear bag—except for your weight belt, tank, and BC. When you have to carry your equipment, put your BC on your tank, and carry the tank on your back. Carry your gear bag in one hand, and carry your weight belt in the other hand. Equipment-carrying devices with roller wheels can reduce the work of moving your diving equipment (see figure 6.11).

Assembling Equipment

Today's backpacks are part of the BC and have one or more bands to secure the scuba cylinder. Many of the bands are made of webbing, which stretches when wet. Soak a fabric tank band in water for a couple of minutes before securing it around a scuba tank. The soaking softens the webbing and allows it to stretch when you tighten the band. A dry fabric belt may allow the tank to slip when the band gets wet and stretches. A tank that slips from a pack can be a hazard.

Orient your backpack with the opening of the tank valve facing the backpack. Stand the tank up with the valve handle facing to your right. Slide the tank band over the tank with the tank between you and the pack. Tighten the band so the valve opening points directly toward the pack (see figure 6.12).

The height of the tank band on the tank varies with the type of backpack. Generally, the top of the pack is even with the base of the tank valve. After you attach the pack

Figure 6.11   A gear bag with wheels can make transporting equipment easier.

Figure 6.12   Strapping the backpack to the tank.

and before you attach the regulator, don the scuba tank and check the height adjustment by slowly tilting your head backward. If your head hits the tank valve, the tank is too high in the pack. Reach over your shoulder for the tank valve. If you cannot touch it, the tank is too low in the pack. Adjust the height as needed. When you become familiar with the correct height adjustment, you will not need to test it before completing the assembly of the scuba unit, but you should check it before entering the water.

Tighten the band as much as possible before securing it, and test the tightness by grasping the tank valve with one hand and the top of the pack with the other hand. Try to move the pack up and down on the tank. If there is movement, the band needs to be tighter.

Attach the regulator assembly to the scuba tank. The tank valve should have a valve protector or a piece of tape over the valve opening. Remove the cover or tape (but do not litter—put the tape in a trash container or in your gear bag). Make sure that the O-ring remains in place and is free of debris. Loosen the regulator yoke screw, and remove the dust cover. If your regulator second stages have purge depressors, release the purges. Expel any water or dirt from the valve by opening the tank valve slightly and momentarily before you attach the regulator to the tank.

Your regulator has several hoses. Orient the hose to your primary second stage toward the same side of the tank as the handle of the tank valve so that the hose will come over your right shoulder. When you orient the hose this way, the other hoses are properly oriented automatically as long as they are untangled and can hang freely.

Carefully seat the inlet opening of the regulator on the tank valve outlet, and then turn the yoke screw or DIN fitting until it is snug but not tight. Tighten the fittings using only your fingers and thumb. See figure 6.13 for an example of a regulator attachment.

Attach the various regulator hoses to the scuba unit. It is easier to attach the low-pressure hose to the BC before you pressurize the hose. Attach your instrument console to the BC, but do not attach your extra second stage yet.

Turn on the air. Hold the SPG with the front facing away from you and others so it will not cause an injury if it fails when pressurized. The SPG blowout plug should prevent an explosion from occurring, but holding the gauge is a good precaution. Open the tank valve slowly in a counterclockwise direction. Open the valve all the way; then close it one-quarter turn. You should feel the hoses stiffen under pressure. Listen for leaks in the system. If the regulator free-flows, cover the mouthpiece opening with your thumb to stop the flow. If air leaks

Figure 6.13 Your regulator and hoses should look like this if attached correctly to the cylinder.

from the tank valve seal, turn the air off, remove the regulator, and inspect the seal. You may have to replace the O-ring. Solve all air leakage problems before you use the scuba unit.

Testing the unit is the final step. Use your SPG to make sure the tank is full. Reset instruments in your console as needed. While looking at the SPG, depress the regulator purges momentarily to test the second stages and clear them of any debris; then breathe deeply through each second stage several times. The tank pressure reading should remain constant while you breathe from the regulator. If the pressure reading drops when you inhale, you have not opened the tank valve sufficiently. Do not open the valve partially to check the pressure of the tank. When you have finished testing the regulators, attach the extra second stage to the BC. Depress the low-pressure inflation valve on the BC for one or two seconds to make sure the valve functions correctly. When you have completed the assembly and testing of the unit, lay it on its side with the regulator and instruments on top.

Equipment assembly procedures are the same for both new and experienced divers. Always assemble and test your scuba equipment before you suit up. Practice will help you recall the assembly procedures.

Donning and Inspecting Scuba Equipment

With skin diving equipment, you don the weight belt after the skin diving vest, but with a jacket-type BC, you should don the weight belt before the scuba unit.

A good way to don a scuba unit out of the water is for your buddy to hold the system and help you into it. Once your arms are through the shoulder straps, you should bend forward and balance the unit on your back while you secure the waistband. Place the regulator hoses over your shoulders while you fasten the waistband so the hoses are not trapped beneath the waistband. Some dive boats have vertical tank racks on seats to allow you to sit while donning the system. Do not sit on the deck or ground to don a scuba tank, however, because the tanks of other scuba divers can strike you in the head.

Some divers prefer to don the scuba unit in the water—this is a good practice if you dive from a small boat or have a minor back problem. Put the scuba unit into the water first. Make sure that it does not float away! To don a jacket BC unit in the water the way you would don a coat, inflate it fully, sit on it, put your arms through the arm holes, and slide off and into the unit. Or you may put your scuba unit on over your head. Maneuver the tank in front of you with the valve facing you and the backpack facing up. Place the regulator in your mouth and keep the hose of the primary second stage between your arms. (If you place your right arm inside the loop of the hose, the hose will wrap around your arm when you try to lift the tank over your head.) Place your forearms completely through the arm holes just past your elbows, and begin to lift the scuba unit over your head. Rather than lift the unit, you should push yourself down in the water and duck beneath the scuba unit. Lower the tank into position on your back. Use your left hand to pull your snorkel clear of your BC as the tank lowers into position. When the tank is in place, lean forward and secure the waistband.

When you have donned your scuba equipment and the remainder of your diving equipment, inspect all your equipment to make sure it is positioned, adjusted, and functioning correctly. Your buddy should do likewise. Then inspect each other's equipment.

Do a head-to-toe buddy check. Specific checks for each item of equipment are listed in the Head-to-Toe Buddy Check sidebar.

Equipment inspections are important. Solving problems is easier before you enter the water than afterward. It does not take much time to inspect each other's equipment, but the practice can save a lot of time later. Make predive inspections a habit.

Scuba Diving Skills

To be a scuba diver and enjoy diving with minimum risk of injury, you need to learn the proper procedures for entering and exiting the water, controlling your buoyancy, descending and ascending, monitoring your instruments, and coordinating with a buddy. This section provides a helpful introduction to these skills, but you must learn them by doing. You will learn the skills in pool-like conditions and then apply them in open water.

Using Entry Techniques

The four basic types of water entries for divers are wading, seated, feetfirst, and back roll. You need to learn when to use each type and the procedures for each. The objective of any entry is to get into the water as easily as possible without injuring yourself or losing any equipment. After you enter the water and are under control, switch from your regulator to your snorkel if you are going to swim or remain at the surface.

You can make open-water entries from the shore or from a boat. You can wade in from the shore, or you can enter from an artificial structure such as a dock, pier, or jetty. The conditions vary greatly, and so do the entry techniques. Surf may be a factor at some locations. Bottom conditions can range from smooth and soft to rough and firm. The bottom may slope gradually or steeply, and there

■ Head-to-Toe Buddy Check

Mask	In place, flush on face, no hair under skirt, not fogged
Snorkel	Attached to left side of mask
Scuba cylinder	Valve open all but a quarter turn, valve facing user's right side, height OK, snug in pack
SPG	Full pressure, not damaged or leaking
Scuba regulator	Primary and alternate air sources function OK, both buddies know the placement of the alternate air systems, regulator hoses oriented properly and free for use
Buoyancy compensator	Inflates and deflates properly
Weighting system	In place, proper amount of weight, right-hand quick release accessible, weights clear to drop, both buddies familiar with weight release system
Exposure suit	Properly positioned and zipped
Dive knife	Attached properly, easy to access, secured
Fins	Securely strapped or worn
Instruments	Watch, dive timer, or dive computer ready for use

may be holes and drop-offs. Plants, animals, and rocks may be present in the entry area. A good entry technique for one location may be inappropriate for another. It takes experience and knowledge of the area to determine an effective entry procedure.

You need to know some general techniques when making wading entries at an open-water site. A wading entry sounds simple, but keep in mind that diving equipment affects your center of gravity, your mobility, and your peripheral vision. You must walk backward or sideways when wearing fins.

If there is little or no surf, you can wade in, don your fins, and begin your dive. Breathe through your regulator and have your BC inflated partially. Shuffle your feet to detect holes and rocks and to chase away bottom-dwelling creatures (see figure 6.14). When the water reaches your thighs, lie down in the water and start swimming. In some areas with muddy bottoms, you should not wade because you can sink deeply into the mud and lose a fin when you try to extract your foot. When the bottom is firm and the water is calm, you can wade into the water without your fins and don them in the water. It is helpful to have information about the bottom conditions of a dive site.

In most areas where there is surf, you should don your fins before you enter the water, and you should not remove them until you are clear of the water after the dive. Time your entry to coincide with small waves (see the discussion of waves and surf in chapter 5). Keep all equipment in place, and breathe through your regulator. Deflate your BC because you need to duck beneath breaking waves when they are higher than your waist. If you inflate your BC, you will be unable to duck beneath the waves, and a large wave could lift and toss you. Hold your mask with one hand at all times; spread your fingers and curl them over the top of the mask so you can see. Keep your knees bent and shuffle sideways into the waves to minimize your profile to the moving water. Stop moving just before a wave hits you, allow the wave to pass, and then resume your shuffling until the water is deep enough for you to swim. Allow incoming waves to pass over you, and move through the surf zone quickly.

From a commercial dive boat, you can enter the water from the side or from a water-level platform at the back of the boat. Have all equipment in place, breathe

Figure 6.14 When entering surf, shuffle sideways (keeping knees bent), hold your mask, and lean into waves.

Courtesy of Fred Humphrey.

from your regulator, and hold your mask securely. Have any specialty items, such as a camera, handed to you after you are in the water; another option is to retrieve these items from an equipment line. When entering from the side of a boat, note the direction of boat movement. Wind will cause an anchored boat to swing from side to side. If you enter the water on the side of the boat when the boat is moving in that direction, the boat may pass over you after you enter.

You can do a controlled, seated entry from a dock, from a swimming platform on a boat, or from any surface where you can sit close to the water, whether the water is only a few feet deep or too deep for standing. With all equipment in place, turn and place both hands on one side of your body on the surface that you are seated on. Then lift yourself slightly, move your body out over the water, and lower yourself into the water. A controlled, seated entry is a simple and easy entry (see figure 6.15).

Use feet-first entries when the distance to the water is too high for a seated entry, such as when entering from a commercial charter boat. Two types of feet-first entries can be used: giant stride and feet together.

Use the giant-stride entry, shown in figure 6.16, when the distance to the water is about 3 to 5 feet (1 to 1.5 m) and you want to remain at the surface during the entry. Stand at the entry point with your equipment in place and your BC partially inflated. Observe the point of entry and make sure the area is clear. Hold your mask firmly with one hand, spreading your fingers so you can see. Look straight ahead while stepping out with one leg. The entry is a step, not a hop or a jump. If you step out as far as you can, your trailing leg follows automatically. Keep one leg extended forward and the other leg extended backward until you hit the water; then pull your legs together quickly to stop your downward momentum. As soon as you stabilize at the surface, turn and signal that you are OK, and then move away from the entry point so that the next diver can enter.

Figure 6.15   Entering the water from a seated position.

Figure 6.16   Giant-stride entry.

Use the feet-together entry to avoid discomfort from the impact when the distance to the water is too high for a giant-stride entry. The procedures are the same as for the giant-stride entry, except that after you step out from the entry point, you bring your legs together before you hit the water. A feet-together entry submerges you. After you bob back to the surface and stabilize, signal the next diver and clear the entry area.

A back-roll entry can be done from either a seated or squatting position. Use the seated back-roll entry from a low, unstable platform, such as a small boat. You can also use a back-roll entry when the distance to the water is too high for a regular seated entry and the platform is too unstable for you to stand. To do a seated back roll, sit with all equipment in place and your back to the water. Move your bottom to the very edge of the surface on which you are sitting. Have someone make sure the entry area is clear. Hold your mask with one hand and your mask strap with the other hand. If you do not hold the mask strap, the force of the water may wash it up over your head, and your mask may fall off. Lean backward to begin the entry. Hold your knees to your chest as you roll backward; if you don't, you may clip your heels on the edge of the surface you were seated on (see figure 6.17). You are likely to do a backward, disorienting somersault in the water with this entry. You can reorient yourself when you bob back to the surface.

A squatting back roll is used when there is no suitable surface on which to sit. The thin side of a small, rocking boat is a good example of an unsuitable seat. For a squatting back-roll entry, prepare yourself while sitting on an adequate seat immediately adjacent to the entry area. Make sure the entry area is clear, then stand partially, turn your back to the entry area, and literally sit down into the water (see figure 6.18). Pull your knees to your chest as you enter so that you do not catch your heels.

Figure 6.17 Entering with legs extended risks clipping the heels on the boat. Tuck the legs into the chest instead.

Christian Wheatley/Getty Images

Figure 6.18 Squatting back-roll entry.

Surface Snorkeling With Scuba Equipment

You may use your snorkel for surface swimming in order to conserve the air in your scuba tank. This procedure is used in areas where divers need to swim from shore to reach the dive area. If you use air from your cylinder for surface swimming, you will reduce the amount of time you can remain underwater. When snorkeling while wearing scuba equipment, you should inflate your BC partially. Excessive air in your BC combined with the weight of your scuba tank

Three Important Scuba Diving Rules

1. Equalize pressure in your ears early and often.
2. Always breathe; avoid breath holding.
3. If the scuba regulator is out of your mouth, exhale continuously.

can cause you to roll sideways when swimming facedown. It is better to swim on your back or side; these positions allow wider kicks than when swimming facedown, and the tank weight is not a factor. If you swim on your back, you can breathe without the snorkel. Swim beside—not behind or in front of—your buddy. Move slowly and steadily, pacing yourself. If you feel short of breath after snorkeling, rest before beginning your descent.

Recovering and Clearing the Regulator

When you are in the water wearing scuba equipment and have removed your regulator second stage from your mouth—such as when snorkeling or talking at the surface—you need to recover it from behind your right shoulder (where it falls naturally). The second stage will have water inside, and you must clear the water before you breathe. If you start with the regulator in your mouth, you need to place the regulator in the water. The task is more difficult than it sounds because if you place the second stage in the water with the mouthpiece facing up, the regulator free-flows. Place the second stage in the water with the mouthpiece facing downward to prevent free-flow.

Two methods can be used to recover the regulator second stage from behind your shoulder. The most popular technique is the sweep method. Lean to the right side so gravity swings the second stage away from you. Reach back with your right hand until you touch the bottom of your scuba tank, and then extend your arm and sweep it forward in a large arc. The hose will lie across your arm, where you can retrieve the second stage easily.

The second method of recovering the second stage is the over-the-shoulder reach. Reach back toward your regulator first stage with your right hand while lifting the bottom of your scuba tank with your left hand. Grasp the second-stage hose where it attaches to the first stage and follow it down to the second-stage end. Some divers find this recovery method difficult or impossible.

Clearing the regulator can be as simple as exhaling into it. As long as the exhaust valve is at the lowest point, the water inside the second stage will be displaced. If the exhaust valve is not at the lowest point when you exhale, only part of the water may be exhausted, and you may inspire some water when you inhale. To avoid choking on inhaled water, find out where the exhaust valve is on your regulator, be sure to make it the lowest point when you clear your regulator, and inhale cautiously after clearing the regulator.

Another way to clear a regulator second stage—the purge method—involves using low-pressure air to clear the water from the chamber. If you insert the mouthpiece into your mouth and depress the purge, you may blow water down your throat. You can prevent this in two ways. One way is to depress the purge lightly as you place the bubbling regulator in your mouth, and to use back pressure from your lungs to keep water out of your mouth and throat. The other method is to place the regulator into your mouth, block the opening with your tongue, and depress the purge momentarily to clear the chamber. Either method is acceptable. If you are purging the regulator while placing it in your mouth, release the purge the moment the regulator is in place to avoid overinflating your lungs. Develop the habit of blowing a continuous stream of tiny bubbles any time the regulator is out of your mouth to avoid holding your breath while breathing compressed air.

Performing Snorkel–Regulator Exchanges

You must be able to switch from breathing from your snorkel to breathing from your regulator and vice versa. When you prepare to descend for diving, you exchange your snorkel for your regulator; when you surface after a dive, you exchange your regulator for your snorkel. Do both exchanges with your face in the water. Take a breath, exchange one mouthpiece for the other, and clear the new breathing device.

Inflating and Deflating the BC

You should be familiar with two ways to inflate a BC and two ways to deflate it. The easiest and most commonly used means of inflation is the low-pressure inflator, which is used to add air to the BC in short bursts. Inflating the BC for several seconds can cause serious buoyancy control problems if the inflator valve sticks. By adding air a little at a time, you have better control of your buoyancy.

If your low-pressure inflator or your integrated second stage develops a problem while you are diving, you may need to disconnect the low-pressure hose. When you disconnect the hose, the low-pressure inflator no longer functions, so you have to control buoyancy by orally inflating the BC. The mouthpiece of a BC is usually more elaborate than the mouthpiece of a skin diving vest. To help keep water out of a BC, the mouthpiece has a purge so that the water inside can be cleared before you open the valve to the BC. To clear the BC mouthpiece and orally inflate the BC, follow this procedure:

1. Insert the mouthpiece into your mouth.
2. Exhale a small amount of air into the mouthpiece to clear it.
3. Keep the mouthpiece in your mouth.
4. Depress the manual inflator-deflator valve.
5. Exhale into the BC.
6. Release the manual inflator-deflator valve.
7. Repeat the procedure until you achieve the desired amount of buoyancy.

You can use the same bobbing technique at the surface that you learned for the skin diving vest (see the previous explanation in this chapter), but oral inflation procedures are different underwater. To inflate a BC orally underwater, follow these steps:

1. Grasp the inflation valve with your left hand, and grasp your regulator second stage with your right hand.
2. Take a breath.
3. Insert the BC mouthpiece into your mouth.
4. Clear the mouthpiece.
5. Exhale most of the air in your lungs into the BC.

6. Save enough air to clear the regulator, which fills with water when you remove it from your mouth.

7. Repeat the procedure until you achieve the desired amount of buoyancy.

You can deflate your BC with the manual inflator-deflator valve or with a dump valve. If you do not use a dump valve, you must open the deflator valve at the lower end of the BC hose and hold it higher than the highest point of the BC. Using a dump valve is more convenient than using the deflator valve. Note that you can deflate your BC only when the exhaust port is the highest point. Air cannot escape if you try to deflate a BC in a horizontal or inverted position, so you need to be in an upright position to deflate your BC.

Testing Buoyancy

Similarities exist between buoyancy testing for skin diving and buoyancy testing for scuba diving, but there are also some important differences. Buoyancy varies more when you scuba dive than when you skin dive. The volume of air in your lungs varies more in scuba diving. You dive deeper, so suit compression affects your buoyancy more. As you use air from your scuba tank, your buoyancy changes. You need to sense buoyancy changes quickly to maintain control of your buoyancy.

Your initial buoyancy test for scuba diving can be the same as your buoyancy test for skin diving. Begin by testing your BC at the surface. Inflate it fully and then deflate it. Make sure the low-pressure inflator and all deflation valves function correctly. With your regulator in your mouth and your BC completely deflated, relax and breathe slowly. When your lung volume is high, you should remain at the surface with your eyes just below the surface–water interface. If you sink with your lungs full of air, you need to remove some weight. When you exhale completely, you should sink. If you cannot sink after a complete exhalation, you need additional weight. Test your buoyancy while you are close to your point of entry, and correct any buoyancy problems before you attempt to dive.

As you descend in open water, you may need to add air to your BC in order to maintain neutral buoyancy. Strive to maintain neutral buoyancy continuously. Add air to your BC in small amounts, and test your buoyancy by stopping all motion and observing what happens. If you are sinking, inhale and add air to your BC. If you are rising in the water, exhale and release air from your BC. With experience you will know when to add air to your BC, when to vent air from your BC, and how much air to add or release.

You can learn buoyancy control in a swimming pool by assuming a rigid, face-down position with your arms at your sides. If your buoyancy is correct, a slow, full inhalation raises your shoulders while your fin tips remain on the bottom; a slow, complete exhalation causes your shoulders to sink. Some people call this buoyancy evaluation **diver's push-ups** (although you do not use your hands). If you do not rise with a full inhalation, you should add a small amount of air to your BC and try again. Figure 6.19 illustrates a diver doing diver's push-ups.

As a scuba diver, you need enough weight to get down at the beginning of a dive and enough weight to allow you to remain in control when you ascend at the end of the dive. The precise weight for scuba diving is the amount you need to hover at a depth of 15 feet (4.6 m) with 300 psi (20 atm) of air in your tank and no air in your BC. This amount may overweight you slightly at the beginning of a dive. Test your buoyancy at a depth of 15 feet at the end of a dive to see if you need to make an adjustment for your next dive.

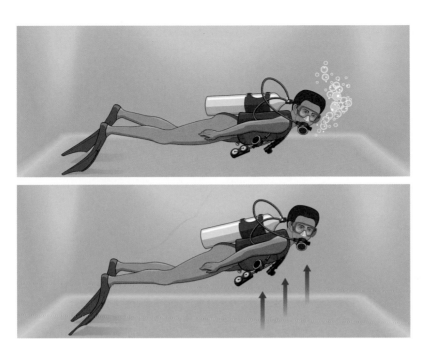

Figure 6.19   Executing proper diver's push-ups ensures good buoyancy control.

Controlling Buoyancy

No skill identifies a scuba diver's ability as much as buoyancy control. The ability to finely control buoyancy is important for safety, for enjoyment, and for the welfare of the environment. When your buoyancy is out of control, a hazard exists for both you and the environment around you.

With your buoyancy adjusted to the point where you can pivot slightly up and down on your fins on the bottom (in a pool) while inhaling and exhaling, push yourself about 2 feet (0.6 m) off the bottom and remain motionless. You may or may not remain in a horizontal position, but that is not important. Maintain your depth by controlling your average lung volume, but remember to breathe continuously. If you are sinking, keep more air in your lungs. If you begin rising, reduce the amount of air in your lungs. With practice, you will be able to hover motionless just off the bottom.

To demonstrate mastery of hovering, assume a vertical position in the water. Cross your legs at the ankles, grasp one wrist with the opposite hand, and remain motionless. Find an eye-level reference and develop the ability to hover motionless while upright in the water. Pay attention to the buoyancy effects of breathing. Once you master hovering both horizontally and vertically, you will realize several benefits. Your air will last longer, swimming will not tire you as much, you will need fewer buoyancy adjustments, and you will do less damage to the diving environment. Your buoyancy control continues to improve with practice until you become a highly experienced diver.

A useful skill for maintaining neutral buoyancy during ascent is a BC venting technique called an **open-valve ascent**. When you ascend, air in your BC expands and affects your buoyancy. You must release the expanding air to control buoyancy. If you vent the air from time to time, your buoyancy is in a constant state of change: You may not release enough air, or you may release too much. The open-valve ascent is a better alternative. Hold the BC inflator-deflator valve just below the level of your shoulder, point the mouthpiece of the inflator-deflator valve downward, and open the deflator valve. Air cannot escape because the opening is lower than the exhaust port on the BC. While you hold the mouthpiece downward and the deflation valve open, raise the inflator-deflator slowly until air just begins to bubble from the mouthpiece. Bubbling occurs when the mouthpiece and the exhaust port on the BC are at the same level. If you hold the inflator-deflator valve at the bubbling level while ascending, the expanding air inside the BC bubbles out through the open valve, and your buoyancy remains constant. If you need to release additional air to control buoyancy, raise the inflator-deflator slightly; if you need to decrease the amount of air you release, lower the assembly slightly.

Using the Dive Flag

You should display the appropriate dive flag or flags when diving. Authorities in some areas require you to use a flag, and flag use is encouraged in all areas. Follow these conventions when you use a dive flag: Display the flag only when divers are in the water, and surface within 100 feet (30 m) of your flag—the closer the better. The flag does not guarantee your safety from boaters, who are supposed to give the flag a berth of at least 100 feet; however, the flag does serve as a signal to many boaters who recognize that the flag means there are divers in the vicinity. Figure 6.20 shows a boat anchored with a dive flag indicating there are divers in the area.

If you support your flag with a surface float, you need to tow your float to the area where you wish to dive. In areas lacking underwater plants, you can tow the float while you dive. In areas with plants, you need to anchor the float to keep it from drifting away, and you must navigate back to the flag at the end of your dive. When entering through surf, you should tow the surface float behind you. Push the float ahead of you when exiting through surf.

Figure 6.20 Surface as close as possible to the dive flag to keep you safe from other boaters.

Descending

Scuba descents are different from skin diving descents. You usually descend headfirst as a skin diver, but scuba divers descend feet-first. A feet-first descent allows better control of buoyancy, provides better orientation, allows buddies to maintain contact during descent, helps prevent the swallowing of air, and allows easier pressure equalization of air spaces.

Descending involves several procedures, which seem complex at first but become routine with practice. The process of descending includes preparing to descend, initiating the descent, and completing the descent.

1. Preparing to descend
   - Check your instruments. Orient yourself at the surface and set a reference on your compass. Be sure your underwater timer and depth gauge are zeroed.
   - Confirm that your buddy is ready to begin.
   - Exchange your snorkel for your regulator.
   - Pressurize your ears slightly to begin the equalization process (see chapter 3).
   - Hold your BC deflator valve in your left hand.
   - Give or acknowledge the signal to descend.

2. Initiating the descent
   - Begin the descent by venting your BC. It is better to do this with the dump valve than by holding the deflator valve above your head. Hold the inflator-deflator valve in your left hand throughout the descent so you can add or release air from your BC at any time. Exhale fully to help get started downward.
   - Breathe shallowly for the first 10 feet (3 m).
   - Equalize pressure in your ears about every 2 feet (0.6 m) for the first 15 feet (4.6 m). If you experience equalizing problems, ascend a few feet to reduce the pressure, equalize again, and descend again. Exhale some air into your mask to prevent a mask squeeze. (See chapter 3 for a description of pressure equalization.)
   - Keep your fins still while you descend so that you do not stir up silt on the bottom.
   - Control your rate of descent by the average amount of air you keep in your lungs. When you begin sinking while your lungs are full, add a short burst of air to your BC to regain neutral buoyancy.

3. Completing the descent
   - Remain with your buddy throughout the descent.
   - Avoid contact with the bottom.
   - Hover above the bottom, level off to a swimming position, agree on a direction with your buddy, and begin your exploration.

Two types of descents are performed in open water: **reference descents** and **nonreference descents**. A reference descent is one that you control by following a line or the slope of the bottom. You should do a reference descent whenever possible. A descent made vertically in water without any external reference is a nonreference descent, which is more difficult to control than a reference descent.

Clearing the Mask

To clear a mask while scuba diving, you need to develop the skill of breathing through your mouth with your nose exposed to water. With concentration and practice, you can master this skill quickly. First, try inhaling through your mouth and exhaling through your nose. Next, try inhaling and exhaling through your mouth. If you feel any water going up your nose, exhale immediately to keep the water out.

To practice clearing a mask, you need to flood it with water. This is not difficult, but a few tips make it easier. If you exhale lightly while tilting the mask forward on your face to break the seal at the top, the mask releases from your face easily, and the air escapes at the highest point. When you reseat your mask to begin clearing it, be sure to hold back any strands of hair with one hand while you reseat the mask with the other. Hair under the mask causes leakage. If you are wearing a hood, make sure that the hood is clear of the mask before you attempt to clear water from the mask.

Buddy Diving

You should always dive with a companion, using the **buddy system**. A buddy provides reminders and assistance and sees things that you might not see. Buddies inspect each other's equipment, provide feedback based on observations, and work as a team. Dive buddies should remain close enough to each other that one can immediately assist the other in the event of an emergency. The more turbid the water and the greater the depth, the closer buddies should remain to each other. During your training, you should strive to remain within touching distance of your buddy at all times; learn to keep track of your buddy. Maintaining contact with a dive buddy in open water is not difficult when you follow a few standard procedures.

Agree on a position relative to one another and maintain that position as much as possible. That way, your buddy will know where to look for you, and you will know where to look for your buddy. The best dive team configuration is side by side; the least desirable is for one diver to be above and behind the other. Looking up and back is difficult when you are hampered by your equipment.

Agree on a direction of movement. Both parties should maintain that direction until both agree to proceed in a different direction. When you follow this practice, there are fewer directions to consider if you and your buddy become separated.

Confirm your buddy's position every few seconds. If you scan the areas ahead from side to side while swimming, you should get a glimpse of your buddy each time you turn your head in your buddy's direction.

When visibility is poor, physical contact can keep you and your buddy together. Holding hands is appropriate. Or you can use a short line—a **buddy line**—to keep in contact with each other. If you become separated from your buddy underwater, look for your buddy for up to one minute. If you are unable to locate your buddy, ascend slightly and turn in a circle while looking for bubbles. The visibility is often better a few feet above the bottom than it is at the bottom. If you do not see your buddy's bubbles, ascend to the surface and wait for your buddy, who should also duplicate this procedure. When you have reunited at the surface, you can descend again and continue your dive. Obviously, it is better to remain together underwater than to surface to reunite.

The Buddy System

Teaming up with a qualified partner is appropriate for activities that involve risk, such as swimming, rock climbing, and skin and scuba diving. Safety is the primary purpose of the buddy system, but having a dive buddy also makes diving more enjoyable. The following list describes the duties and responsibilities of a good dive buddy:

- Helps to plan the dive in advance and after arrival at the dive site
- Reviews signals and emergency procedures
- Assists with the donning of the scuba unit
- Inspects equipment
- Maintains contact while diving and follows procedures for reuniting if separation occurs
- Provides reminders concerning depth, direction, time, air pressure, and ascent rate
- Points out items of interest
- Identifies problems that you are unaware of, such as an air leak
- Provides reassurance and assistance as needed
- Summons additional assistance as needed
- Provides first aid as needed
- Assists with exits and the removal of the scuba unit

If you are unable to relocate your buddy underwater and your buddy does not surface promptly, look at your surroundings to mark your position so that you will know the approximate location where your buddy was last seen. If someone is overseeing the diving operations, notify this person that your buddy is missing so that a search can be initiated. If you are alone, try to locate bubbles that could indicate your buddy's position.

Underwater Swimming

When you swim along the bottom, your fins can raise a cloud of silt that harms the environment and reduces visibility. Silting is more of a problem when you are overweighted because the excess weight angles your fins toward the bottom when you swim (see figure 6.21). The first step in reducing silt is to weight yourself properly. In areas where the bottom silt is thick, add air to your BC to make yourself slightly buoyant underwater. The buoyancy forces you to swim at a slight downward angle and keeps the thrust of your fins directed upward. Another way to reduce silt is to remain far enough from the bottom to keep from disturbing it.

Figure 6.21 Overweighting can cause divers to stir up a cloud of silt.

Finally, consider changing your kick if you boil up silt with your kick strokes. You should also consider redistributing your weight by placing a small portion of it higher on your body to achieve level trim as described in the "Mobility Adjustments" section of chapter 3.

When you kick something while swimming, you must overcome the tendency to want to get away from whatever you kick. Your kicks are strong and can damage the environment or another diver. As soon as you feel something with a fin, stop kicking, look back to see what you have hit, and maneuver yourself clear before proceeding.

Navigating

To find your way underwater, you can use natural navigation and compass navigation. You can best determine your relative position with a combination of both types of navigation.

With natural navigation, you use your natural surroundings to determine where you are. Light, shadows, plants, formations, water movement, depth, and other indicators can help you navigate. As you move, note your surroundings. Observe which way you are going relative to the movement of the water, the sand ripples on the bottom, the depth contour, and the angle of the sun. By noting natural aids to navigation, you can find your way underwater.

A dive compass increases the accuracy of navigation. Figure 6.22 shows two types of dive compass. You need to be able to set a direction (called a **compass heading**) and to determine which way you are going relative to the directional reference you have set. Your compass should have a reference line, called a lubber line, that you point in the direction of travel. The north-seeking needle or card of the compass establishes a position relative to the lubber line as long as you hold the compass in a level position. Many dive compasses have index marks on a movable bezel. You set the index marks to indicate the heading. Electronic compasses allow you to set a heading and use arrows to indicate the direction that you need to turn to remain on course.

Figure 6.22 Traditional dive compass (left) and electronic dive compass (right).

To go in the direction set on the compass, you must hold the compass so the lubber line is directly in line with the centerline of your body. If the lubber line points to one side, you will not be on course even though the north reference is at the correct point on the dial. Figure 6.23 shows a compass lock position.

A **compass course** is a series of headings that leads to a destination. Many types of compass courses may be used. One frequently used course is the **square compass course**. To navigate a square course, set your initial heading and proceed in that direction for a given distance, which can be measured by time, tank pressure, or fin kicks. Stop and turn 90 degrees to the right while continuing to keep the lubber line aligned with the centerline of your body. Note the relative position of north on the compass, and proceed in the new direction for the same distance as you covered on the first leg of the course. Stop again, and turn another 90 degrees to the right. Note the position of north on the compass, which should be opposite your initial heading. Proceed along the third leg of the course for the same distance as before. Stop once more, turn again 90 degrees to the right, note the relative position of north, and follow the new heading back to your starting point.

Figure 6.23 The compass-lock position.

Divers also frequently follow a **reciprocal compass course**—an out-and-back course. Set the initial heading on the compass. At the midpoint of the dive, turn 180 degrees until north on the compass is directly opposite the original heading. Then follow the reciprocal heading back to your starting point. Advanced scuba diving courses provide additional compass navigation training.

If you do not know precisely where you are when the end of a dive approaches, you may need to surface, find a reference for your exit, and set a compass heading that leads directly to the end-of-dive location. Be especially careful if you surface more than 100 feet (30 m) from your dive flag.

A compass provides correct directional reference information when it is not affected by nearby objects. Metal objects, other compasses, and electrical fields within a couple of feet of a compass can cause it to deviate from its correct reading. Keep metal, magnets, dive lights, and other compasses away from your compass to help ensure accuracy.

Monitoring Instruments

Most diving instruments are passive; that is, they do not provide information unless you look at them. Some instruments emit an audible beep, but most require observation to provide information. Develop the habit of checking your instrumentation frequently while diving so that you can control your depth, dive time, and direction. This will also help you avoid running out of air. You should be able to accurately estimate your tank pressure at any time during training. If you cannot estimate the pressure within 300 psi (20 atm) at any time, you need to monitor your SPG more frequently.

When you are planning to dive in open water, you should look at your instruments when you assemble your equipment. Look at your instruments again when you inspect your equipment. Look at your instruments again before you descend and again while you are descending. Refer to your compass for directional reference before you begin moving underwater. Monitor your gauges every few minutes while diving, and compare your air pressure with your buddy's several times during a dive. At any given time during a dive, you should be able to accurately estimate your depth, your dive time, your direction, your tank pressure, and your buddy's tank pressure. If you cannot do this, you need to improve your instrument-monitoring skills.

Using Scuba Diving Hand Signals

Scuba divers use several hand signals that are not used for skin diving. The signals specific to scuba diving relate to air supply. Learn and use the standard hand signals shown in figure 6.24. Remember to display hand signals clearly and deliberately and also to acknowledge the hand signals you receive.

Ascending

Scuba ascents are different from skin diving ascents, although there are a few similarities. The procedures you need to learn become automatic with practice and experience.

To initiate an ascent, one member of a buddy team gives the ascent signal, which the other acknowledges. Always obey the ascent signal. Prepare to ascend by noting your time, depth, and remaining air. Locate your BC inflator-deflator assembly, and hold it in your left hand. Begin the procedures for the open-valve ascent previously described (see "Controlling Buoyancy").

Begin ascending slowly with your buddy while breathing continuously. Monitor your depth gauge and keep tabs on your buddy. The maximum rate of ascent is 0.5 feet (0.15 m) per second, which is quite slow. Some instruments warn you when your rate of ascent is too rapid. You need training, practice, and awareness to avoid exceeding the maximum rate of ascent.

Stop and decompress (outgas) when indicated by your dive computer. Whether or not you make a "deep stop," you should stop for one to three minutes at a depth of 15 feet (4.6 m) to help prevent decompression sickness (DCS). The procedures for decompression are described in chapter 7. As you ascend, look up and around. Extend one hand above your head for protection against overhead obstacles. Make one full rotation to view the surrounding area as you near the surface. When you reach the surface, make another rotation to view the area, and then inflate your BC to establish buoyancy. Exchange your regulator mouthpiece for your snorkel.

Handling Equipment

Sometimes you will need to remove, adjust, and replace scuba equipment while you are in the water. You may need to remove equipment to exit the water onto a boat, to make an adjustment, or to free the equipment from an entanglement. With training and practice, you should be able to handle your equipment easily.

Removal of the scuba unit is easy because it is similar to removing a coat. Open the releases, slip your left arm free, swing the scuba tank forward under your right arm, hold the scuba unit with your left hand, and pull your right arm free. Freeing your left arm is easier if you insert your hand and wrist through the armhole of the BC first and remove it hand first (instead of pulling your arm through first). If you are at the surface in water too deep for you to stand when you want to remove your scuba unit, you should remove your weight belt first and place it on a surface float or support station. Don the scuba unit in the water according to the in-water donning procedures previously presented in this chapter.

1. Descend

2. Ascend

3. Stop

4a. OK

4b. OK

4c. OK

5. Something's not right

6. Emergency

7. Low on air

8. Out of air

9. Give me air

10. Look

11. Danger

12. Watch me
(finger pointing to chest)

13. You lead, I follow

14. Get with your buddy

Figure 6.24 Scuba diving hand signals.

Using Exit Techniques

The technique you use to exit the water depends on the situation. To exit from shallow water in a swimming pool, begin by removing your weight belt, tank, and fins, in that order. Carefully place the equipment on the side of the pool; then climb out by using the ladder or lifting yourself up onto the edge of the pool.

To exit from the deep end of a swimming pool (as shown in figure 6.25), begin with your BC inflated partially. If you exit on a ladder, grasp the ladder with one hand and remove your fins with the other; maintain contact with the ladder at all times. Place your fins on the edge of the pool, or slide the heel straps over your wrists; then climb the ladder to exit the water. Clear the exit area at once, and take your fins with you. Remove your scuba system and weight belt when you are well clear of the exit area.

Figure 6.25 Exiting from the deep end using a ladder.

To exit from deep water without a ladder, begin by removing your weight belt and carefully placing it out of the water. Remove the scuba unit and use one hand to trap the regulator hose against the surface onto which you will exit. Use your other hand to remove your fins, and place them out of the water. Place both hands on the exit edge. With the regulator hose trapped under one hand, lower yourself to about chin level in the water while you extend one leg forward and one leg backward. Pull yourself upward with your arms, and pull your legs together forcefully in a strong scissors kick to provide upward momentum. Pull with your arms until you are far enough out of the water to push downward and lift yourself from the water (see figure 6.26). Immediately after your exit, turn around and pull your scuba unit from the water carefully.

If you are boarding a boat that has a ladder, you should keep your tank and mask on and keep your regulator in your mouth in case you fall back into the water (see figure 6.27). Use the ladder exit technique described for exiting the deep end of the pool. Maintain contact with the ladder at all times when you

Figure 6.26 Exiting from the deep end without a ladder.

are in the water. If the boat has a platform at the rear, you usually swim onto the platform, remove your fins, and then stand on the platform and board the vessel.

Techniques for wading exits in open water vary with the environment. You should usually wear all your equipment until you are clear of the water. Shuffle your feet along the bottom while moving backward. Surf exits require training and practice. Stop outside the breaking waves and evaluate the surf. Approach the surf zone with your regulator in your mouth and your BC deflated. Hold your mask continually in the surf zone. Follow a breaking wave, and allow additional waves to pass over you until the water is only a couple of feet deep. If the surf is mild, you can stand at that point and back out of the water. If the surf is strong, swim until you can crawl; then crawl clear of the water (see figure 6.28).

When you are clear of the water, work with your buddy to remove your fins. The buddy system is in effect even when you are out of the water.

Figure 6.27   Boarding a boat with a ladder.

Disassembling Equipment

The first step in disassembling your scuba equipment is to turn off the air by turning the valve in a clockwise direction. Release the pressure in the hoses by depressing the purge on the regulator second stage. Keep the purge depressed until you bleed all the air from the system. Next, disconnect all hoses that are connected to the scuba unit: the low-pressure inflator, the extra second stage, and the SPG. Loosen the yoke screw and remove the regulator from the tank. Dry the first-stage dust cover thoroughly and replace it. Loosen the tank band and remove the BC from the scuba tank. Be sure to rinse and care for your equipment as soon as possible (following the procedures described in chapter 4).

Figure 6.28   Using a crawling exit in strong surf.
Courtesy of Fred Humphrey.

Managing Physiological Problems

If you do everything you are trained to do as a scuba diver, you can avoid problems. But it is not a perfect world. If you fail to pay attention or forget to do something, a problem can occur. Good divers can deal with nearly any problem. This section introduces you to proven ways of dealing with potential diving difficulties. Do not be overly concerned about the problems presented. You can prevent them, but knowing how to deal with them helps reduce your apprehension.

Difficulties affecting your physiology include seasickness, dizziness, stress and panic, overexertion, coughing, and cramping. When you have one of these problems, your body sends messages that something is wrong. You need to know the messages and the actions you can take to overcome physiological difficulties.

Seasickness

The best strategy is to try to prevent seasickness (see "Equilibrium Adjustments and Seasickness" in chapter 3) because taking medication after you are seasick is usually ineffective. If you do get seasick, you are likely to vomit. Vomiting underwater can be dangerous because of involuntary gasping that can cause you to choke. Only you can determine your degree of nausea. If you throw up or feel as if you are on the verge of doing so, do not dive. If you feel queasy, getting into the water may help you overcome the feeling. Some divers who feel slightly nauseated find that they feel better if they get into the water quickly and dive. After that first dive, they are fine for the remainder of the day.

You should surface if you feel nauseated while diving. If you must vomit underwater, do not vomit through your regulator. Hold the second stage against one corner of your mouth, and depress the purge fully while you vomit. You should get air instead of water if you gasp. When you have finished throwing up, place the second stage in your mouth, clear it, and resume breathing. The purge method should be a last resort. Vomiting through the regulator is not recommended because this method sometimes results in clogging.

If you are seasick and have to throw up while aboard a boat, do it over the rail on the side of the vessel opposite the wind. Do not use the restroom (or head, as it is called on a boat). The best remedy is to get to land, rest until you feel better, and take seasickness medication before returning to the vessel. If you are ill from motion sickness—and if the dive boat has a dinghy and there is land nearby—you should request to be taken to shore for a while.

Dizziness

The absence of visual clues in a weightless environment can cause temporary dizziness. Visual references can help you prevent disorientation (see chapter 3). Injury, temperature changes, and pressure changes affecting the inner ear can also cause a whirling feeling called vertigo, which may be more difficult to overcome than dizziness caused by disorientation.

To cope with either dizziness or vertigo, you should first seek a fixed visual reference. If possible, make physical contact with something solid for a point of reference. If there is nothing to see or to grasp, close your eyes and hug yourself. In most cases, dizziness passes in a minute or two. If you then move slowly and keep your head still, you should be able to surface. A good buddy can recognize your difficulty and assist you.

Stress and Panic

Stress is the perception of a substantial imbalance between environmental demand and a person's response capability, and it occurs under conditions where failure to meet demand is perceived as having serious consequences. Stressors are conditions or attitudes that cause stress. Dive stressors, which can be internal or external, include cold, illness, exhaustion, injury, fear, equipment problems, loss of air supply, buddy separation, depth, darkness, currents, and disorientation. Stress is not always bad. Moderate stress can cause a feeling of exhilaration, improve performance, and lead to a positive condition called eustress. Excessive stress causes anxiety, decreases performance, and leads to a negative condition called distress.

Knowledge and appraisal of a situation affect your reaction to stress. Training, experience, and your predisposition toward a situation affect your knowledge and appraisal. Thus, your perception of the circumstances is determined by what you know and are able to do, by what you have done, and by any inherent fears about the circumstances that you might have.

The problem with stress in diving is that it can lead to panic—a sudden, uncontrolled, irrational reaction to a perceived danger. Divers who panic often perish. You must manage stress in order to prevent panic. Dr. Tom Griffiths, who has researched stress, said the following: "The most critical factor in the progression of panic after stress increases is whether or not a problem arises." Divers who can recognize and manage stress can overcome problems and are far safer than those who cannot cope with the effects of stress.

Stress has both physiological and psychological components. Anxiety causes involuntary physiological changes. When stress leads to anxiety, your breathing rate and heart rate increase, your nervous system becomes more active, and your awareness decreases. These factors decrease your performance and increase your anxiety. Then heightened anxiety begins the cycle again. Unless you interrupt the cycle, anxiety escalates into panic. Psychological difficulty is every bit as critical as the physical problems. Frank Pia, a chief lifeguard, says, "Much of the distress that a person experiences when difficulty arises stems from what the person tells himself about the situation." You can be exhilarated by a situation or allow it to cause anxiety and distress. Pia continues, "The difference between panic and a heightened physiological state is the thought process."

Michael J. Asken, who has written books about stress, encourages the use of task-relevant instructional self-talk (TRIST). You determine your emotional state when in distress by what you tell yourself. Asken says that in a stressful situation, "Success is not achieved by focusing on the outcome, hoping for a good outcome, or even telling yourself that the outcome will be OK. The most effective self-talk involves imagining that your instructor is sitting on your shoulder guiding you through your response."

With the previous concepts in mind, you can recognize and manage stress. The first steps are to sense your breathing rate and identify your self-talk when a problem occurs. If your breathing rate is fast and you are having negative thoughts about the situation, it is time to break the stress cycle. Stop all physical activity, establish buoyancy, and breathe deeply. Divers in distress usually have an adequate supply of air! As you gain control of respiration, you can think more clearly. Take control of your thoughts before they take control of you. Imagine that you are telling someone else how to deal with this situation. Assess your options, determine the best course of action, and then take deliberate action. As you begin to overcome the difficulty, your confidence increases and your physiological condition begins to return to normal. Figure 6.29 shows how to break the stress cycle that leads to panic.

Now you can understand why some divers are thrilled by the same situation that causes another diver to panic. Remember that stress is simply a matter of perception and that you can change your perception with training and experience.

You can also learn to manage difficult situations by imagining them vividly in your mind. Your body cannot distinguish the difference between an actual event and one that you imagine. As you learn to solve problems in your mind, you can learn to recognize and manage stress.

Overexertion

If you work too hard while scuba diving, the equipment may not be able to supply enough air to meet your respiratory needs. You experience a sudden feeling of suffocation, and you may suspect that your equipment has malfunctioned. It is unlikely that scuba equipment will cease to function suddenly in a way that restricts airflow. More likely than not, overexertion is causing the feeling that you cannot get enough air. You can manage overexertion similarly to the way you manage stress. Stop all physical activity and breathe deeply; you should overcome your respiratory problem within a minute or two.

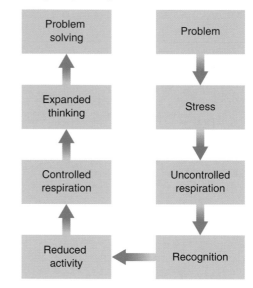

Figure 6.29 The panic cycle and how to break it.

Coughing

When water strikes your larynx, a reflex coughing action tries to clear the foreign matter from your airway. When you cough while in water, you may inhale additional water, which can complicate the situation. You need to overcome the reflex as quickly as possible. The best way is to swallow hard three times in rapid succession. If you must cough, try to do so through a regulator so that you inhale air rather than water if you gasp. You can lose buoyancy as you expel air when coughing, so you may need to establish positive buoyancy if you cough excessively.

Cramps

When your muscles get cold or when circulation to your muscles is inadequate, cramping can occur. A cramp is a sudden, strong, involuntary, persistent, painful muscle contraction. Divers tend to get cramps in the lower legs and the feet. To alleviate a cramp, stretch the affected muscle and rub it to increase circulation. Pounding a cramped muscle is ineffective and causes tissue damage. If you experience a cramp in your leg or foot in the water, you may be able to get rid of it by grasping the tip of your fin and pulling it toward you. Another technique to help release a leg cramp is to contract the muscles of the opposite leg. This action can inhibit nerve impulses to the cramped muscles. Buddies should assist one another with getting rid of cramps. Figure 6.30 shows a diver relieving a cramp.

Figure 6.30 Your diving buddy can help you relieve a cramp by rubbing and stretching the cramped muscle.

Managing Physical Problems

Potential physical difficulties in diving include entanglement; loss of buoyancy control; loss of air supply; and a distressed, injured, or incapacitated buddy. As with physiological problems, you can overcome these problems, but it is better to avoid them.

Entanglement

You will probably encounter fishing line, nets, wire, string, and rope in the water—and these items can entangle you. Underwater plants can also entangle divers in some areas. Streamlining your equipment to minimize places where things can get caught helps reduce the chance of entanglement. Being aware also helps. When you encounter something that can entangle you, swim around it or push it beneath you and swim over it. Avoid swimming beneath things that can cause entanglement. The area of your tank valve and regulator first stage is one of the easiest places to become entangled and also one of the most difficult areas to free from entanglement.

If you become entangled underwater, you should stop. Then try to examine the problem without turning because turning often compounds the problem. If you can reach the entanglement, you should free yourself. If not, signal your buddy to help you get free. If you can see what you are doing, you can use your dive knife to cut yourself free. Trying to cut yourself free from something in the area of your tank valve is an obvious mistake. If your tank is entangled and you can't reach the entanglement—and your buddy is not nearby to lend assistance—you should remove your scuba unit, free it from the entanglement, and put it back on.

Loss of Buoyancy Control

You can lose control of buoyancy underwater if you lose weights or if a low-pressure inflator on your BC or dry suit sticks. You can take steps to prevent loss of buoyancy control. Check your weight system from time to time while you are diving to make sure it is secure. Inspect your low-pressure inflators before each use, and have them serviced at the first sign of unusual operation.

If your weights fall off while you are underwater, immediately maneuver yourself into an inverted position, swim down forcefully, and retrieve the weights. If you are successful, you can avoid an uncontrolled ascent; if you are unsuccessful, you will float to the surface. Your rate of ascent depends on how buoyant you are without your weights, the type of exposure suit you are wearing, the amount of air in your BC at the time, your depth, and the amount of surface area you can expose to the direction of motion. You learned in chapters 2 and 3 that the greater the cross-sectional area of an object moving in a given direction, the greater the resistance to movement in that direction. If you lose control of buoyancy and your ascent is uncontrolled, you can slow your rate of ascent by **flaring**—arching your back, extending your arms and legs, and positioning your fins parallel to the surface. Flaring (shown in figure 6.31) is the method recommended to slow a buoyant ascent.

Unless you care for your BC inflator carefully and have it serviced annually, the inflator valve will eventually stick. If your low-pressure inflator sticks in the open position, you should first hold your BC deflator valve in the open position. Modern BCs vent air faster than the low-pressure inflator admits air. If the inflator valve remains stuck, disconnect the low-pressure hose. If an uncontrolled ascent results, flare to slow your rate of ascent.

Loss of Air Supply

You are unlikely to have air supply difficulties if you have your regulator serviced annually, if you maintain your regulator properly, and if you monitor your SPG. Potential problems include a regulator that free-flows, low air pressure, and no air to breathe. Divers have ways to deal with each of these difficulties.

Figure 6.31 Flaring is an excellent way to slow a rapid ascent.

Sand, dirt, vomit, and freezing can cause regulator free-flow. If free-flow occurs, your best course of action is to switch to your extra second stage. You could also use your buddy's extra second stage. If there is no source of air except the regulator that is free-flowing, you can breathe from it by pressing your lips lightly against the mouthpiece, taking the air you need, and allowing the excess air to escape. Look down while you breathe from the regulator to keep the escaping air from causing your mask to leak.

You are supposed to end a dive with at least 500 psi (34 atm) of air in your tank. If you are inattentive and breathe nearly all the air from your cylinder while diving, it will become difficult to get air from your regulator. Divers often refer to this situation as being "out of air," but, in reality, they are out of air only at the depth at which breathing is difficult. As you ascend, the lower ambient pressure allows you to obtain additional air from your tank. When breathing becomes difficult and your tank is nearly empty, you should use your buddy's alternate air source (AAS) or ascend while continuing to breathe shallowly through your regulator.

In the rare event that you should completely lose your primary source of air while underwater, you have five ascent options. Figure 6.32 shows the order of preference of these options.

An extra-second-stage-assisted ascent closely approximates a normal ascent. You ascend while breathing from your buddy's extra second stage. When you require air underwater, get your buddy's attention and give the signals for "out of air" and "give me air," if possible. If your buddy's extra second stage and primary second stage are similar, your buddy will hand you the extra second stage, or you may take it. If your buddy's extra second stage is integrated into the BC low-pressure inflator, your buddy will hand you the primary second stage and breathe from the integrated second stage. If you cannot get your buddy's attention, take the extra second stage, begin breathing, and then signal your buddy

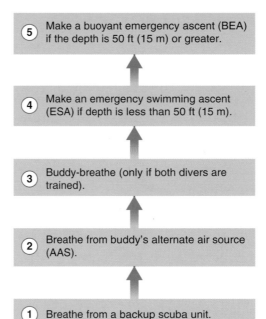

Emergency ascent option hierarchy

⑤ Make a buoyant emergency ascent (BEA) if the depth is 50 ft (15 m) or greater.

④ Make an emergency swimming ascent (ESA) if depth is less than 50 ft (15 m).

③ Buddy-breathe (only if both divers are trained).

② Breathe from buddy's alternate air source (AAS).

① Breathe from a backup scuba unit.

Figure 6.32 Loss-of-air options.

that you have no air. After you establish a breathing rhythm, grasp each other's right forearm or BC and ascend normally (see figure 6.33).

An emergency swimming ascent (ESA) is a scuba ascent you do using only the air in your lungs. The ascent rate of an ESA is faster than a normal ascent, but it is not rapid. Retain your regulator in your mouth, and try to breathe from it from time to time. Do not hold your breath or you risk a lung overexpansion injury. If you exhale too much air, you will have a strong urge to inhale. The key to a successful ESA is to exhale enough air that your lungs remain at a comfortable volume. When you do an ESA correctly, you can ascend 50 feet (15 m) easily without an overwhelming desire for air. If the depth is over 50 feet, discard your weights to initiate a buoyant emergency ascent (BEA). Swim

Figure 6.33   Air sharing involves cooperation and coordination with your buddy.

for the first portion of the ascent, but allow yourself to drift up when buoyancy can replace swimming. Flare during the last 15 feet (4.6 m) of a BEA, and keep your lungs at a comfortable—but not maximum—volume.

Buddy breathing—the sharing of a single regulator second stage by two divers—is not a desirable loss-of-air option because it jeopardizes the safety of two people. You and your buddy should practice buddy breathing at the surface before beginning a dive if buddy breathing is a loss-of-air option for the dive. Not all divers are trained to buddy-breathe, and buddy breathing attempted by two divers who are not proficient with the skill can result in disaster. However, those who are proficient buddy breathers can make a loss-of-air situation a mere nuisance.

Initiate buddy breathing with the "out-of-air" signal followed by the signal for "give me air." Your buddy holds the regulator second stage in the right hand and grasps your shoulder strap with the left hand. Your buddy extends the second stage toward you and holds it in such a way that you have access to the purge. You grasp your buddy's wrist (not the regulator) with your left hand and grasp your buddy's shoulder strap with your right hand. Guide the second stage to your mouth and push your lips against the mouthpiece to make a seal instead of inserting the mouthpiece into your mouth. By not putting the mouthpiece into your mouth to breathe, you can exchange the regulator quickly and reduce mask leakage caused by facial movements. Take several quick breaths initially; then pass the regulator back to your buddy. Exhale a small amount of air continuously when you are not breathing from the regulator. The exhalation helps prevent a lung overexpansion injury during ascent. After the initial contact, you and your buddy each take two breaths before passing the regulator. Do not inhale fully when buddy breathing because full breaths can cause buoyancy problems or lung injuries. A medium inhalation is adequate because you receive air every few seconds. You should exhale fully after each first breath that you take. The complete exhalation helps expel carbon dioxide and reduces your urge to breathe.

As soon as you and your buddy establish a breathing rhythm, you should swim to the surface, holding on to each other throughout the ascent. Blow bubbles continuously when the regulator is not in your mouth. Remember to control your buoyancy.

Skills for loss-of-air situations require proficiency, so they must be learned well and renewed periodically. Discuss the procedures for a loss-of-air situation with your buddy, and agree on the options you will use. You should both be familiar with the signals, positions, and techniques.

Assisting Your Buddy

You have read about many ways to assist your buddy and how your buddy can assist you, so you should realize the importance of the buddy system while diving.

In addition to helping your buddy handle entanglements, cramps, equipment problems, and loss-of-air situations, you may need to provide assistance if your buddy is incapacitated from exhaustion, illness, or injury.

A buddy who becomes agitated at the surface needs assistance in regaining control. Help such a buddy establish buoyancy, calm down, and breathe slowly and deeply. When the situation is under control, you may be able to help your buddy resolve the difficulty that caused the agitation.

If your buddy becomes exhausted, provide assistance at the surface with a biceps push, a fin push, or a do-si-do (arm-under-arm) push. The three types of pushes are illustrated in figure 6.34. Use the biceps push when your buddy can help, and use the fin push when your buddy is too exhausted to help at all. Monitor your buddy and offer encouragement while you provide assistance. (Note: Scuba rescues require techniques different from surface assistance.)

Figure 6.34 Providing assistance to an exhausted buddy using the (a) biceps push, (b) fin push, and (c) do-si-do push.

Managing Emergencies

Diving accidents occur when divers do not exercise good judgment or when they fail to follow recommended practices. If you do what you are supposed to do, the chances of a diving accident are extremely small. But you may have to render aid to someone else who violates safety rules. This section identifies the aid you should be capable of providing.

Training and Preparation

Three types of emergency preparedness training are recommended for all divers: first aid, cardiopulmonary resuscitation (CPR), and diving rescue techniques. You can get first aid and CPR training from various public service organizations. You'll learn some diving rescue techniques in your entry-level course, but you should also complete a rescue specialty course.

Emergency preparedness includes having emergency equipment and information available. The emergency equipment available at a dive site should include these items:

- Diving first aid kit (see the checklist of kit items in chapter 4)
- Oxygen delivery system
- Blanket (if appropriate)
- Drinking water

You may not have all of the emergency equipment yourself, but you can determine whether it is available aboard a boat or as part of an organized dive.

Have a means of communication—a telephone, cellular phone, CB radio, or marine radio—to summon assistance. Have contact information for local emergency medical assistance and for the emergency treatment of divers at the dive site. Have phone numbers and radio frequencies for local emergency support services. Examples of numbers to have include the Coast Guard, paramedics, hospital, ambulance, police or sheriff's office, recompression facility, and the Divers Alert Network (DAN). The Divers Alert Network has a 24-hour emergency number 919-684-8111 to assist with the coordination of responses to diving accidents.

Scuba Lifesaving

The principal elements of scuba lifesaving are cognizance, assessment, rescue, and evacuation (CARE). Cognizance is the ability to detect signs that identify or predict an accident. Trained and experienced divers can recognize situations that can lead to accidents before divers enter the water, when they enter the water, at the surface, during descents, underwater, during ascents, and during exits. As your experience increases, you will become more cognizant of potential difficulties.

Assessment is an ongoing evaluation of various factors that can affect a lifesaving situation. Rescuers need to consider their own ability to rescue the victim, the victim's condition, the environmental conditions, the equipment available, and additional resources.

Rescue techniques include approaches, extensions, throws, assists, establishing buoyancy, defenses, towing, deep-water rescue breathing, equipment removal, and removing the victim from the water. The ability to rescue both conscious and unconscious divers at the surface and underwater is an important skill to develop; you should take a scuba lifesaving or rescue specialty course as soon as possible after completing basic scuba training.

An unconscious diver underwater can drown unless rescued immediately. Illness, drugs, and blows to the head can cause loss of consciousness. If a diver loses consciousness underwater, make the diver buoyant and get her to the surface immediately. You do not need to concern yourself about expanding air if the diver is not breathing because an unconscious person exhales automatically regardless of head position. Do not concern yourself about the diver's decompression status; she can be treated for DCS but will die after about four minutes without air. Do not jeopardize your own safety when attempting to rescue another diver.

A diver who is not breathing needs air quickly and must get it at the surface. This is where your CPR skills and diving rescue techniques are invaluable. Open the victim's airway. Often this is all an unconscious person needs to be able to breathe. To open the airway, tilt the head and lift the chin. Turn the person's head to the side to drain water from the mouth and throat. Vomiting is common, so be prepared for it. Clear vomit from the victim's mouth and throat at once or the person may inhale it and choke.

A person who is not breathing after you have opened the airway requires rescue breathing and medical assistance. Shout for help. If you can remove the victim from the water quickly, you should do so. If removal will be delayed by even a couple of minutes, begin rescue breathing while you remain in the water. Keep the victim's airway open and lightly pinch the victim's nostrils to seal them. Seal your mouth over the other person's mouth and fill the person's lungs with air until the chest rises gently. Give the victim one breath every 5 seconds or two breaths every 10 seconds while swimming to safety. A gurgling sound from the victim indicates water or vomit in the airway. Roll the person to the side and drain the fluid before continuing rescue breathing. The preferred method of in-water artificial respiration involves using a rescue-breathing mask, which you can carry in the pocket of your BC. Figure 6.35 shows a person doing rescue breathing using such a mask.

You will probably not be able to detect a pulse in the water, so don't bother trying. You cannot administer CPR in the water; you must remove the victim from the water and position her on a firm surface.

Evacuation is the final element of scuba lifesaving. Evacuation procedures include accident preparedness, communications, and transportation options. Advance planning is essential to evacuate an injured diver to a medical facility.

First Aid

Some aspects of diving first aid are not taught in standard first

Figure 6.35   Rescue breathing with a breathing mask.

aid courses. This section touches on those aspects, but you need the additional study and training that you can get in rescue specialty and oxygen administration courses.

Nothing is more important than attending to basic life support: airway, breathing, and circulation. The next priority for any serious diving injury is treatment for shock. Lay an injured diver who is breathing on his side, keep the person warm (but avoid overheating), and administer sips of water if he is conscious. If you suspect an air embolism, DCS, or near drowning, have the person breathe oxygen in the highest possible concentration. Keep any diver who has lost consciousness or who has symptoms of DCS lying down until he can be evaluated at a medical facility. Monitor the victim continuously.

You should be able to recognize signs and symptoms that indicate a serious diving illness. The following signs and symptoms indicate an injury that requires the prompt administration of oxygen and medical treatment:

- Confusion
- Seizure
- Loss of consciousness
- Nausea or vomiting
- Shortness of breath
- Sudden, extreme weakness
- Numbness or a pins-and-needles sensation
- Inability to do simple motor skills
- Paralysis
- Unequal pupils

Venomous marine animals may be encountered in some parts of the world. A few venomous animals can inflict life-threatening wounds (see chapter 5). The wounds can cause pain, weakness, nausea, shock, mental confusion, paralysis, convulsions, depression, arrest of breathing, and even cardiac arrest. Fortunately, such wounds are rare.

Venomous injuries are either punctures or stings. First aid for venomous puncture wounds involves removing all foreign matter from the wound, applying hot packs to the injured area for half an hour, and keeping the injured area below the level of the heart. The injured person should obtain medical attention.

First aid for a venomous sting includes killing any stinging cells that are in contact with the skin, removing any residue, cleansing the area, applying an analgesic ointment for pain relief, and seeking medical attention. Vinegar is a good solution to apply to all stings to neutralize stinging cells initially.

You may not recall the appropriate first aid procedures in the event of an accident; therefore, you should bring along a diving first aid book to help you identify an injury and administer the appropriate first aid. A wilderness first aid book is also strongly recommended because diving often occurs in remote areas.

Managing Accidents

If a serious diving accident occurs, and no supervisory personnel are available to take charge, you have to manage the situation to the best of your ability. Summon help, but do not leave a seriously injured diver unattended. Enlist the aid of others. Try to locate the injured diver's identification and medical information. Write down what happened, as well as the person's dive profile,

SCUBA WISE

People are creatures of habit, and habits are the result of repetition. If you repeat an action correctly enough times, you form a good habit. On the other hand, if you repeat an action incorrectly enough times, you create a bad habit. Divers need good habits to avoid accidents, but sometimes they fail to take the time to develop them. I often watch divers on charter boats and at dive sites as they prepare to dive. I notice that some fail to inspect their equipment adequately, some fail to plan their dive properly, and some fail to follow the practices outlined in this chapter. They usually know what to do, but because they have bypassed many steps every time they go diving, they have a habit of skipping important items. How safe is a pilot if he ignores the preflight checklist? Taking the correct action requires concentration initially, but when repeated until the action becomes a habit, the process becomes automatic. People can make complex processes simple by repeating them. When a skill is executed properly every time, it not only becomes habit but also is easier to recall when you really need it, such as in an emergency. I strongly encourage you to take the time to form good diving habits. If you do, I assure you that the odds of being injured are extremely small.

symptoms, dive times, and so forth. Pin the information in a conspicuous place, and send it with the injured diver to the medical facility. Accompany the diver to the medical facility, if possible.

Summary

The skills of diving range from simple skin diving procedures to complex scuba skills to problem management. You need to learn the skills correctly the first time, practice them until you can do them easily, and renew them frequently to stay proficient. You also need to be trained and prepared to handle a diving emergency. As mentioned previously, visualization of skills can help you develop skills. This is especially important for problem-management skills. Some problems are not common, and you may never encounter them; but you need to be prepared to manage them. If you visualize a problem vividly in your mind, you will be able to remain relatively calm when that problem occurs because you will know what actions to take. Knowing what to do helps you remain relatively calm, which allows you to think and to better manage your situation.

Application-of-Knowledge (AOK) Questions

1. What are ways in which you can control buoyancy?
2. What do you need to remember to do while ascending from a scuba dive?
3. What can you do to minimize the chances of becoming separated from your buddy while scuba diving?
4. The inflator valve on your BC sticks when you open it to add air. What actions can you take to prevent a rapid ascent?
5. What should you do if your regulator begins free flowing while you are underwater and cannot be stopped?
6. When preparing to exit the water into a small boat, what is the correct order for the removal of your equipment?
7. While swimming against a current at the bottom in 40 feet (12.2 m) of water, you begin to experience air starvation. What is the proper way to manage this problem?
8. If you become entangled underwater, what can you do to get free of the entanglement?

Sunset at Grand Cayman

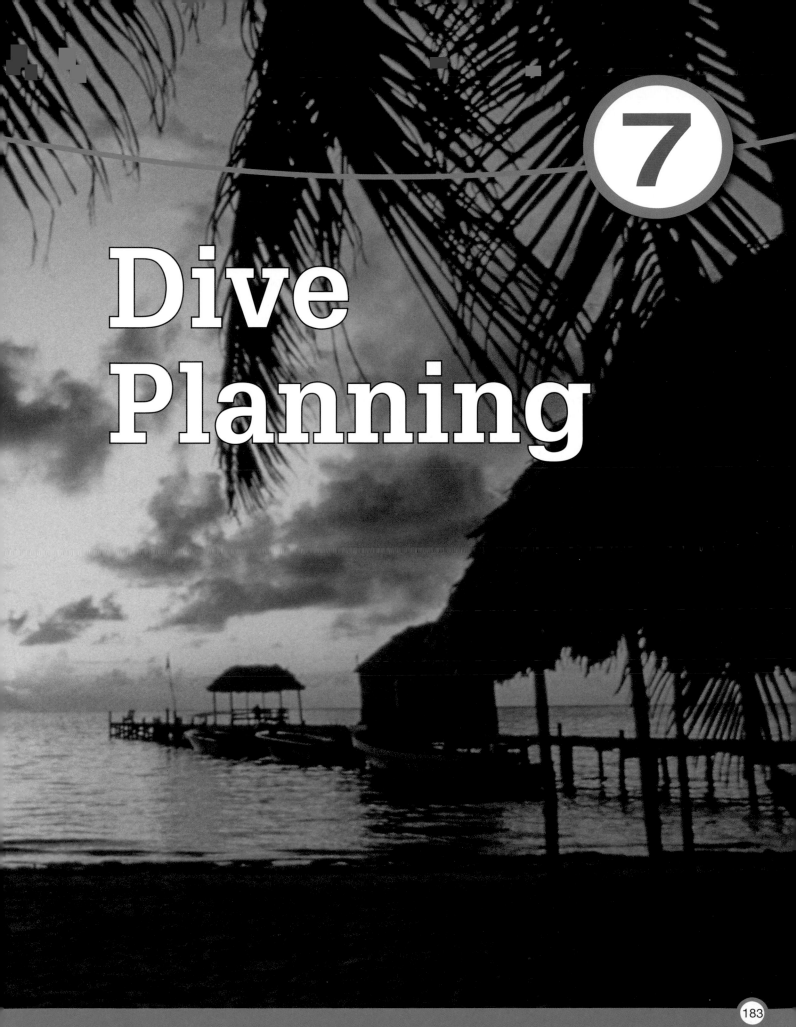

Dive
Planning

7

Dive In and Discover

By the end of this chapter, you will be able to do the following:

- List at least nine factors to consider in dive planning.
- Explain the why, who, where, when, how, and what of advance planning.
- Explain the on-site planning procedures for a dive.
- List at least five methods of obtaining area orientations for scuba diving.
- Use dive tables to plan repetitive dives that do not require decompression.
- Explain the planning procedures for cold or strenuous dives, variations in ascent rate, multilevel dives, omitted decompression, diving after required decompression, going to altitude after diving, exceeding maximum time when doing precautionary decompression, and a repetitive-dive residual nitrogen time that exceeds the absolute bottom time of the previous dive.
- Define the terms *residual nitrogen*, *repetitive dive*, *surface interval time*, *maximum bottom time*, *decompression stop*, *repetitive group*, *safety stop*, *residual nitrogen time*, *actual bottom time*, *total bottom time*, *emergency decompression*, *no-decompression-stop limit*, *dive profile*, *step dive*, *spike dive*, *multilevel dive profile*, *sawtooth dive profile*, *scrolling*, and *contingency plan*.
- Explain contingency planning for scuba diving.
- Compare the advantages and disadvantages of dive computers.

In this chapter, you will learn about all phases of dive planning: advance planning, short-term planning, on-site planning, and postdive planning. You will also learn about area orientations and how to do dive profile planning. An essential part of dive planning is scheduling your time and depth to avoid DCS (decompression sickness).

A well-planned dive increases enjoyment and satisfaction and decreases the risk of injury. A poorly planned dive can result in disappointment, embarrassment, and discomfort. By the end of this chapter, you will understand the significance of the expression "Plan your dive, and then dive your plan."

Dive-Planning Factors

Many factors affect your plans for a dive or a diving trip. Keep the following considerations in mind when you are looking ahead to a dive outing:

- Health and fitness are important. Illnesses, required medications, and recent operations probably disqualify you for diving. If your health is not normal, consult a diving physician. If there is any doubt about your physical condition, refrain from diving until you are in good health. If you are prone to motion sickness, take steps to try to prevent it.
- Climate is a big factor affecting dive planning. If you dive close to where you live, dive planning is easier than if you intend to dive thousands of miles away. A difference in climate usually means a big difference in diving conditions, which means a difference in your equipment requirements.
- The distance you travel to a diving destination affects your planning. If you travel far to reach the destination, allow a day to rest and recover from travel before you dive. After even one day of repetitive diving, wait one full day before flying home.
- Weather affects diving conditions significantly. Storms and sudden changes in the weather can make diving dangerous. Know the weather forecast, and reschedule your dive if poor weather is predicted. Know the expected wind speed, air temperature, and water conditions.
- Seasonal changes affect water movement, water visibility, air and water temperatures, entry and exit areas, and the presence of certain types of animals. You

First you learn the theory of diving, then the skills of diving, and then you apply what you have learned. Your training objective is to qualify to dive without supervision, which involves planning your underwater excursions.

Fish in a Red Sea coral cave

should know what to expect at a dive site at different times of the year. It helps to know the visibility, water temperatures, tides, surf, surge, currents, bottom composition, silt conditions, plants, and animals.

You need to be physically and mentally fit for diving. Fitness for diving implies that you are well rested, are well nourished, have the physical strength and stamina to meet the requirements of the environment and the activity, are qualified for the activity, are not apprehensive about your plans, are not goaded into doing something you are not prepared to do, and do not allow pride to affect good judgment.

Your objective for the dive affects your planning. Different diving activities require different plans and different equipment. The planning of an underwater photography dive is not the same as the planning of a dive where you intend to hunt for game.

You must know and observe laws, regulations, and customs. Some areas have laws that require the use of a dive flag. Obey fish and game regulations. Some diving professionals discourage the taking of any living thing in an area. You need to know the behavior expected of you. Knowing the expectations in advance can help you avoid being embarrassed at the dive site.

Etiquette is important. Will early-morning diving activities be offensive to residents near the dive site? Will the parking of vehicles at a site irritate people? Be considerate of others who may be in the area where you intend to dive, including those who are fishing nearby. Consider the impact of noise, changing clothes, and dive site access. Then make your plans using good etiquette.

Advance Planning and Preparation

The first phase of dive planning is the determination of why, who, where, when, how, and what.

Why?   Determine the objective of the dive. What do you want to do? Take photos? Explore? Look for artifacts?

Who?   Determine with whom you want to dive. Select a buddy who is interested in your dive objective.

Where?   Determine a primary and an alternative site. If conditions at the primary site are unfavorable, go to the alternate site.

When?   Determine the best time to dive. The water at most areas is usually calmer in the morning than it is in the afternoon. Tidal currents and height may affect the best time to dive.

How?   Decide how to reach the dive site. Who will drive? What are the directions?

What?   Determine what equipment is needed for the dive. Who will bring the float and flag? How many tanks do you need? Are there any special needs for the intended activity?

Advance preparation can include

- making reservations,
- paying deposits,
- buying or renting equipment,
- having equipment serviced or repaired,
- getting tanks filled,
- obtaining a fishing license or permit,
- preparing equipment for photography, and
- obtaining emergency contact information.

Fresh water diving at Lake Mead, Nevada

Your preparations will usually include a trip to your local dive facility. Inspect your equipment before you go. You may discover a needed repair that requires some time to complete. Identify your equipment needs early.

Short-Term Planning and Preparation

The day and evening before you intend to go diving, you need to take three actions. First, you should find out the weather forecast and current water conditions so you can determine if conditions will be acceptable for your diving activities. Call your dive buddy to discuss and confirm your plans. Last-minute revisions, such as going to the alternative site, may be necessary. If you anticipate poor diving or weather conditions, reschedule the dive.

The second step of short-term preparation is packing your diving equipment and your personal items. (See chapter 4 for an equipment checklist.)

The third step of short-term planning is to write down your dive plans and schedule. Leave this information with a friend. Instruct your friend to notify the authorities if you fail to return by a certain time.

On-Site Planning and Preparation

When you and your buddy arrive at the dive site, you must determine whether the conditions are acceptable for diving. If not, go to an alternative site. If the conditions at the alternative site are also unacceptable, abort the dive.

An important step in the assessment of a dive site is the estimation of the current. Look for telltale signs such as kelp bent over from water movement, a wake around the anchor line or behind an anchored boat, or objects drifting on the surface. Determine the velocity of moving water by measuring how long it takes a floating object to move a known distance, such as the length of your boat. When an object moves 100 feet (30 m) in one minute, the speed of the object is approximately 1 knot (1.15 miles or 1.85 km per hour). When a current exceeds about 1/3 knot (0.4 miles or 0.6 km per hour), you must heed it because you can swim at a speed of only about 3/4 knot (0.86 miles or 1.4 km per hour). Plan the dive so that the current assists you in swimming to your exit point at the end of the dive. Figure 7.1 includes a table that can help you estimate current velocity.

If the diving conditions are favorable, you should then determine the diving area. Select the entry and exit areas for the dive, and discuss the entry and exit procedures. Agree on the course to be followed during the dive. Agree on time, minimum air pressure, and landmarks for changes in direction. You and your buddy should know in advance approximately where you will be at any time during the dive.

An important part of your planning is discussing and agreeing on the procedures for the buddy system. Decide who is in charge of the team, where you will position yourselves relative to each other, how you will move (steadily or start and stop), and what reunion procedures you will follow in the event of separation. Remember that communication is much easier on land than it is underwater, so take advantage of the opportunity you have to communicate and coordinate while preparing for a dive.

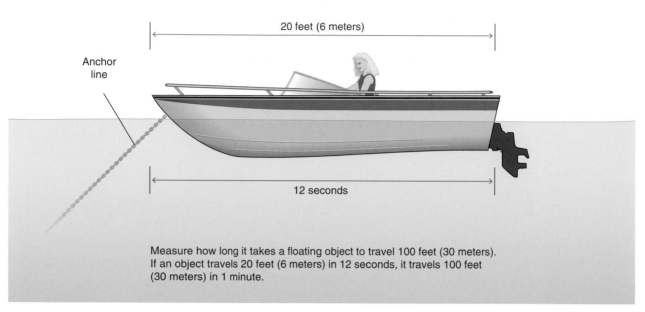

Current velocity estimation

20 feet (6 meters)

Anchor
line

12 seconds

Measure how long it takes a floating object to travel 100 feet (30 meters).
If an object travels 20 feet (6 meters) in 12 seconds, it travels 100 feet
(30 meters) in 1 minute.

Current velocity table
(time to travel 100 feet or 30 meters)

Time (seconds)	Speed (knots)	Time (seconds)	Speed (knots)
5	12.0	95	0.62
10	6.0	100	0.59
20	3.0	110	0.54
30	2.0	120	0.49
40	1.5	130	0.46
50	1.2	140	0.42
60	1.0	150	0.39
70	0.84	160	0.37
80	0.74	170	0.35
90	0.66	180	0.33

Figure 7.1 You can estimate the velocity of a current if you time how long it takes a floating object to move the length of your boat.

Always review your plans for emergencies. Agree on air-sharing procedures. Discuss what to do in the event of a serious diving emergency. Know where, how, and whom to call for help. Make sure you both have access to a first aid kit and other emergency equipment. A few minutes spent coordinating procedures before an emergency can save precious seconds if an accident occurs.

Scuba diving requires dive profile planning. You and your buddy need to agree on the maximum time and depth for your dive. You must limit time and depth to avoid decompression illness. Dive profile planning is discussed later in this chapter.

Area Orientations

You should recognize the importance of learning about a dive site before diving there. Because orientation is vital and because you want to be a responsible diver, you need to learn how to obtain orientations. Area orientations can be formal or informal. A formal orientation is provided as a service by a diving professional. The professional will tell you what to look for and what to look out for in the area and will lead you on a dive. A professional dive guide provides suggestions and points out items of interest and potential hazards. When you have completed a formal orientation, ask the professional to sign and stamp your logbook. A continuing education dive course is another excellent form of formal orientation to a new area.

Formal orientations are ideal, but if you cannot arrange to have a professional introduce you to a new region, consider some or all of the following options for an informal orientation:

- Read books, articles, and brochures about diving in the area. Learn as much about an area as you can before you go there.

- Write to dive stores in the region where you intend to dive. Ask if you can participate in a dive class session for your orientation to the area.

- Write to dive clubs in a region where you intend to dive. Ask if you can participate in a club-sponsored dive when you are in the area. Ask for contact information for several club members who dive regularly and may be willing to allow you to go diving with them.

- When you arrive in a new area, find local dive sites and visit them when divers are likely to be there. Ask the divers about the sites while they are preparing to dive or after they exit from a dive. If you have your equipment ready, you may be able to accompany them on a dive. Make sure they have experience in diving at the site.

SCUBA WISE

Having reviewed dive accident reports for many years, I have found that failure to adequately plan or to carry out the plan for a dive is a common cause of accidents and injuries. I have been able to avoid serious injury during decades of diving. However, I have had some bad experiences. These experiences occurred when I failed to plan adequately, when I attempted activities without first completing training for the activity, or when I did not have adequate knowledge of a new dive site.

I dived from shore in California on a beach with a steep incline without taking the time to research the dive. I was used to donning my fins, wading into the water, and swimming beneath the oncoming waves. When I attempted this procedure on this type of beach, I found that there was a trough created by plunging waves, and that the trough was a dropoff. The trough is also where the waves break suddenly and violently. As I waded into the water, I lost my footing at the trough at the same time that a large breaker suddenly formed and pounded me into the trough. I managed to kick past the trough before the next wave hit, but I was humbled by the experience. A key part of dive planning is to understand the terrain and learn the local procedures. After the dive, I watched a local diver literally run into the water after a wave broke, jump over the trough, turn onto his back, pull on one fin, and kick beyond the area where the waves broke. I have used that technique on steep beaches ever since that day when the plunging surf taught me a lesson. Avoid surprises that could be dangerous by learning about any new location before diving there.

○ Purchase a space on a diving charter boat. When you board the vessel, tell the crew you are new to the area. Ask for advice about diving procedures, and ask to be introduced to an experienced diver who can provide additional information.

When you dive with local divers, allow them to go first. Do as they say and do as they do. Procedures vary from region to region. A procedure you use in your area may be inappropriate in a different area. For example, in your normal diving environment, you may be able to enter the water from a boat in a current without holding on to a line. But if you tried to do so in a different area, you might be swept away at once. Be humble, listen to others, and follow their example to avoid embarrassment.

Dive Profile Planning

There are limits on how long you may remain at various depths. The amount of nitrogen absorbed by your body determines the limits. You need to be aware of the effects of **residual nitrogen**, which is nitrogen remaining in your system from a dive made within the past 12 hours. Whether you do one dive or a series of dives, it takes time to eliminate nitrogen from your body. If you dive again before the excess nitrogen has had time to outgas, you add to the nitrogen already in your body, and you reach critical nitrogen levels faster than if you had not already absorbed excess nitrogen. A **repetitive dive** is any dive made within 6 to 24 hours (depending on the dive-planning device) of a previous dive. Figure 7.2 shows how the amount of residual nitrogen in the body builds from repetitive dives. A **rest stop**—a precautionary decompression stop during ascent—reduces the risk of decompression illness.

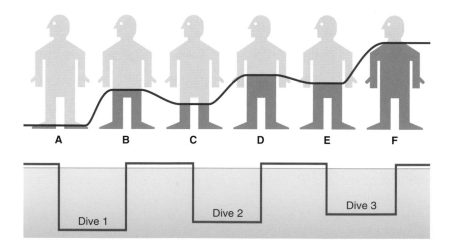

A—Normal amount of nitrogen in body
B—Amount of nitrogen in body after first dive
C—Amount of nitrogen in body after first surface interval
D—Amount of nitrogen in body after second dive
E—Amount of nitrogen in body after second surface interval
F—Amount of nitrogen after third dive

Figure 7.2 If you make a repetitive dive before allowing the residual nitrogen to leave your body, the nitrogen continues to accumulate.

Decompression experts use complex mathematical calculations and field testing to establish time limits for various depths for single and repetitive dives. The time limits are published in tables and programmed into calculators and dive computers. You need to know how to use these dive-planning devices to plan your dive profile so that you can minimize the risk of decompression illness.

No dive-planning device can guarantee that you will not develop decompression illness. Dive tables, calculators, and computers provide information based on statistics acquired through testing. If a diver adheres to the profile limits of a device, the statistical probability that the diver will develop decompression illness is small. The devices assume that you are in good health, that you do not get cold during the dive, that you do not exert strenuously, and that you ascend at the correct rate.

If you dive to the maximum time limits indicated by any dive-planning device, you increase the likelihood of decompression illness. Reducing your exposure to pressure reduces the likelihood of decompression illness.

Dive Tables

The U.S. Navy (USN) developed tables for dive planning. The recreational diving community adopted the military tables in 1980 and has used modified versions successfully. Although the tables were designed for military diving rather than recreational diving, many decompression experts still consider the USN dive tables—with reduced maximum dive times—appropriate tables for recreational use. New Doppler-tested dive tables developed by the USN are the basis for the dive tables presented in this chapter.

The USN tables use compartments with half times of 5 minutes, 10 minutes, 20 minutes, 40 minutes, 80 minutes, and 120 minutes. The amount of nitrogen remaining in the 120-minute (2-hour) compartment determines the **repetitive group designations** of the tables, which are represented by letters. Because outgassing of a compartment takes six half-times, you can see why the USN tables define a repetitive dive as any dive within 12 hours (6 × 2 hours) of a previous dive.

The tables include four sets of dive tables:

A. Total bottom timetable

B. Surface interval timetable

C. Residual nitrogen timetable

D. Decompression timetable

Dive Table Modifications

Diving organizations and manufacturers have modified the dive tables to make them more appropriate for recreational diving. Here are some typical differences between standard dive tables and the modified dive tables presented in this chapter:

○ Reduced time limits—Dive-planning devices today include maximum time limits that are less than the no-decompression-stop limits of the USN dive tables.

○ Reduced depth limits—The USN dive tables provide dive-planning information for depths to 190 feet (58 m). The recommended maximum depth limit for recreational diving is 100 feet (30.5 m). New divers should limit diving to

AIR DIVING TABLES

READ BEFORE PLANNING A DIVE

SEI & PDIC International Air Diving Tables are designed to enhance diver safety and assist in dive planning. The Air Diving Tables should be used only by persons properly trained in their use. SEI & PDIC International Air Diving Tables provide a conservative safety margin to help avoid decompression sickness. Use of these Air Diving Tables is not guaranteed to eliminate the possibility of decompression sickness. To gain the greatest conservative margin from these tables, divers must carefully plan their dives in accordance with the No-Decompression Stop Limits and ascend no faster than 30 feet per minute with appropriate safety stops. Do not exceed the No-Decompression Stop Limits. Do not dive deeper than 100 feet. Do not use these tables for high altitude diving without calculating an adjustment for high altitude. Susceptibility to decompression sickness varies in accordance with a diver's physical wellness and readiness, environmental conditions, ascent rates, and many other situations and conditions.

© 2009 Scuba Educators International Revised 10-2013

Table A
TOTAL BOTTOM TIME (TBT) IN MINUTES

No-Decompression Stop Limit ↓

Meters	Feet																
3	10		57	101	158	245	426									
4.6	15		36	60	88	121	163	217	297	449					
6.1	20		26	43	61	82	106	133	165	205	256	330	461		
7.6	25	354	20	33	47	62	78	97	117	140	166	198	236	285	354
9.1	30	223	17	27	38	50	62	76	91	107	125	145	167	193	223
10.7	35	168	14	23	32	42	52	63	74	87	100	115	131	148	168
12.2	40	135	12	20	27	36	44	53	63	73	84	95	108	121	135
13.7	45	102	11	17	24	31	39	46	55	63	72	82	92	102	
15.2	50	80	9	15	21	28	34	41	48	56	63	71	80		
16.7	55	63	8	14	19	25	31	37	43	50	56	63			
18.3	60	51	7	12	17	22	28	33	39	45	51				
21.3	70	42	6	10	14	19	23	28	32	37	42				
24.4	80	32	5	9	12	16	20	24	28	32					
27.4	90	24	4	7	11	14	17	21	24						
30.5	100	18	4	6	9	12	15	18							
33.5	110	16	3	6	8	11	14	16							
36.6	120	10	3	5	7	10									
39.6	130	6	2	4	6										

Repetitive Group Designation

Repetitive Group Designation ↓
A B C D E F G H I J K L M

Table C
RESIDUAL NITROGEN TIME (RNT) IN MINUTES

Repetitive Dive Depth in Feet/Meters

35/11	40/12	45/14	50/15	55/17	60/18	70/21	80/24	90/27	100/30	110/33	120/36	130/39	
15/153	13/122	12/90	11/69	10/53	9/42	8/34	7/25	6/18	5/13	5/11	5/5	4/2	← A
24/144	21/114	18/84	17/63	15/48	14/37	12/30	10/22	9/15	8/10	8/7	7/3	6	← B
33/135	29/106	25/77	23/57	20/43	19/32	16/26	14/18	12/12	11/7	10/6	9/1	9	← C
43/125	37/98	32/70	29/51	26/37	24/27	20/22	18/14	16/8	14/4	13/3	12	11	← D
53/115	45/90	40/62	35/45	32/31	29/22	25/17	22/10	19/5	17/1	16	14	13	← E
64/104	55/80	48/54	42/38	38/25	35/16	29/13	25/7	22/2	20	18	17	15	← F
75/93	64/71	56/46	49/31	44/19	40/11	34/8	29/3	26	23	21	19	18	← G
88/80	74/61	64/38	57/23	51/12	46/5	39/3	33	29	26	24	22	20	← H
101/67	85/50	73/29	65/15	58/5	52	44	38	33	30	27	24	22	← I
116/52	97/38	83/19	73/7	65	58	49	42	37	33	30	27	25	← J
132/36	109/26	93/9	81	72	65	54	46	41	36	33	30	27	← K
149/19	122/13	104	90	80	72	59	51	44	40	36	32	30	← L
169	136	115	99	88	79	65	55	48	43	39	35	32	← M

Note: For repetitive dives less than 35 feet use the RNT values for 35 feet

37	Minutes of Residual Nitrogen (RNT) Added to Actual Bottom Time to Compute TOTAL BOTTOM Time
98	Calculated Maximum ACTUAL BOTTOM TIME (ABT) in minutes. If This Number is Exceeded, a Decompression Stop is Required

New Repetitive Group

Table B
SURFACE INTERVAL TIME (SIT) IN HOURS AND MINUTES

	A	B	C	D	E	F	G	H	I	J	K	L	M
A	2:20/0:10	3:36/1:17	4:31/2:12	5:23/3:04	6:15/3:56	7:08/4:49	8:00/5:41	8:52/6:33	9:44/7:25	10:36/8:17	11:29/9:10	12:21/10:02	13:13/10:54
B		1:16/0:10	2:11/0:56	3:03/1:48	3:55/2:40	4:48/3:32	5:40/4:24	6:32/5:17	7:24/6:09	8:16/7:01	9:09/7:53	10:01/8:45	10:53/9:38
C			0:55/0:10	1:47/0:53	2:39/1:48	3:31/2:38	4:23/3:30	5:16/4:22	6:08/5:14	7:00/6:07	7:52/6:59	8:44/7:51	9:37/8:43
D				0:52/0:10	1:44/0:53	2:37/1:45	3:29/2:38	4:21/3:30	5:13/4:22	6:06/5:14	6:58/6:07	7:50/6:59	8:42/7:51
E					0:52/0:10	1:44/0:53	2:37/1:45	3:29/2:38	4:21/3:30	5:13/4:22	6:06/5:14	6:58/6:07	7:50/6:59
F						0:52/0:10	1:44/0:53	2:37/1:45	3:29/2:38	4:21/3:30	5:13/4:22	6:06/5:14	6:58/6:07
G							0:52/0:10	1:44/0:53	2:37/1:45	3:29/2:38	4:21/3:30	5:13/4:22	6:06/5:14
H								0:52/0:10	1:44/0:53	2:37/1:45	3:29/2:38	4:21/3:30	5:13/4:22
I									0:52/0:10	1:44/0:53	2:37/1:45	3:29/2:38	4:21/3:30
J										0:52/0:10	1:44/0:53	2:37/1:45	3:29/2:38
K											0:52/0:10	1:44/0:53	2:37/1:45
L												0:52/0:10	1:44/0:53
M													0:52/0:10

	0:52	Maximum Time For This Interval
	0:10	Minimum Time For This Interval

SEI & PDIC INTERNATIONAL ACCEPTS NO RESPONSIBILITY FOR ACCIDENTS ARISING FROM THE USE OF THESE TABLES

Courtesy of Scuba Educators International.

REPETITIVE DIVE PROFILES

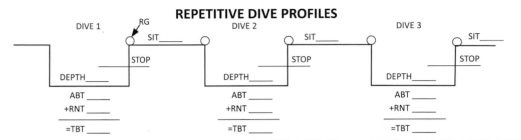

DEFINITIONS

BOTTOM TIME (BT). The elapsed time in minutes, starts when the diver leaves the surface in descent and stops when the diver begins safety stop or surfaces (round up to next whole minute). On repetitive dives this is Actual Bottom Time (ABT).

DEPTH. The depth of a dive; use the maximum depth attained during the dive in feet or meters of seawater. When depth is not indicated on the table use the next greater depth available.

NO-DECOMPRESSION STOP LIMIT. The longest amount of time a diver can spend at depth without requiring a decompression stop. Table A lists these for all depths. For repetitive dives the Residual Nitrogen Time (RNT) must be added to the Bottom Time (BT) and the Total Bottom Time (TBT) must not exceed the No-Decompression Stop Limit.

REPETITIVE DIVE. Any dive conducted within the time period specified by the surface interval table (Table B) of a previous dive with a minimum surface interval of 10 minutes. For repetitive dives of less than 35 feet, use the RNT (Table C) values for 35 feet to calculate Total Bottom Time (TBT).

REPETITIVE GROUP DESIGNATION (RG). Letters that relate to the amount of residual nitrogen in a diver's tissues for the time specified in the Surface Interval Table.

RESIDUAL NITROGEN TIME (RNT). Located in Table C, an amount of time, in minutes, which must be added to the Bottom Time (BT) of a repetitive dive to calculate Total Bottom Time (TBT). Represents residual nitrogen still in a diver's tissues from previous dives.

SAFETY STOP. A 3 minute minimum safety stop at 15-25 feet is recommended at the end of all dives.

SURFACE INTERVAL TIME (SIT). Located In Table B, the elapsed time from when a diver surfaces following a dive to the time (next whole minute) that diver starts the descent of the next dive. SIT must be a minimum of 10 minutes.

TOTAL BOTTOM TIME (TBT). Calculated by adding the Bottom Time (BT) and the Residual Nitrogen Time (RNT). For times not indicated at a particular depth, use the next longer time available for that depth.

RULES

ASCENT RATE. Divers should ascend at 30 feet per minute or slower.

DIVES LESS THAN 25 FEET. Dives less than 25 feet do not have a specific No-Decompression Stop Limit. However, if conducted as repetitive dives, they must be calculated as a 35 foot dive for Residual Nitrogen Times (RNT), Table C.

EXCEEDING THE NO-DECOMPRESSION STOP LIMITS. If divers err and stay longer than the times allowed on the No-Decompression Stop Limit, Table A, the divers have exposed themselves to an increased decompression requirement and must refer to the Decompression Stops Table, Table D, for required decompression stops to complete the dive. Once on the surface these divers should not dive again for at least 12 hours or fly for at least 24 hours.

FLYING AFTER DIVING. The longer the surface interval before flying the less likely a diver will experience decompression sickness. A minimum surface interval of 12 hours is required before ascent to altitude (or a ground altitude of 1000 feet above sea level). Divers who plan to make multiple dives for several days or computer assisted dives should take extra precaution and wait an extended surface interval of greater than 12 hours before flying or ascending to altitude. Divers who have made dives requiring decompression stops should wait a minimum of 24 hours before flying or ascending to altitude.

HIGH ALTITUDE DIVING. These Air Diving Tables are not to be used for diving at altitudes greater than 1000 feet above sea level without calculating altitude adjustments.

ORDER OF DIVES. All repetitive dives should be conducted with each successive dive equal in depth or shallower than the previous dive.

SPORT DIVING MAXIMUM DEPTH. Sport divers should not exceed 100 feet of depth.

SPORT DIVING TIME LIMIT. On any dive the Total Bottom Time (TBT) should not exceed the No-Decompression Stop Limit. Dives requiring mandatory decompression stops should not be planned.

Table D
DECOMPRESSION STOPS TABLE

Depth Feet Meters	Bottom Time (min.)	Time to First Stop (min:sec)	Decompression Stops (min) @ 20ft.	Total Ascent (min:sec)	Repetitive Group
40 12.2	135		0		M
	150	0.40	6	7:20	O
	160	0.40	14	15:20	Z
	170	0.40	21	22:20	Z
	180	0.40	27	28:20	Z
50 15.2	80		0		K
	90	1:00	2	3:40	M
	95	1:00	4	5:40	N
	100	1:00	8	9:40	O
	110	1:00	21	22:40	O
60 18.3	51		0		I
	60	1:20	2	4:00	L
	65	1:20	7	9:00	L
	70	1:20	14	16:00	N
	80	1:20	23	25:00	O
70 21.3	42		0		I
	50	1:40	9	11:20	L
	55	1:40	14	16:20	M
	60	1:40	24	26:20	N
	70	1:40	44	46:20	O
80 24.4	32		0		H
	35	2:00	1	3:40	J
	40	2:00	10	12:40	K
	45	2:00	17	19:40	M
	50	2:00	24	26:40	M
90 27.4	24		0		G
	30	2:20	4	7:00	J
	35	2:20	14	17:00	L
	40	2:20	23	26:00	M
	45	2:20	31	34:00	N
100 30.5	18		0		F
	25	2:40	3	6:20	J
	30	2:40	15	18:20	L
	35	2:40	26	29:20	M
	40	2:40	36	39:20	N
110 33.5	16		0		F
	20	3:00	3	6:40	I
	25	3:00	14	17:40	K
	30	3:00	27	30:40	M
	35	3:00	39	42:40	N
120 36.6	10		0		D
	15	3:20	2	6:00	H
	20	3:20	8	12:00	J
	25	3:20	24	28:00	L
	30	3:20	38	42:00	N
130 39.6	6		0		C
	10	3:40	1	5:20	G
	15	3:40	4	8:20	I
	20	3:40	17	21:20	K
	25	3:40	34	38:20	M

Dive Table Terms

Actual Bottom Time (ABT)—The elapsed time in minutes (rounded up to the next whole minute) from when a diver leaves the surface in descent until the diver begins a rest stop or surfaces.

No Decompression Stop Limit (NDSL)—The maximum time that a diver may stay at a specified depth (indicated in table A). For repetitive dives, the residual nitrogen time (RNT) from table C must be added to the actual bottom time (ABT) to obtain the total bottom time (TBT), which must not exceed the NDSL specified in table A. Table C also indicates the maximum ABT for various depth and repetitive group combinations that will prevent the TBT from exceeding the NDSL.

Repetitive Dive—Any dive conducted within 12 hours of a previous dive with a minimum 10-minute surface interval. For repetitive dives of less than 40 feet, use the 40-foot (12 m) values in table C (RNT table) to determine the TBT.

Repetitive Group Designation (RGD or RG)—A letter that indicates the amount of residual nitrogen in a diver's tissues for 12 hours after diving.

Residual Nitrogen Time (RNT)—An amount of time (in minutes) that must be added to the actual bottom time (ABT) of a repetitive dive to determine the total bottom time (TBT). RNT compensates for residual nitrogen remaining in a diver's tissues from previous dives.

Surface Interval Time (SIT)—The elapsed time (rounded up to the next whole minute) from when a diver surfaces after a dive to the time the diver begins the descent of a repetitive dive. The minimum SIT is 10 minutes.

Total Bottom Time (TBT)—The sum of ABT and RNT. For times not indicated at a particular depth, use the next longest time available for that depth.

depths of about 60 feet (18 m). Advanced divers qualify to dive to approximately 100 feet. Divers who complete a deep-diving specialty course qualify to dive to 130 feet (39 m). Technical divers qualify to dive at even greater depths. Depth in water is similar to speed on land. When you qualify for a driver's license, you may drive at speeds up to the legal limit. Driving at much higher speeds is hazardous and requires specialized training, special equipment, and controlled situations to minimize the risk of serious injury or death. Deep diving (beyond 100 feet) is similar to race car driving in many respects. Deep diving is a professional endeavor that unqualified recreational divers should not attempt.

○ Revised **surface interval times**—In 1983, a USN study reported a number of errors in the surface interval timetable. The errors usually do not affect the type of diving that recreational divers do, but some modified versions of the tables include the corrections.

○ Combined tables—Modified versions of the USN dive tables often combine information to make the tables easier to use. Tables may include the **total bottom time** (TBT) for repetitive dives along with the **residual nitrogen time** (RNT). Tables may include required decompression information to eliminate a separate decompression timetable.

Dive Table Use

In this section we'll take a closer look at some of the individual elements comprising the combined dive tables.

Table A provides the NDSL, without required decompression stops for various depths. This table also provides a letter designation for various dive profiles. The letter designation indicates the amount of excess nitrogen remaining in your body after a dive.

Table A

TOTAL BOTTOM TIME (TBT) IN MINUTES

START HERE →

Meters	Feet	No-Decompression Stop Limit	A	B	C	D	E	F	G	H	I	J	K	L	M
3	10		57	101	158	245	426								
4.6	15		36	60	88	121	163	217	297	449					
6.1	20		26	43	61	82	106	133	165	205	256	330	461		
7.6	25	354	20	33	47	62	78	97	117	140	166	198	236	285	354
9.1	30	223	17	27	38	50	62	76	91	107	125	145	167	193	223
10.7	35	168	14	23	32	42	52	63	74	87	100	115	131	148	168
12.2	40	135	12	20	27	36	44	53	63	73	84	95	108	121	135
13.7	45	102	11	17	24	31	39	46	55	63	72	82	92	102	
15.2	50	80	9	15	21	28	34	41	48	56	63	71	80		
16.7	55	63	8	14	19	25	31	37	43	50	56	63			
18.3	60	51	7	12	17	22	28	33	39	45	51				
21.3	70	42	6	10	14	19	23	28	32	37	42				
24.4	80	32	5	9	12	16	20	24	28	32					
27.4	90	24	4	7	11	14	17	21	24						
30.5	100	18	4	6	9	12	15	18							
33.5	110	16	3	6	8	11	14	16							
36.6	120	10	3	5	7	10									
39.6	130	6	2	4	6										

Repetitive Group Designation → **A B C D E F G H I J K L M**

Dive table courtesy of Scuba Educators International.

Table B, the surface interval timetable, provides letter group information based on your surface interval time (SIT). You begin a surface interval with one letter group designation; as you outgas nitrogen, you acquire lower letter group designations.

Table B

SURFACE INTERVAL TIME (SIT) IN HOURS AND MINUTES

New Repetitive Group (across top) → Repetitive Group Designation

Each cell shows maximum SIT (top) / minimum SIT (bottom).

Repetitive Group	A	B	C	D	E	F	G	H	I	J	K	L	M
A	2:20 / 0:10	3:36 / 1:17	4:31 / 2:12	5:23 / 3:04	6:15 / 3:56	7:08 / 4:49	8:00 / 5:41	8:52 / 6:33	9:44 / 7:25	10:36 / 8:17	11:29 / 9:10	12:21 / 10:02	13:13 / 10:54
B		1:16 / 0:10	2:11 / 0:56	3:03 / 1:48	3:55 / 2:40	4:48 / 3:32	5:40 / 4:24	6:32 / 5:17	7:24 / 6:09	8:16 / 7:01	9:09 / 7:53	10:01 / 8:45	10:53 / 9:38
C			0:55 / 0:10	1:47 / 0:53	2:39 / 1:45	3:31 / 2:38	4:23 / 3:30	5:16 / 4:22	6:08 / 5:14	7:00 / 6:07	7:52 / 6:59	8:44 / 7:51	9:37 / 8:43
D				0:52 / 0:10	1:44 / 0:53	2:37 / 1:45	3:29 / 2:38	4:21 / 3:30	5:13 / 4:22	6:06 / 5:14	6:58 / 6:07	7:50 / 6:59	8:42 / 7:51
E					0:52 / 0:10	1:44 / 0:53	2:37 / 1:45	3:29 / 2:38	4:21 / 3:30	5:13 / 4:22	6:06 / 5:14	6:58 / 6:07	7:50 / 6:59
F						0:52 / 0:10	1:44 / 0:53	2:37 / 1:45	3:29 / 2:38	4:21 / 3:30	5:13 / 4:22	6:06 / 5:14	6:58 / 6:07
G							0:52 / 0:10	1:44 / 0:53	2:37 / 1:45	3:29 / 2:38	4:21 / 3:30	5:13 / 4:22	6:06 / 5:14
H								0:52 / 0:10	1:44 / 0:53	2:37 / 1:45	3:29 / 2:38	4:21 / 3:30	5:13 / 4:22
I									0:52 / 0:10	1:44 / 0:53	2:37 / 1:45	3:29 / 2:38	4:21 / 3:30
J										0:52 / 0:10	1:44 / 0:53	2:37 / 1:45	3:29 / 2:38
K											0:52 / 0:10	1:44 / 0:53	2:37 / 1:45
L												0:52 / 0:10	1:44 / 0:53
M													0:52 / 0:10

Repetitive Dive Depth in Feet/Meters scale (left axis): 130/39, 4/2, 6, 9, 11, 13, 15, 18, 20, 22, 25, 27, 30, 32

Dive table courtesy of Scuba Educators International.

Table C, the residual nitrogen timetable, provides adjusted (reduced) no-stop time limits based on the amount of nitrogen in your body from a previous dive or dives. The table also converts your residual nitrogen to an amount of time for each depth. This residual nitrogen time (RNT) must be added to your actual dive time to obtain the total bottom time (TBT) for the repetitive dive.

Table C

RESIDUAL NITROGEN TIME (RNT) IN MINUTES

Repetitive Dive Depth in Feet/Meters (top) →

Each cell shows residual nitrogen time (top) / adjusted no-stop time limit (bottom).

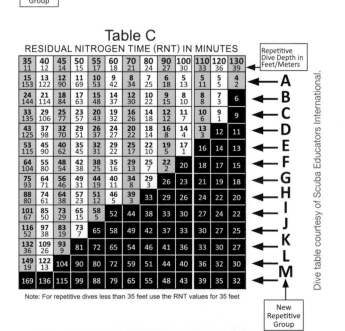

	35/11	40/12	45/14	50/15	55/17	60/18	70/21	80/24	90/27	100/30	110/33	120/36	130/39
A	15 / 153	13 / 122	12 / 90	11 / 69	10 / 53	9 / 42	8 / 34	7 / 25	6 / 18	5 / 13	5 / 11	5 / 5	4 / 2
B	24 / 144	21 / 114	18 / 84	17 / 63	14 / 48	13 / 37	12 / 30	11 / 22	9 / 15	8 / 10	8 / 8	7 / 3	6
C	33 / 135	29 / 106	25 / 77	23 / 57	20 / 43	19 / 31	16 / 26	14 / 19	12 / 12	11 / 7	10 / 6	9 / 1	9
D	43 / 125	37 / 98	32 / 70	29 / 51	26 / 37	24 / 27	20 / 22	18 / 14	16 / 8	14 / 4	13 / 3	12	11
E	53 / 115	45 / 90	40 / 62	35 / 45	32 / 31	29 / 22	25 / 17	22 / 10	19 / 5	17 / 1	16	14	13
F	64 / 104	55 / 80	48 / 54	42 / 38	38 / 25	35 / 16	29 / 13	25 / 7	22 / 2	20	18	17	15
G	75 / 93	64 / 71	56 / 46	49 / 31	44 / 19	40 / 11	34 / 8	29 / 3	26	23	21	19	18
H	88 / 80	74 / 61	64 / 38	57 / 23	51 / 12	46 / 5	39 / 3	33	29	26	24	22	20
I	101 / 67	85 / 50	73 / 29	65 / 15	58 / 5	52	44	38	33	30	27	24	22
J	116 / 52	97 / 38	83 / 19	73 / 7	65	58	49	42	37	33	30	27	25
K	132 / 36	109 / 26	93 / 9	81	72	65	54	46	41	36	33	30	27
L	149 / 19	122 / 13	104	90	80	72	59	51	44	40	36	32	30
M	169	136	115	99	88	79	65	55	48	43	39	35	32

Note: For repetitive dives less than 35 feet use the RNT values for 35 feet

New Repetitive Group (bottom)

Dive table courtesy of Scuba Educators International.

Table D, the decompression stops table, provides the amount of time that you must decompress if your total bottom time (actual dive time plus residual nitrogen time) exceeds the maximum no-stop time (NDSL) limit.

Now you are ready to learn how to plan dives using the air diving tables. Use table A to determine the maximum no-stop time (NDSL) for a dive. This is the maximum time you can spend underwater for the deepest depth you reach during a dive. If your total bottom time exceeds the NDSL time, you must complete mandatory decompression using table D (this will be discussed later). Your goal is to avoid exceeding the NDSL.

Rows are horizontal, and columns are vertical. Enter table A on the row corresponding to the deepest depth you plan to reach during a dive, and then move across to the end of the row to find your maximum NDSL. After your dive, reenter the row and find the first number (in minutes) that does not exceed your actual dive time. Proceed downward on the column containing your dive time and locate the repetitive group

Table D
DECOMPRESSION STOPS TABLE

Depth Feet Meters	Bottom Time (min.)	Time to First Stop (min:sec)	Decompression Stops (min) @ 20ft.	Total Assent (min:sec)	Repetitive Group
40 12.2	135		0		M
	150	0.40	6	7:20	O
	160	0.40	14	15:20	Z
	170	0.40	21	22:20	Z
	180	0.40	27	28:20	Z
50 15.2	80		0		K
	90	1:00	2	3:40	M
	95	1:00	4	5:40	N
	100	1:00	8	9:40	O
	110	1:00	21	22:40	O
60 18.3	51		0		I
	60	1:20	2	4:00	L
	65	1:20	7	9:00	L
	70	1:20	14	16:00	N
	80	1:20	23	25:00	O
70 21.3	42		0		I
	50	1:40	9	11:20	L
	55	1:40	14	16:20	M
	60	1:40	24	26:20	N
	70	1:40	44	46:20	O
80 24.4	32		0		H
	35	2:00	1	3:40	J
	40	2:00	10	12:40	K
	45	2:00	17	19:40	M
	50	2:00	24	26:40	M
90 27.4	24		0		G
	30	2:20	4	7:00	J
	35	2:20	14	17:00	L
	40	2:20	23	26:00	M
	45	2:20	31	34:00	N
100 30.5	18		0		F
	25	2:40	3	6:20	J
	30	2:40	15	18:20	L
	35	2:40	26	29:20	M
	40	2:40	36	39:20	N
110 33.5	16		0		F
	20	3:00	3	6:40	I
	25	3:00	14	17:40	K
	30	3:00	27	30:40	M
	35	3:00	39	42:40	N
120 36.6	10		0		D
	15	3:20	2	6:00	H
	20	3:20	8	12:00	J
	25	3:20	24	28:00	L
	30	3:20	38	42:00	N
130 39.6	6		0		C
	10	3:40	1	5:20	G
	15	3:40	4	8:20	I
	20	3:40	17	21:20	K
	25	3:40	34	38:20	M

Dive table courtesy of Scuba Educators International.

designation letter (from A to M) for your dive. For example, a dive of 50 feet (15 m) for 30 minutes assigns you to group E. Remember that whenever the depth or duration of your dive exceeds a listed number in the table, you must use the next larger number.

Next, you use table B, the surface interval table, to determine your letter group for a repetitive dive. Your group designation depends on the amount of time that you remain at the surface until you dive again. The longer your surface interval, the closer to the beginning of the alphabet your letter group will be.

Enter table B using the group designation you obtained from table A. Move downward along the column until you find the time range (expressed as hours: minutes; for example, 1:26 is 1 hour and 26 minutes) that your surface interval time (SIT) falls into. Remember that when you exceed a number on the dive tables, you must use the next larger number. Follow the row to the left to find your ending letter group designation. For example, if your letter group was E at the beginning of a 2:00 surface interval, you would be in group C at the end of the surface interval. You would be in group C after a surface interval ranging from 1:45 to 2:39.

Use table C, the residual nitrogen time (RNT) table, to determine both your adjusted maximum no-stop time for a repetitive dive and your residual nitrogen time (which must be added to your actual dive time) for your planned depth. For example, if your repetitive group letter from a previous dive is C and your planned depth for your next dive is 50 feet, your actual bottom time (the smaller, lower number for the depth column coordinate) must not exceed 57 minutes. Additionally, the residual nitrogen time (RNT) for the depth (the larger, upper number for the depth column coordinate) must be added to your actual bottom time. If you dived to 50 feet for 40 minutes as a group C diver, you would add 23 minutes of RNT to your actual bottom time to obtain a total bottom time (TBT) of 63 minutes.

After a repetitive dive, you return to table A and use your total bottom time (TBT) to obtain a new repetitive group designation. For example, your dive to 50 feet for 40 minutes as a group C diver yielded a TBT of 63 minutes. According to table A, 63 minutes of TBT at a maximum depth of 50 feet would assign you to repetitive group I at the beginning of your next surface interval.

Table D is for emergency use only when you exceed the maximum no-stop time (NDSL) for a depth. Avoid dives that require planned decompression. If you unintentionally allowed your total bottom time (TBT) to exceed the NDSL, you would refer to table D to determine the required decompression. For example, if your TBT for a depth of 60 feet (18 m) was more than 51 minutes (the NDSL), but less than 61 minutes, you would need to decompress at a depth of 20 feet (6 m) for 2 minutes. Your total ascent time, including the decompression, would require 4 minutes. Your repetitive group after the decompression dive would be L. This example is for emergency purposes only. You should never plan a decompression dive unless you complete specialty training and meet every requirement for safety.

Special-Equipment Dive Planning

You must use special dive tables if you dive using oxygen-enriched air (nitrox); you learn how to use these tables when you take a nitrox specialty course. Do not attempt specialized diving without proper training. Exceeding the 130-foot (39 m) depth limit by a few feet when breathing compressed air is not particularly dangerous, but exceeding the maximum depth limit (which varies with the gas mixture) when breathing mixed gases can cause seizures and drowning. Gas mixtures other than compressed air are only for divers who have the prerequisite training and equipment.

Dive Profile Terms and Rules

Divers use several types of **dive profiles**, which are created by plotting the time and depth of a dive. Figure 7.3 shows a diagram of a standard profile. A dive to a constant depth for a given period of time is typically depicted as a profile with square corners. A **multilevel dive profile** is a dive that progresses from deep to shallow during a given period of time. When you make a dive in a series of steps, you can refer to it as a **step dive**. A **sawtooth dive profile** is a dive that progresses from deep to shallow and back to deep. Avoid this type of dive. Another profile is the bounce profile. This represents a dive with a short ABT,

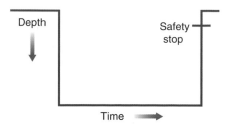

Figure 7.3 Standard dive profile.

such as a dive to free a fouled anchor. You should also avoid this profile, which is depicted graphically as a spike. Bounce profiles are also called **spike dives**. Figure 7.4 graphically depicts these four profiles.

Dive Profile Diagramming

Diagram your dive profiles when planning and recording your dives. Include planned and actual depths, rest decompression stops, bottom times, repetitive group letter designations, and surface interval times. For repetitive dives, include RNTs and TBTs. A simple method for diagramming dive tables is to use a worksheet like the one shown in figure 7.5. Some dive computers automatically record a profile of your dive that may be displayed for review.

Try the following exercise, which combines diagramming with the dive table procedures you have learned. Use the blank diagramming worksheet in figure 7.5 as a template. If you have any difficulties, refer to the preceding section about the use of the dive tables. Assume that all dive times include three-minute rest

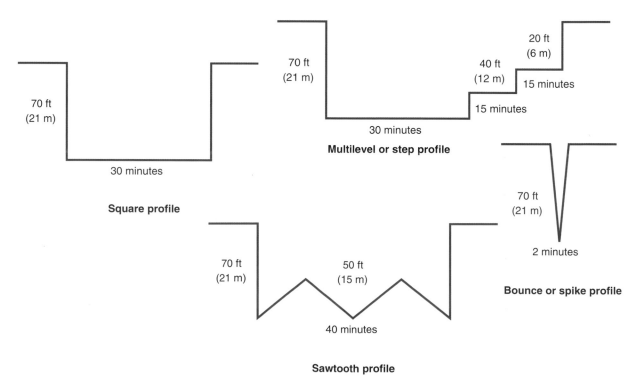

Figure 7.4 Types of dive profiles.

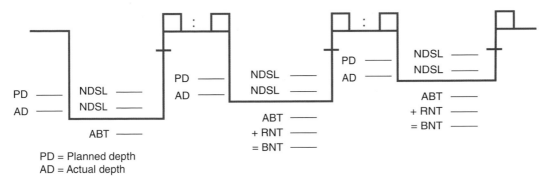

PD = Planned depth
AD = Actual depth

Figure 7.5 Use a worksheet like this to plan your dives.

stops. Calculate and diagram the following series of dives (the answers to the diagramming problem are in the next paragraph and in figure 7.6):

○ The first dive is to 78 feet (24 m) with an ABT of 20 minutes, followed by a surface interval of 1.5 hours.

○ The second dive is to 55 feet (16.8 m) with an ABT of 25 minutes, followed by a surface interval of 2 hours.

○ The third dive is to 40 feet (12 m) with an ABT of 25 minutes.

Solution: The repetitive group after the first dive is E. After the surface interval, the repetitive group changes to D. The RNT for a D diver at 55 feet (16.8 m) is 26 minutes. The TBT (ABT + RNT) for the second dive is 51 minutes (25 + 26). The repetitive group after the second dive is I. After the second surface interval, the group changes to G. The RNT for a group G diver at 40 feet is 64 minutes. The TBT for the third dive is 89 minutes (25 + 64). The repetitive group after the third dive is J.

The following tips help make dive profile diagramming easier:

○ Enter the repetitive group letter at every upper corner of a profile except the first corner.

○ Add ABT and RNT to obtain TBT for every repetitive dive. Use the recall word ART to help remember that you add ABT and RNT to obtain TBT.

Now combine the dive table procedures to plan a series of dives. Use the blank diagram shown in figure 7.5. Assume that the depth of the first dive—the deepest dive—is 60 feet. The NDSL, according to table A, is 51 minutes. Plan an ABT

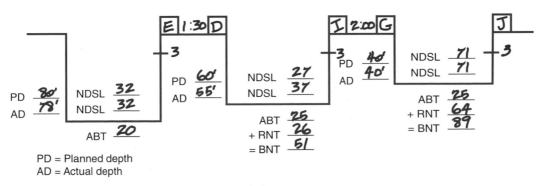

PD = Planned depth
AD = Actual depth

Figure 7.6 Completed diagramming worksheet.

Rules

Ascent Rate. Divers should ascend at 30 feet per minute or slower.

Dives Less Than 25 Feet. Dives less than 25 feet do not have a specific No Decompression Stop Limit. However, if conducted as repetitive dives, they must be calculated as a 35 foot dive for Residual Nitrogen Times (RNT), Table C.

Exceeding the No Decompression Stop Limits. If divers err and stay longer than the times allowed on the No Decompression Stop Limit, Table A, the divers have exposed themselves to an increased decompression requirement and must refer to the Decompression Stops Table, Table D, for required decompression stops to complete the dive. Once on the surface, these divers should not dive again for at least 12 hours or fly for at least 24 hours.

Flying After Diving. The longer the surface interval before flying, the less likely a diver will experience decompression sickness. A minimum surface interval of 12 hours is required before ascent to altitude in a pressurized aircraft (or a ground altitude of 1000 feet above sea level). Divers who plan to make multiple dives for several days or computer-assisted dives should take extra precaution and wait an extended surface interval of greater than 12 hours before flying or ascending to altitude. Divers who have made dives requiring decompression stops should wait a minimum of 24 hours before flying or ascending to altitude.

High Altitude Diving. These Air Diving Tables are not to be used for diving at altitudes greater than 1000 feet above sea level without calculating altitude adjustments.

Order of Dives. All repetitive dives should be conducted with each successive dive equal in depth or shallower than the previous dive.

Sport Diving Maximum Depth. Sport divers should not exceed 100 feet of depth.

Sport Diving Time Limit. On any dive, the Total Bottom Time (TBT) should not exceed the **No Decompression Stop Limit.** Dives requiring mandatory decompression stops should not be planned.

Definitions

Bottom Time (BT). The elapsed time in minutes starts when the diver leaves the surface in descent and stops when the diver begins safety stop or surfaces (round up to next whole minute). On repetitive dives, this is Actual Bottom Time (ABT).

Depth. The depth of a dive; use the maximum depth attained during the dive in feet or meters of seawater. When depth is not indicated on the table, use the next greater depth available.

No Decompression Stop Limit. The longest amount of time a diver can spend at depth without requiring a decompression stop. Table A lists these for all depths. For repetitive dives, the Residual Nitrogen Time (RNT) must be added to the Bottom Time (BT) and the total bottom time (TBT) must not exceed the No Decompression Stop Limit.

Repetitive Dive. Any dive conducted within the time period specified by the surface interval table (Table B) of a previous dive with a minimum surface interval of 10 minutes. For repetitive dives of less than 35 feet, use the RNT (Table C) values for 35 feet to calculate Total Bottom Time (TBT).

Repetitive Group Designation (RG). Letters that relate to the amount of residual nitrogen in a diver's tissues for the time specified in the Surface Interval Table.

Residual Nitrogen Time (RNT). Located in Table C, an amount of time, in minutes, which must be added to the Bottom Time (BT) of a repetitive dive to calculate Total Bottom Time (TBT). Represents residual nitrogen still in a diver's tissues from previous dives.

Safety Stop. A 3-minute minimum safety stop at 15-25 feet is recommended at the end of all dives.

Surface Interval Time (SIT). Located in Table B, the elapsed time from when a diver surfaces following a dive to the time (next whole minute) that diver starts the descent of the next dive. SIT must be a minimum of 10 minutes.

Total Bottom Time (TBT). Calculated by adding the Bottom Time (BT) and the Residual Nitrogen Time (RNT). For times not indicated at a particular depth, use the next longer time available for that depth.

of 28 minutes (including rest stop) for the dive. Your repetitive group designation after the first dive is E. Now plan a repetitive dive to the same depth. Refer to table C to plan the dive because table C provides the maximum allowable times for various letter group designations. If your surface interval is less than 52 minutes, you remain in the E group, your RNT is 29 minutes, and your ABT must not exceed 22 minutes. Your surface interval should be at least 1 hour, as recommended. If you wait an hour between the first and second dive, your repetitive group changes to D, your RNT is 24 minutes, and your ABT cannot exceed 27 minutes. If you want to dive for 28 minutes, you need to extend your surface interval to at least 1 hour and 45 minutes to obtain repetitive group C.

Assume that you repeat the first dive as a group C diver. Your RNT is 19 minutes and your ABT is 28 minutes, so your TBT is 47 minutes. Your repetitive group after the second dive is I.

Assume that the dive site is so good that you want to make a third dive to 60 feet. No ABT minutes are allowed for a diver with a group I designation. Proceed up the column of the table. If you want to dive to 60 feet again for 28 minutes, you need to attain repetitive group C, which allows 32 minutes of diving without required decompression. When you know the group that you need to attain as well as your starting group, you can plan your surface interval. Table B tells you that you must wait at least 5 hours and 14 minutes to move from group I to group C. It would be wise to consider a shallower dive at this point.

Use the tables to plan dives that enable you to avoid emergency decompression. You have three options for planning repetitive dives that do not require mandatory decompression. If your RNT prevents you from making a desired dive, you can (1) reduce the duration of the dive, (2) reduce the depth of the dive, or (3) increase the surface interval preceding the dive.

Special Procedures

Unusual circumstances may arise that require special procedures. You should know the procedures for dive profile planning for each of the following situations:

- A cold or strenuous dive—When a dive is particularly cold or strenuous, use the next greater time for the dive. If the dive is both cold and strenuous, use the next greater time and depth.

- Variations in the rate of ascent—If you ascend faster than 30 feet (9 m) per minute, extend your rest stop by at least two minutes. The faster you ascend, the more you should increase the stop time.

- Multilevel dives—Treat dives to multiple levels as square-profile dives, as if all the time of the dive was at the deepest depth of the dive. Do not attempt to extrapolate the dive tables.

- Omitted decompression—If you need to decompress but fail to do so, use the following procedure for omitted decompression. If you have no symptoms of decompression illness after the dive, remain out of the water, breathe oxygen in the highest concentration possible, rest, drink water, and be alert for symptoms of decompression illness. Wait 24 hours before diving again. If you suspect decompression illness, proceed at once to a hyperbaric facility for a medical examination. The USN has a procedure for in-water decompression, but diving medical experts agree that this procedure is inappropriate unless there is no alternative.

- A rest stop that causes your ABT or TBT to exceed NDSL—If a rest stop causes ABT or TBT to exceed the maximum time limits, determine your repetitive group letter designation using the NDSL for the profile.

- Diving after mandatory decompression—After a dive that requires decompression, wait at least 24 hours before diving again.

- A repetitive dive with an RNT that exceeds the ABT of the previous dive—If the RNT for a repetitive dive exceeds the ABT of the previous dive, use the RNT for planning the repetitive dive.

- Altitude after diving—Ascending to altitude after diving increases the likelihood of decompression illness because of further reduction in pressure. Driving in the mountains or flying after diving can cause decompression illness that would not occur if you remained at sea level until you eliminated the excess nitrogen.

The Divers Alert Network (DAN) recommends that divers wait a minimum of 12 hours before ascent to altitude in a commercial jet airliner (higher than 8,000 feet, or 2,438 m) after a single no-decompression dive. If you make multiple dives for several days, wait at least 18 hours before flight. If your dive requires decompression, a preflight interval substantially longer than 18 hours is required. Lengthening your preflight time interval reduces the chance that you will experience decompression illness.

DAN does not have a recommendation for flying or driving at lower altitudes. The most extensively tested tables for altitudes are the Swiss dive tables. The Swiss tables use a compartment with a much longer half-time than the USN tables. A reasonable approach to altitude delays after diving makes the surface intervals of the USN dive tables equivalent to those of the Swiss tables. Converted USN minimum surface intervals in table 7.1 specify the minimum time required to attain permissible nitrogen levels for various altitudes.

Altitude is any elevation above 1,000 feet (305 m). The altitude delay timetable provides recommended time delays for altitudes up to 10,000 feet (3,048 m). To use the altitude delay timetable, enter the table horizontally on the top line and

Table 7.1 Altitude Delay Timetable

Starting repetitive group

Altitude (ft/m)	ABC	D	E	F	G	H	I	J	K	L	Group*
2,000/610	0:00	0:00	0:00	0:00	0:00	0:00	0:00	0:00	0:00	2:26	K
3,000/914	0:00	0:00	0:00	0:00	0:00	0:00	0:00	0:00	2:37	4:08	J
4,000/1,219	0:00	0:00	0:00	0:00	0:00	0:00	0:00	2:53	4:30	5:51	I
5,000/1,524	0:00	0:00	0:00	0:00	0:00	0:00	3:04	4:57	6:29	7:44	H
6,000/1,829	0:00	0:00	0:00	0:00	0:00	3:20	5:24	7:12	8:38	9:54	G
7,000/2,134	0:00	0:00	0:00	0:00	3:41	6:02	8:06	9:43	11:10	12:36	F
8,000/2,438	0:00	0:00	0:00	4:08	6:50	9:11	11:04	12:41	14:19	15:40	E
9,000/2,743	0:00	0:00	4:57	8:06	10:48	12:58	14:51	16:39	18:11	23:09	D
10,000/3,048	0:00	6:18	10:37	13:25	15:56	18:05	20:10	21:18	23:24	24:50	C

Note: Times represent the minimum recommended time delay before ascending to the listed altitude and are USN surface interval times with a delay factor of 5.4. Times are in hours:minutes (for example, 5:24 is 5 hours 24 minutes).

*Recommended minimum repetitive groups for indicated elevations.

find your starting repetitive group. Next, find the altitude to which you wish to ascend. If you exceed a number, use the next greater one. The time at the coordinates of the desired altitude and your starting repetitive group indicates the minimum time delay recommended before ascending to the altitude selected.

Profile Contingency Planning

When you plan a dive profile, you should also plan for contingencies. You should know what to do in case you unintentionally exceed your planned depth or time or both. A simple matrix, such as that depicted in figure 7.7, is helpful. When diving using dive tables, you should prepare a contingency matrix in advance of your dives and carry it with you while diving. Dive computers automatically provide contingency information.

Not all dive-planning information displayed by a computer can be accepted at face value. You must learn to apply the dive computer guidelines included in this section.

After you complete your plans, you need to implement them. The first rule of dive planning is to plan your dive, and then dive your plan. You and your buddy should make every effort to do as you agreed to do before the dive. When circumstances force changes in your plans, it helps to have **contingency plans**.

Times in boxes are emergency decompression times.

Sample	Planned time 30 minutes	Next greater time 40 minutes	Next greater time 50 minutes
Planned depth 60 ft	0	0	0
Next greater depth 70 ft	0	0	5
Next greater depth 80 ft	0	5	10

	Planned time ___	Next greater time ___	Next greater time ___
Planned depth ___			
Next greater depth ___			
Next greater depth ___			

Figure 7.7 A contingency matrix helps you plan ahead for unexpected events.

These plans need to address many possible contingencies for a dive. For example, you should know what to do if you

- surface downcurrent from a boat when you had planned to surface in front of it,
- are unable to reach or use the exit point you had selected on shore,
- end the dive a long distance from your exit location,
- exceed the maximum allowable bottom time (ABT or TBT) for a dive,
- experience a failure of your dive computer while diving, or
- ascend directly to the surface without precautionary decompression.

Dive Calculators and Dive Computers

The benefits of a dive computer outweigh the potential problems associated with the use of these devices. Because dive computers simplify dive planning, you should obtain a dive computer as soon as you can. However, make sure you learn how to use dive tables and dive calculators so that you will know how to plan a dive if you do not have a dive computer. Although dive computers have minimized the use of dive tables, divers must be able to use dive tables as a backup in case the dive computer fails to work.

Dive calculators are circular planning devices that eliminate the mathematics required with the dive tables. Dive calculators provide precalculated numbers, and they eliminate the need to add and subtract times. Guides on the calculators help eliminate line-jumping errors frequently made when using dive tables.

Dive tables have 5- or 10-foot (1.5 or 3 m) increments and require all the time of a dive to be counted at maximum depth of the dive. If the first part of your dive is deeper than the remainder of the dive, you suffer a penalty because the tables treat the entire dive as if it took place at the deepest depth (see figure 7.8). At the end of the dive, you receive a repetitive group designation that is higher than you deserve. Dive tables are advance-planning devices, while dive computers provide constant information on decompression status.

Dive computers use 1-foot (0.3 m) increments for profile planning, and they calculate nitrogen absorption continuously. As you vary depth during a multilevel dive, you are charged only for the nitrogen you absorb. You do not incur the maximum-depth penalty (see figure 7.8) of the dive tables, so your residual nitrogen time after a multilevel dive is less than when calculated using dive tables. The penalty avoidance is the primary advantage of a dive computer as a planning device. Dive computers also provide advance-planning information by **scrolling** a sequential display of time limits for various depths. You

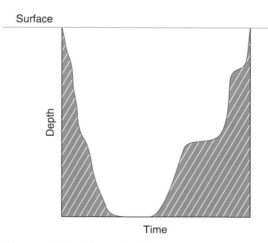

Figure 7.8 The striped area represents penalty time imposed by dive table procedures.

must carry your dive computer with you when you dive because it provides information about your decompression status continuously and keeps track of your residual nitrogen.

Regardless of the type of dive computer you choose, you need to understand some basic principles. First, be sure to read the instruction manual that comes with your computer. Wait 24 hours after diving with dive tables before using a dive computer to ensure that you eliminate all residual nitrogen from your body. Do not exceed the ascent rate specified by the manufacturer, and do a five-minute rest stop at a depth of 15 to 20 feet (4.6 to 6.1 m) at the end of every dive. If you exceed the rate of ascent specified for your computer, extend the duration of your precautionary stop by at least the amount of time it should have taken you to ascend to the stop depth. Do not make repetitive dives deeper than 80 feet (24 m). Keep your dive computer activated until its outgassing is complete. If your computer fails at any time while you are diving at a depth in excess of 30 feet (9 m), terminate the dive immediately with a rest stop. If your computer fails or if you switch it off accidentally, discontinue diving for 24 hours.

If you exceed the maximum time limit for a dive, decompression is mandatory. The computer displays a ceiling—the minimum depth to which you may ascend. As you decompress, the ceiling becomes shallower until the computer indicates that you may surface. After a minimum interval at the surface, the computer begins scrolling—displaying the time limits for various depths sequentially. Wait 24 hours before diving again after any dive for which a ceiling was displayed.

The concept of backup planning with dive tables is good for square profiles; however, for multilevel dives planned with a computer, the use of the dive tables for backup planning is not feasible.

Modern dive computers offer many features. Here are some examples of the features that a computer may include:

- Operating modes for various breathing gases
- Decompression stop data
- A wireless transmitter that provides both cylinder pressure and remaining air data
- Dive profile lifetime history memories

Dive Computers

Advantages

- The maximum-depth penalty of the dive tables is avoided.
- Dive profile information is accurate.
- Dive computers store a record of the dive profile.
- You can eliminate common errors made when using manual dive planners.
- Dive computers offer additional features, such as an ascent rate indicator.

Disadvantages

- Dive computers are electronic instruments that can fail.
- Dive computers are expensive to purchase and service.
- Each diver must have a separate computer.
- The mathematical model varies from one type of computer to another, so some confusion results when each diver of a buddy team uses a different type of computer.

- A multiple-step ascent rate indicator
- Altitude adjustment
- A dive-planning mode
- Backlighted displays
- Audible alarms

An integrated, wireless-transmitting, digital-compass dive computer provides dive-planning information before, during, and after your dives. This type of computer is a highly desirable device. Central processing units (CPUs) in closed-circuit rebreathers (CCRs) are also sophisticated dive computers that provide highly technical dive-planning information.

The advantages of dive computers greatly outweigh the disadvantages, and computers have become an almost essential item for scuba divers.

Postdive Review

After a dive, you and your buddy should reflect on your experience. How closely did the actual dive match the dive that you planned? If there were deviations from the plan, what caused them? Could you have prevented the deviations with a different plan or approach? What changes can you make to improve the next dive? Some problems require research, or you may need to ask the advice of a diving professional. The experience of each dive should affect your plans for future dives. Your dives with your buddy should progress more smoothly each time you dive together. Each time you visit a dive site, your dive procedures should improve. A review of each dive with your buddy and a discussion about future diving are valuable parts of dive planning. Even if you have a new dive buddy for a dive, you should plan your dives together and discuss the experience afterward. It is a good idea to keep notes about your dives on a waterproof slate and transfer unusual experiences to your dive log along with the usual data. Reflecting on past experiences from time to time will help you become a better diver.

Summary

The saying "If you fail to plan, you plan to fail" is true for scuba divers. All phases of dive planning are important and help ensure enjoyable and successful underwater experiences. Follow the recommended steps for planning, get area orientations when appropriate, have contingency plans, and discuss your dives with your buddy.

Dive profiles are a large portion of dive planning. Plan to dive conservatively. No dive-planning device can guarantee that you will not develop decompression illness after diving. The deeper, longer, and more frequently you dive, the greater your risk of decompression illness. Limit multiple-day and multilevel dives because repetitive multiple-depth profiles make you more susceptible to decompression illness. Make a rest stop at the end of every dive, avoid improper profiles, and have surface intervals of an hour or more. After three consecutive days of repetitive diving, wait a full day before diving again. Exercise good judgment and common sense.

Application-of-Knowledge (AOK) Questions

1. What is the most difficult task of dive planning?

2. How can you make dive planning easier and be more likely to accomplish it?

3. You have a dive planned, the weather and water conditions are good, and you catch a cold virus the day before your dive. Cold medicine minimizes your congestion. What should you do?

4. A friend who has more diving experience than you invites you to dive on a shipwreck that is located at a depth of 120 feet (36.6 m). How should you respond to his invitation?

5. Would you rather plan a dive by using a dive computer or by using dive tables? What is the advantage of each approach?

6. You have been diving at a resort for a week. None of your dives have required decompression other than safety stops. Your plane leaves the day after tomorrow at 10 a.m. When should you stop diving?

7. If you have to go over a mountain pass with an altitude of 5,000 feet (1,525 m) to return home after diving, what action do you need to take?

Sergeant major fish in Cozumel

Diving Opportunities

8

Continuing Education

A good diver never stops learning. You cannot learn everything you need to know about diving during a single course of instruction. After you complete your entry-level course, you can enroll in an intermediate or advanced scuba course immediately. These courses allow you to gain additional experience under supervision, help you develop important skills (such as navigation), and introduce you to special interest areas of diving. When you have identified a diving specialty you would like to pursue, you should complete a specialty course for that topic. A specialty course helps you begin enjoying the special area from the outset and helps you avoid mistakes and injury. Specialty areas that are of interest to new divers include the following:

- Underwater photography
- Underwater hunting and collecting
- Underwater environment
- Scuba lifesaving and rescue
- Night diving
- Boat diving
- Dry suit diving
- Drift diving
- Cavern diving
- Altitude diving
- Nitrox diving (enriched air)

Chestnut cowry by a starfish in California

As a qualified scuba diver, you can do many things. You can learn more, dive in different areas, be recognized for expertise, help others, or earn money, just to name a few. Opportunities abound.

The following specialty courses may be of interest to experienced scuba divers with advanced training:

- Wreck diving (penetration)
- Ice diving
- Cave diving
- Deep and wall diving
- Light salvage
- River diving
- Search and recovery
- Rebreather diving
- Mixed-gas diving

Courses are only one way to learn about diving. Many diving seminars, workshops, and conferences are also available. Check the calendar section of diving publications to learn of events scheduled in your area. Diving changes constantly, so you need to keep updating your knowledge of diving medicine, diving equipment, and diving procedures. Continuing education programs give you the opportunity to learn from professionals who are continually involved in diving.

You can learn more about scuba diving by reading books, magazines, and newspapers. Subscribe to a scuba periodical and read all you can about diving. The appendix contains a list of scuba periodicals. You can also visit websites by and for scuba divers.

Another good way to continue your diving education is to join a dive club. Dive clubs offer many benefits to divers, including education. A talk on an interesting subject by a good speaker is usually part of the monthly meeting of a local club.

Continuing your education is important for your safety and enjoyment. When you have increased your knowledge about diving, you may become interested in helping others to learn.

Local Opportunities

You do not need to live in a coastal area to dive regularly or to get involved in diving. You can dive nearly anywhere you can find water, and there are dive stores, dive clubs, and diving events in noncoastal areas. Get involved in diving in your area right away. Find all the diving-related businesses and groups in your area: dive clubs, dive stores, dive boats, diving events, and diving publications. Join a dive club, attend the meetings, and participate in club dives. Find a local diving website to make contact with other divers in the area. Complete continuing education courses. Attend local diving seminars, workshops, con-

Underwater photography at Cozumel.

ferences, and shows. Talk to other divers when you attend diving events. Seize every opportunity to learn and every opportunity to dive with those who are more experienced than you.

Dive Travel

Many divers enjoy taking dive trips to exotic destinations, and there are thousands of beautiful and exciting diving locations to choose from around the world. If you plan to travel somewhere to dive, you need to know how to arrange dive travel, how to prepare to travel, and how to enjoy your trip.

Travel agencies that specialize in dive trips provide valuable information, so it is a good idea to book your trip through one of them. You might want to consider a dive package that includes accommodations and diving. Dive resorts advertise these packages in diving publications and often offer packages for bargain prices at dive shows. Many resorts have toll-free numbers you can call to obtain information about dive packages. To ensure the best value for your money, compare several packages before you book a trip. If a brochure from a dive resort is out of date, check with the resort for current offers.

When planning a dive travel trip, you need to decide whether you want to dive from a live-aboard dive boat or from a shore-based dive resort. A live-aboard trip allows you to dive in a variety of locations. The vessel moves from place to place throughout the day. You dive in remote areas that only a few divers visit. You may find a live-aboard dive trip to be a wonderful experience if diving is the only objective of your trip and you are not affected by motion sickness.

Consider a shore-based dive trip if you do not care for confinement and if you want to participate in activities other than diving. Many beautiful islands and resorts offer a variety of things to do in addition to diving. Nondiving members of your travel party can usually find many sources of enjoyment at a land-based diving destination.

Many diving publications and diving websites are available to help you decide where to dive, although making a choice from all the fantastic destinations available can be difficult. Recommendations from other divers, trips sponsored by your dive club or dive store, and travel presentations can help you decide.

When you have decided on the region for your dive trip, get as much information as possible about diving in the area. Obtain and review brochures, books, articles, videos, and any other materials about the region. The Internet is another excellent resource for information on dive locations. Talk to divers who have been to the location where you plan to go. The more you know in advance, the more enjoyable you can make your experience.

After you select your diving destination, you should make your reservations well in advance, confirm all arrangements in writing, and get clarification concerning cancellations, refunds, and so forth.

Research and plan your dive trip by learning about the water temperature for the time of year when you will be diving. Then obtain the appropriate exposure protection. Remember that too much insulation is better than too little. Also make sure that all your equipment is in good working order.

Plan to avoid sunburn. Sunlight in tropical areas is more intense than in other climates. Use a sunscreen, and unless you are well tanned, keep yourself covered at all times, even while in the water. Use lip balm with a sunscreen ingredient.

Underwater salvage operations.

You cannot develop a tan in a few days, so it is silly to try if you do not already have one. Sunburn can ruin an expensive vacation, and donning an exposure suit is painful when you are burned. It takes only a few minutes for an untanned person to get burned in the tropics, so be careful!

Obtain all required documentation well in advance. Obtaining passports and visas can take months. Be sure to find out whether the country to which you are traveling requires immunizations.

Learn what to expect when you arrive at your destination. Know the frequency and voltage of the electricity; take converters if you are bringing electrical devices that operate on a different voltage. Know the monetary exchange rate. Consider taking a small pocket calculator to help compute the conversion of money.

If you have an expensive camera, video equipment, or jewelry, take your property to a customs office before you leave the country and have it documented to avoid being charged duty on the items when you return home.

Do not procrastinate in making your preparations. Procrastination can cause a cancellation of your trip, a forfeiture of your deposit, and a great deal of frustration. Consider travel insurance.

Limit what you pack for your trip. You do not need much clothing for a dive trip unless you plan to attend formal events. A few pairs of shorts and T-shirts, some swimsuits, and a couple of sets of nice clothes for dinner should suffice. Experienced dive travelers travel light when it comes to clothing and personal effects.

Diving destinations provide tanks and weights, so you do not need to take those items with you. When you pack for your trip, keep in mind that there may be weight limitations for your baggage. Excess baggage costs can be very high. To guard against theft, avoid flaunting expensive diving, photography, and video equipment. Use inconspicuous containers to ship your equipment, and it will be less likely to disappear. Insure luggage that contains expensive equipment. Items I always take with me are mask, snorkel, fins, exposure suit, boots, gloves, regulator, buoyancy compensator, and dive computer. I rent tanks and weights. My gear can be packed in a dive bag, but I prefer to use a suitcase for better protection of the equipment. I pack a dive gear bag in the suitcase because I don't want to use a suitcase at the dive site. There are also dive gear bags that have wheels, which are useful when you can roll the bag.

Be prepared for travel illnesses. Obtaining medications for nausea, diarrhea, and colds is easier before a trip than it is if you become ill in a foreign land.

Flying is the most common method of transportation for dive travel. Air travel usually produces jet lag and dehydration. A viral illness a couple of days after reaching your destination is common because many virus germs are concentrated inside the cabins of airliners. Here are some tips and suggestions concerning air travel:

Schedule your flight to arrive the day before you start diving. It is unwise to plan to dive the same day you arrive.

Drink a full glass of water or fruit juice every hour during your flight to avoid dehydration. Avoid alcohol, milk, and drinks containing sugar. The humidity in an aircraft is about 8 percent, so you will become dehydrated unless you drink plenty of fluids.

Avoid eating heavy meals and salty foods when flying. Light foods cause less dehydration than fatty foods. Consider ordering a special meal of salad and fruit, or bring your own food if meals aren't served on the flight.

Wash your hands frequently when traveling. Germs from your hands can get into your eyes and nose and lead to viral infections.

Remember that baggage compartments on airliners are unpressurized and that the reduced atmospheric pressure can damage your gauges. Therefore, you should either bring your gauges inside the cabin in your carry-on luggage or store them in airtight containers.

As soon as possible after reaching your destination, get some exercise and drink plenty of liquids. Limit your consumption of alcohol, which causes dehydration. Getting intoxicated at the outset of a diving vacation is one of the worst things you can do because you increase your chances of getting DCS.

Confirm your return air reservations as soon as you arrive, especially if you travel to another country. If you fail to do this, you are likely to lose the reservations. You could end up arriving at the airport to go home and discovering that your tickets are not valid.

Your first dive at your destination should be an orientation dive. In addition to learning about diving in the area, you should use the dive to check your buoyancy and make any needed adjustments. Work out any equipment problems during a dive in shallow, still, calm water. Avoid deep dives or moving water until you have acclimated to the area.

After three days of repetitive diving, refrain from diving for a day so that your body can outgas. Go shopping or take a land tour for a refreshing change of pace. Allow one day between your final scuba dive and your scheduled flight home.

Scuba equipment is a means to an end—a mechanism that enables you to go to areas that are otherwise unreachable by the average person. I think of scuba diving as a means of transporting myself to a destination where I can explore or participate in a special activity. Scuba diving without an objective loses its thrill after only a few dives. You need to develop an interest area, which can be anything from bottle collecting to wreck diving. When you have an objective for your dives, diving can be extremely rewarding. Over the years, I have participated in many different diving activities. My favorite underwater pursuit is photography. I can collect priceless memories without removing anything from the environment. In my opinion, underwater photography is the most challenging and the most satisfying dive activity. Select a diving activity that appeals to you, complete training for the activity, and then pursue it. You may choose several different activities. No matter what you choose to do while diving, I hope that your experiences will be as wonderful as mine have been.

The nondiving day before flying helps prevent DCS caused by altitude, and it gives you the opportunity to rinse, dry, and pack your diving equipment. Snorkeling is a good last-day activity, and your mask, snorkel, and fins dry quickly for last-minute packing.

Dive travel can be fun, exciting, and memorable when you plan it well. You can avoid unpleasant, frustrating, and disappointing experiences by researching your destination and preparing properly. Good diving to you!

Dive Destinations

One of the great pleasures of scuba diving is visiting different regions of the country and the world. Fantastic dive sites can be found nationally and internationally. The following areas are popular dive destinations that you might want to visit. The pictures throughout this book were taken at these destinations.

California

Dense kelp beds that form surface canopies make diving in California an unforgettable experience. The kelp provides shelter for many forms of life. Rock formations provide anchorage for the buoyant kelp and support additional life-forms, such as abalone, lobster, and moray eels. An expedition on a live-aboard dive boat to one or more of California's offshore islands during the summer months is an extremely worthwhile scuba experience. Shore diving in California can be difficult because of surf and low visibility. An area orientation is essential before attempting to dive through surf.

Washington

Puget Sound, which was carved into the landscape by glaciers, forms a gigantic body of ocean water that is much more protected than the coastal waters. The Sound contains many shipwrecks and artificial reefs, which are havens for many life-forms. Puget Sound is the home of the world's largest octopus as well as giant lingcod, monkey-faced eels, and beautiful orange and white anemones called metridians. The water is cold, but the visibility is 15 to 20 feet (4.5 to 6.1 m) most of the time. Dry suits are recommended.

Florida

Florida features some of the best and most diverse diving in the United States. From crystal clear springs and rivers to the Keys, there are many spectacular dive sites. Cavern and cave diving are popular, but training for these specialties is mandatory. The Florida coast has abundant shipwrecks. The Keys boast coral reefs and colorful fish. All scuba divers should definitely have a dive excursion to Florida included in their dive log.

New England

The cold waters of the New England area offer a great variety of diving opportunities. Wrecks, reefs, kelp, and creatures captivate your attention. Lobsters with claws and other interesting life-forms are great attractions. If you are able to schedule some time to dive when you travel to this part of the country, you should try to include the adventure in your itinerary.

Great Lakes

These great bodies of freshwater boast the most well-preserved shipwrecks in the United States. Many of these wrecks are in deep water, so you must have specialty training to explore them. Divers who are unfamiliar with the Great Lakes should use the services of a divemaster. If you like wreck diving, this is one of the places to include on your must-see list.

Hawaii

Hawaii offers exciting diving that includes good visibility, spectacular underwater formations, beautiful reef fish, large turtles, and giant marine mammals. Hawaii is a popular diving destination that you should visit if you get the chance. Aloha!

Caribbean

The Caribbean is one of the world's most popular places to dive, and for good reason. The area includes reefs, wrecks, drop-offs, and life-forms that are unique and breathtaking. Visibility is usually excellent. Many dive resorts in the area offer trips to phenomenal locations. Nearly every experienced diver talks about Caribbean diving experiences.

South Pacific

The islands in the South Pacific offer some of the most beautiful diving to be found anywhere on Earth. Divers can see fantastic soft corals, sea fans, and incredible fish. Visibility is outstanding. Many of the island waters feature wrecks and war artifacts. The beauty found above and beneath the water in this part of the world makes trips to the South Pacific highly desirable for scuba divers.

Underwater photography in Southern California

Middle East

The diving destination in this region is the Red Sea, which is unparalleled for scuba diving. The shear walls, the abundant and colorful life-forms, and the crystal clear waters make this one of the most desirable of all diving destinations. If you can afford a trip on a live-aboard charter boat to offshore islands, you will be treated to unforgettable sights.

To learn details of the world's most popular diving destinations, you can do a search of the topic on the Internet. Many websites provide excellent information. Traveling to exotic dive destinations is one of the most enjoyable aspects of scuba diving.

Career Opportunities

Some people love diving so much that they want it to be their vocation. Career opportunities exist for those who are willing to put forth the effort to achieve their desires. Jobs within the recreational dive industry include resort dive guide, instructor, journalist, dive travel coordinator, retail salesperson, and sales representative for equipment manufacturers. People can also work in nonrecreational scuba jobs, such as scientific research, archaeology, engineering studies, hull cleaning, salvage, and underwater repairs. Two of the same rules that apply to recreational pleasure diving also apply to underwater work: (1) Complete training for an activity before you attempt it, and (2) use complete, proper equipment for the activity. Career training opportunities abound. If you are interested in diving as a vocation, you can find information about training in dive periodicals.

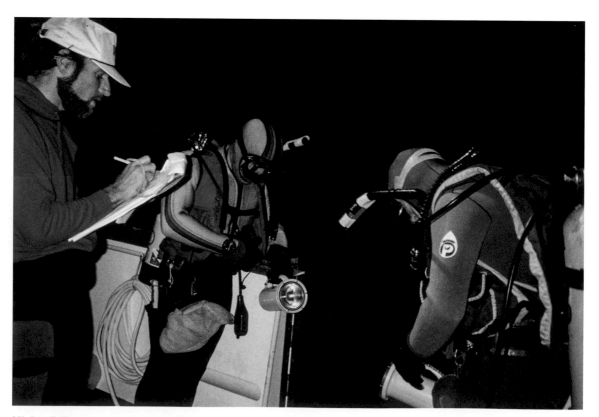

Night diving preparations at Catalina Island, California.

Leadership Opportunities

After you have become an experienced diver, you may want to help others learn and enjoy scuba diving. You can take courses to become qualified as a divemaster, assistant instructor, and instructor. Many people who love diving work part-time in the industry in leadership positions. When you are ready for leadership training, contact your scuba training agency for information.

Summary

Always remember that a good diver never stops learning. You should complete additional training, make sure you are trained for any special activity before you attempt the specialty, read as much as possible, join a dive club, and attend educational events. Take advantage of every opportunity to learn more about diving.

Increase your diving abilities and experience by applying what you learn. Participate in dive trips and charters. Research and plan your excursions thoroughly to maximize your enjoyment and minimize your disappointment. Many opportunities are available for diving adventures throughout the world.

Another opportunity for you as a diver is to make a positive contribution to the diving community. You can do this by conducting yourself in a responsible manner at all times and encouraging other divers to act responsibly. Help establish a good image of diving, get involved in issues that pertain to the diving environment, and help educate people who do not dive. Whether your contribution is small and personal or vast and international, you can make a difference. Decide now that your involvement in the wonderful pursuit of scuba diving will be a positive one.

Application-of-Knowledge (AOK) Questions

1. Why are you learning to dive? Do you just want to investigate a new activity, or are you interested in an activity that requires scuba diving?
2. What do you visualize as your progression of training as a scuba diver?
3. How often do you think you will dive? Will most of your diving be local or related to dive travel?
4. If a nondiving friend asked you what can be done to reduce the risk of injury while scuba diving, what advice would you provide?
5. What causes you the greatest concern about scuba diving? What can you do to minimize your concerns?
6. How do you see yourself as a scuba diver in 5 years? In 10 years?

Appendix A

Associations and Periodicals

Diver Training Organizations

International Diving Educators Association (IDEA): www.ideascubausa.com/home_15.html

Multinational Diving Educators Association (MDEA): http://neptuneshop.wix.com/mdea#!

National Association of Scuba Educators (NASE): http://naseworldwide.org

National Association of Underwater Instructors (NAUI): www.naui.org

Professional Association of Diving Instructors (PADI): www.padi.com/Scuba-Diving

Scuba Diving International: www.tdisdi.com

Scuba Educators International (SEI): www.seidiving.org

Scuba Schools International (SSI): www.divessi.com

Environmental Organizations

Blue Frontier Campaign: http://bluefront.org

Cousteau Society: www.cousteau.org

Earthecho International: http://earthecho.org

Living Oceans Society: www.livingoceans.org

Marine Conservation Society: www.mcsuk.org

Oceana: http://oceana.org

Ocean Defense International: www.oceandefense.org

Oceanic Preservation Society: www.opsociety.org

Reef Check: www.reefcheck.org

Reef Relief: www.reefrelief.org/mission

Save Our Seas: http://saveourseas.com

Sea Shepherd Conservation Society: www.seashepherd.org

Coral Reef Alliance: http://coral.org

Ocean Conservancy: www.oceanconservancy.org

The Ocean Project: http://theoceanproject.org

NOAA National Marine Sanctuary Project: http://sanctuaries.noaa.gov

Scuba Diving Magazines

Advanced Diver: www.advanceddivermagazine.com

Alert Diver: www.alertdiver.com

Dive Training: https://dtmag.com

Diver: http://divermag.com

Scuba Diving: www.scubadiving.com

Undercurrent: www.undercurrent.org

Appendix B
AOK Answers

Chapter 1

1. Some people learn to scuba dive because they seek a new experience or adventure. Scuba diving training opens the gate to a beautiful underwater world, which can provide many pursuits. Scuba diving should be considered a mode of transportation that takes you to places where you can pursue underwater interests such as exploring, photography, and wreck diving. After completion of your basic scuba diver training, continue your education and obtain an advanced scuba diver rating. With the additional skills acquired with advanced training, you will be ready to learn specialty activities and seek the rewards of your chosen endeavors.

2. An open-circuit scuba system allows a diver to breathe compressed air from a pressurized cylinder and exhaust the used gases into the water. It is a simple, reliable, easily maintained air delivery system, which makes it the safest and most popular scuba system. A closed-circuit scuba system allows a diver to rebreathe exhaled air by removing carbon dioxide and adding the correct amount of oxygen without allowing gases to escape from the system. It is a complex air delivery system that requires specialty training and extremely careful maintenance. Closed-circuit scuba systems are very expensive compared to open-circuit systems.

3. A scuba certification card (C-card) indicates that you have completed initial training, but it does not reflect how recently you have been diving. Certification agencies recommend that you complete simple refresher training if you have not dived for a year or longer. This training is a review of your basic skills under the supervision of an instructor during an open-water dive. The confidence you gain from knowing that your skills are refreshed will make your diving safer. A good reason to log your dives is to document your diving activity. Some dive resorts and charter boats will want to review your log book to determine your diving experience, especially your most recent dives. Logged dives also can help you recall many facts that you would otherwise forget.

4. It is logical that the more time you can use your knowledge and skills of scuba diving under the supervision of a certified diving instructor, the better your knowledge and skills will become. Extended training also allows you to ponder your learning between training sessions. You have time to think of questions that will clarify concepts and increase your understanding of principles. Short scuba training courses do not provide these benefits. The goal of learning is to transfer knowledge and skills acquired in a controlled environment to the actual environment in which they will be used. Longer scuba courses develop a greater ability to transfer your

knowledge and skills, which increases your safety for your independent diving after training.

5. A medical exam for scuba diving should be performed by a scuba diving physician who understands medical issues that could be problematic for those considering scuba training. Knowledge of how pressure affects medical conditions can help prevent pain, suffering, and even death.

6. Actions you can take to minimize your risk of injury while scuba diving are to dive only when you are in good health, use well-maintained equipment, dive in good environmental conditions, and adhere to the safety rules of scuba diving.

7. When you are in the process of selecting an instructional course for scuba diving, you need to know the sanctioning national agency, the instructor's experience, the total cost of the course, the course curriculum and duration, and how much open-water (real environment) training is included.

8. You can show that you are a responsible diver if you do only what you are qualified to do, dive within your personal limitations, adhere to safety rules, and remain aware of how your conduct will be viewed by others—divers and nondivers—when you go diving.

Chapter 2

1. Your exertion has used much oxygen, which has produced much carbon dioxide (CO_2), which stimulates you to breathe more to expel the CO_2. The feeling of a lack of air is caused by the need to reduce the amount of CO_2 dissolved in your blood. You need to minimize your activity immediately and breathe deeply until your breathing returns to normal.

2. Rapid, shallow breathing (hypoventilation) moves only a small amount of air in and out of your body. The structures from your mouth to your lungs do not allow gas exchange, so your body is not getting oxygen or ridding itself of CO_2. Gaining control of your breathing by stopping or reducing activity and breathing deeply until you feel better is the correct course of action and can help prevent panic. When your breathing is under control, you can think clearly and manage the difficulty that caused your anxiety.

3. Many factors affect air consumption, but the primary cause of high air consumption is exertion. Relax and move slowly. If you are too buoyant and have to exert to maintain your position in the water, your air supply will be depleted rapidly. If you are wearing too much weight, your attitude in the water will increase your frontal surface area and drag will increase air consumption. Adjust your weight and trim so you can hang suspended in a level position, and then relax and enjoy diving.

4. The first step is to tell yourself that you have time to manage this problem. The next step is to think of the options available to you. The quickest and easiest solution is to switch to your extra second stage or alternate air source. Your buddy's extra second stage is another good choice. The worst way to manage this problem is to spit out your regulator and swim to the surface.

5. Rapid and deep breathing before holding your breath is hyperventilation, which flushes carbon dioxide from your body. The buildup of carbon

dioxide when you hold your breath is what stimulates you to breathe. If you eliminate too much carbon dioxide from your body, you may lose consciousness while breath holding before you are stimulated to breathe. Loss of consciousness underwater can cause drowning. Hyperventilation should be limited to a few breaths before underwater breath holding to avoid what is called shallow-water blackout.

6. Your body loses heat rapidly in water. When you increase your heat production by exercising in cold water, you lose more heat than you would if you had not increased exertion. If you are wearing a wet suit, ascending to shallower water will increase your insulation as the water pressure decreases. Avoid moving directly into a current, which will push cold water through your suit. Your best action is to obtain better insulation for your entire body for future dives.

Chapter 3

1. The current is pushing cold water into and through your wet suit. If you swim at an angle to the current, you will reduce the flow of cold water through your suit and not get as cold. You can also look for places where you can be shielded from the current. You do not need to swim constantly when diving. Most of the life in the ocean is less than 1 inch (2.45 cm), so it is a good idea to stop and look closely at any underwater formations.

2. Some of the best and safest ways to warm yourself after diving are to remove your wet suit, get dry, get out of the wind and into a warmer environment, wrap yourself in a blanket or sleeping bag, eat high-energy food, drink warm drinks, and avoid stimulants. The principle is to warm yourself from the inside out instead of using external heat, which is dangerous. Remember that your core temperature will not be normal until you begin to perspire.

3. Did you think about the density of water and how much resistance to movement it causes? People usually think they will ascend rapidly if they lose their weights, but if you respond quickly, this situation is not difficult to manage. Quickly deflate any air from your BC. Then invert yourself to get your fins above your head, swim downward forcefully for a few kicks, grasp your weight belt, and replace it. (You will learn how to do this skill in chapter 6.)

4. When you ascend 10 feet (3.3 m) to swim over the reef, your buoyancy will increase because your wet suit and the air in your BC will expand. If the upward excursion is brief, you may be able to control your buoyancy just by keeping the amount of air in your lungs minimal. If the excursion is long or you are unable to control your buoyancy by breathing, vent some air from your BC to maintain neutral buoyancy until you descend again.

5. Remember that it is easier to equalize pressure in your ears if you descend feet first. It is good to use an anchor line for reference and control during a descent, but remain upright as you make your way down the line.

6. You should recall that the rate of change of pressure is greatest near the surface. Therefore, you need to equalize pressure in your ears and mask more frequently near the surface than will be required as the depth of

descent increases. If you can keep your air spaces equalized for the first 33 feet (10 m), you are not likely to have problems beyond that depth.

7. If you don't stop swimming, you will experience air starvation. And if you do stop swimming, your buddy will disappear and you may become separated. Prevention is best. Get your buddy to agree that you will swim side by side at all times and that when one of you stops, you both stop. If your buddy is ahead of you and you want or need to stop, use a rock or the butt of your dive knife to bang on your tank to get your buddy's attention. If your efforts fail, stop and get your breathing under control and then surface to reunite with your buddy if he does not return to you.

8. You are out of air, but only at a depth of 50 feet (15 m). As amazing as it sounds, if you start swimming slowly to the surface, there will be additional air to breathe from your tank as the surrounding pressure decreases with ascent. This is not the best option, however. In chapter 6 you will learn other ways to deal with situations involving loss of air supply.

Chapter 4

1. Minimize sun exposure, soak and rinse after use, store in a dark and dry location that is free of smog, inspect your gear regularly, and have your equipment serviced regularly or as needed.

2. The most important concerns for most diving equipment are fit and comfort. Features, colors, and price do not matter if the equipment does not fit well or is uncomfortable to use. If possible, rent equipment before you make a purchase so you will know if an item is right for you.

3. If all of the air escapes from your tank and the valve in your second stage is open (or if you happen to depress the purge button and open the valve), water can enter your tank. You will learn how to minimize the chances that your regulator will free-flow. If you detect water inside you scuba cylinder, take it to a facility for maintenance as soon as possible.

4. Air has weight. The air in a typical scuba tank weighs five to six pounds (~2.25-2.7 kg) when the tank is full. As you deplete the air, your buoyancy increases. The loss of weight may not be apparent at depth if you wear an exposure suit because pressure compresses the suit. You simply add less air to your BC than you would if you were not wearing an exposure suit. Problems arise as you near the surface with a scuba tank that is nearly empty because your suit expands and you are unable to overcome the positive buoyancy caused by the loss of weight from your cylinder. To avoid this problem, you need to adjust your weight to be neutrally buoyant just below the surface while using a tank with approximately 500 psi of air remaining in the tank.

5. You need just enough air in a dry suit to keep it from squeezing you. Any excess air forms a bubble inside the suit, and the bubble rises to the highest point. If you tip upside down to do something, the bubble can rise to your feet, may loosen your fins, and can cause you to float upward in an inverted position. This problem is just one example of why you need special training in the use of a dry suit.

6. A compass is a magnet, and magnets attract one another. Placing your compass near your buddy's compass causes the needles to shift position and the readings to be inaccurate. You need to keep your compass away from any items that can cause the needle to deviate from its natural direction.

7. The best way to clean your diving equipment is to soak it in warm water, rinse it gently with flowing water, and dry it thoroughly before storing it. Some equipment parts, such as dry suit zippers, require scrubbing. Follow the manufacturer's instructions.

8. The attachments to a scuba regulator first stage may include a cylinder pressure gauge, a primary second stage regulator, an alternate air source second stage, a BC inflator hose, and possibly a dry suit inflator hose.

9. The best reasons for having good dive equipment and maintaining it properly are safety and comfort. You will know when your equipment is right when you are not concerned about it while you are diving.

Chapter 5

1. The water temperature affects the equipment you use, your body temperature, your diving procedures, the visibility underwater, and the underwater life, among other things. Water temperature has a profound impact on your diving adventures. Knowing what to expect and how to be prepared for the temperature of the water is essential.

2. Water visibility is affected by depth, pollution, water movement, weather conditions, algae, temperature, your movements, and other factors. Check present diving conditions with your local dive facility and postpone diving when visibility is poor.

3. A good way to manage currents is to know in advance what to expect. Obtaining training for diving in various currents is important. Being aware that the current is weaker at the bottom than at the surface is helpful. Swimming at right angles to a current may help you get out of some currents. Diving against the current is a common practice, but in some situations it is best to drift with the flow of the current.

4. When you encounter a strange animal underwater, respond by stopping movements, respecting the animal, observing it from a distance, and refraining from provoking or feeding the animal. Nearly all marine animals are defensive, not aggressive. Think and respond. The worst action to take when you see a strange or large animal is to panic and ascend rapidly to the surface.

5. No matter how much training or experience you obtain, you will always need to acquire local knowledge about diving in a new area. Watching and mimicking experienced local divers are a good way to avoid embarrassment, but learning in advance about why the divers use the techniques they use is even better.

6. While it may be difficult to accept until you gain experience, the safest and most comfortable place to be while diving is near the bottom. It is much more uncomfortable and dangerous at the surface of the water.

7. The transition from saltwater diving to freshwater diving requires changes that include the amount of weight you wear and perhaps the type and thickness of your exposure suit.

8. When you plan to dive in a new area, you need information about the area. Weather conditions, seasons, forecasts of diving conditions, area hazards, equipment requirements, and local diving procedures are important to know in advance. Chapter 8 provides resources to help you obtain the information that you need.

Chapter 6

1. Buoyancy can be controlled by the amount of weight worn, the amount of air in your BC, and the amount of air in your lungs. Think of these methods as large, medium, and small ways of control, respectively.

2. To ascend properly from a scuba dive, alert your buddy, hold your BC inflator-deflator with the mouthpiece facing down and the valve open, reach up, swim up, ascend slowly, monitor your rate of ascent and your buddy, turn slowly, stop at a depth of 10 feet (3.05 m) for precautionary decompression, ascend to the surface, and make a complete turn to assess your surroundings. Ascending is a complex skill. Learn it well.

3. Successful buddy contact requires predive planning and communications, agreeing on a direction and maintaining that direction until you both agree on a new direction, maintaining the same position (side by side) relative to one another, holding hands or using a buddy line when visibility is poor, and committing to reunite using standard procedures if you become separated.

4. This situation can be frightening unless you respond quickly. All you have to do is raise and open the deflator valve with one hand and disconnect the low-pressure hose with the other hand. You do not need to terminate your dive because you should have the skills needed for manual inflation of your BC.

5. When a regulator free-flows and will not stop, simply switch to your extra second stage and ascend. Remove your tank at the surface and turn off the air supply. If you allow the tank to empty and the second-stage valve is stuck in the open position, water can get inside your cylinder.

6. To exit the water into a small boat, remove your weight belt and place it in the boat, inflate your BC about half full, and remove your scuba unit. Next, grab the rail of the boat and, while holding the regulator hose from your tank under one hand, kick yourself up and into the boat. Remove remaining equipment after you are in the boat.

7. Swimming against a current can be tiring. If there is a nearby obstruction, such as a rock formation, that you can get behind to minimize the current and rest, seek shelter. If there is an outcropping you can grasp that will allow you to rest and catch your breath, use it. If the bottom is sandy, plunge your knife into the bottom to maintain your position while you recover. The most important action is to reduce your exertion and get your breathing under control. If the situation is unmanageable, surface and drift back to your exit point.

8. The assistance of your buddy is the best way to get free of an entanglement, but you can also remove your scuba unit, clear the entanglement, and replace your equipment. Be sure you learn the skills of equipment removal and replacement well so you can manage minor problems that may occur while scuba diving.

Chapter 7

1. The most difficult task of dive planning is getting started! Most people agree that planning is a good idea, but they procrastinate. You can be successful with almost any task if you push yourself to get started. If you keep a list of things to do, consider adding dive planning to that list.

2. To make dive planning easier, find a buddy who would like to dive with you and agree on which items each of you will plan. Set a date to talk again about your plan. By taking responsibility and setting a date, you will have less work to do and will be more likely to meet your goal of developing a good dive plan.

3. If your health is not normal, do not dive. Congestion from a cold can make it difficult to equalize pressure in your ears and sinuses. Pressure can cause the medicine to terminate sooner than it normally would. When decongestants stop working, air passages can swell and close rapidly and trap air. Notify your dive buddy that you need to postpone your dive trip until you are well again.

4. Assuming you are a novice scuba diver, it would be unwise to attempt a dive on a wreck in deep water. Shipwrecks often occur where conditions, such as currents, can be treacherous. Tell your friend that you are extremely interested but that you need to complete advanced and specialty training so you will be adequately prepared for the dive.

5. When you dive using a dive computer, you avoid the dive table penalty rule of having to assume that all of your dive time was spent at the maximum depth. The computer also stores valuable information about your dive, helps you control your rate of ascent, and indicates when you need to stop for decompression. The disadvantage of a dive computer is that it is an electronic instrument that can fail. Dive tables do not need batteries. The best approach to planning time and depth limits is to develop a contingency plan using dive tables, write the plan on an underwater slate, and take it with you when you dive with your computer. If your computer stops working or you inadvertently turn it off, your contingency plan can help keep you safe.

6. You need to plan. After multiple dives, you should wait 18 hours before flying, so your diving needs to end today.

7. When driving decreases pressure with altitude after you have been diving, you need to consult the altitude delay timetable. If your driving altitude reaches 5,000 feet and your starting repetitive-dive group is 1, you need to wait 3 hours 4 minutes before driving over that pass. This requires planning. If your altitude delay timetable is at home in your book, you won't know how long you need to delay your journey.

Chapter 8

1. Some people learn to dive just to experience the activity. They complete training, purchase equipment, make a few dives, and stop diving. Other people continue training, get involved in the diving community, pursue an underwater hobby, and dive for many years. If you think of scuba diving as a means to an end, it can provide wonderful experiences that will keep you involved for many years.

2. You might see yourself completing an advanced diver course and several specialty courses. It helps to gain some dive experience in addition to your training dives. Just be sure that your excursions are limited to the conditions and depths to which you are qualified.

3. If you are not certain that you will dive regularly or that you will dive only locally, consider renting the major equipment (cylinder, regulator, exposure suit, buoyancy compensator, and weight belt). If you find yourself diving frequently, buy your gear. Renting equipment will help you make a good selection. If you plan to dive primarily at dive destinations, rent the major equipment at the destination. When you become an avid scuba diver, you are likely to have full sets of equipment for both cold- and warm-water diving.

4. The best ways to reduce the risk of injury from scuba diving are to be trained for what you do while diving, have the proper equipment for your dive, and gain experience gradually. Making a dive that greatly exceeds your training and limitations without first gaining several experiences that gradually increase your training and limitations is unwise.

5. Phobias are natural, but if something terrifies you and it is related to diving, learn how to deal with the fear before you are exposed to it. For example, many people fear sharks because of what they have seen in media. What you should know is that dangerous shark encounters are rare and most likely occur at the surface of the water. If you see a shark, remain calm, stay on the bottom, and enjoy the exciting experience.

6. When you look to the future, do you envision yourself diving regularly? Are you just going to wait and see what happens, or do you intend to continue your training, get involved, and become a frequent diver with many friends who also enjoy diving? You can dive for a lifetime and not even begin to see everything the underwater world has to offer. May all your diving experiences be enjoyable and memorable!

Glossary of Scuba Diving Terms

absolute pressure—The total pressure exerted on a diver, which is measured by adding atmospheric pressure to gauge pressure.

actual bottom time—The elapsed time in minutes from when a diver leaves the surface in descent until the diver begins a rest stop or surfaces.

alternate air source—A source of compressed air other than the diver's primary scuba regulator. The two primary types of alternate air sources are extra second stages and backup scuba units.

ambient pressure—The surrounding pressure.

Archimedes' principle—This principle states that the force of buoyancy acting on a submerged object equals the weight of the water displaced.

arterial gas embolism (AGE)—An embolism resulting from an air bubble blocking the arterial circulation.

atmospheric pressure—The pressure exerted by the atmosphere.

backpack—The equipment that holds the diver's scuba cylinder.

barotrauma—Trauma or injury caused by pressure.

bends—See decompression illness.

bezel—A movable ring on a waterproof watch (being used as an underwater timer) or compass that you can set to indicate elapsed time or direction.

blooms—Overpopulations of plankton that can color the water, destroy underwater visibility, and form toxins in animals that feed by filtering water.

blowout plug—A plug included in a submersible pressure gauge to relieve pressure in the housing in the event of a high-pressure leak.

Bourdon tube—A type of depth gauge that uses a thin metal tube formed into a spiral. The movement of the coil, linked mechanically to a needle, indicates the amount of pressure exerted on the gauge.

Boyle's law—This law states that for any gas at a constant temperature, the volume varies inversely with the absolute pressure, while the density varies directly with the absolute pressure.

buddy breathing—The sharing of a single regulator second stage by two divers.

buddy line—A short line used by two divers to keep in contact with each other when visibility is poor.

buddy system—The practice of teaming up with a qualified partner for activities that involve risk, such as skin and scuba diving. A buddy provides reminders and assistance and sees things that you might not see.

buoyancy—The upward force of water.

buoyancy compensator—An item of equipment that helps a diver control buoyancy. You can inflate your buoyancy compensator at the surface to increase buoyancy, deflate it to reduce buoyancy for descent, and add air to it to achieve neutral buoyancy underwater.

burst disk—A thin metal disk that is a standard feature of the valves for scuba tanks. If a tank is overfilled or the heat from a fire causes the tank pressure to increase to a hazardous level, the disk will burst and vent the tank to prevent an explosion.

capillary gauge—A type of depth gauge that is made up of a hollow, air-filled, transparent plastic tube sealed at one end and placed around a circular dial. Water pressure compresses the air inside the tube during descent (based on Boyle's law), and the position of the air–water interface inside the tube relative to markings on the dial indicates the depth.

cavern—A large, roomlike opening in a natural formation where light from the surface can be seen.

caves—Openings in a natural formation that extend farther than a cavern where no surface light can be seen.

C-card—The certification card you receive when you complete your training requirements as a scuba diver.

ceiling—The minimum depth that a diver cannot rise above without the risk of DCS.

ciguatera—Fish poisoning that results from eating fish that consume a certain species of algae.

closed-circuit—Refers to a scuba system that eliminates carbon dioxide from exhaled breath and resupplies oxygen without allowing gases to escape from the system.

compartments—Mathematical models used to estimate gas absorption and elimination by various areas of the body.

compass course—A series of headings on a compass that leads to a destination.

compass heading—A direction that is set on a compass.

console—A display unit into which several instruments can be combined. An instrument console attaches to the high-pressure hose coming from the regulator first stage.

continental shelf—An underwater area that extends from land and slopes gradually to a depth of about 600 feet (183 meters).

contingency plans—Plans that address possible circumstances that could force changes in the original plans for a dive.

controlling compartment—The area of the body that determines how long a diver can remain at a given depth. The determination is made by how quickly a gas diffuses from that compartment.

crest—The top of a wave.

Dalton's law—A law stating that the total pressure exerted by a mixture of gases is the sum of the pressures that would be exerted by each gas if it alone were present and occupied the total volume.

decompression illness (DCI)—A serious medical condition in which a diver has neurological symptoms on surfacing. Also known as the bends.

decompression stops—Precautionary stops made during ascent in order to reduce the risk of decompression illness.

defogging—The process of removing the film of oil from the surface of the glass lenses on a scuba mask in order to prevent the mask from fogging underwater. Commercial defogging solutions can help keep your mask clear while you dive.

dehydration—A physical condition resulting from the excess loss of body fluids.

density—Weight per unit volume.

DIN valve—A newer type of threaded outlet for a scuba tank valve that has a recessed O-ring seal and withstands higher pressures than a traditional O-ring valve. Tank pressures in excess of 3,000 psi (204 atmospheres) require a DIN fitting.

dive profiles—Diagrams used to plan a dive by plotting the time and depth of the dive.

diver's push-ups—A buoyancy evaluation used to learn buoyancy control. When the diver is weighted properly, a full inhalation will raise the shoulders while the fin tips remain on the bottom, and an exhalation will cause the shoulders to sink.

dolphin kick—A type of fin kick in which a diver holds both feet together continuously and exerts force against the water using a wavelike up-and-down motion of the body.

downwelling—A compensating downward current that occurs when wind blows along a coast where there is a steep drop-off near shore.

drag—A force that slows movement.

drift—The speed of a current.

drift dive—A dive in which the divers move with the flow of the current.

eardrum—A thin membrane that separates the ear canal from the middle ear and transmits vibrations to the inner ear via a series of small bones that are attached to the membrane.

ebb—The flow of water away from an area because of low tide.

eddies—Swirling currents that result from non-linear water flow

embolism—A blockage of circulation.

emergency decompression—A required delay in ascent that a diver must take if the actual or total bottom time (ABT or TBT) exceeds the no-decompression-stop limit for a dive.

equalization—The process of keeping the pressure inside an air space in or attached to the body equal to the ambient pressure.

eustachian tube—The part of the ear that allows the equalization of pressure in the middle ear.

Farmer Johns—A type of wet suit design where the leg material extends upward to cover the chest and is held in place with shoulder straps

fetch—The area in which waves were created.

fetch length—The distance wind travels unobstructed. The length of water over which a given wind has blown.

flaring—A method of slowing an uncontrolled ascent by arching the back, extending the arms and legs, and positioning the fins so they are parallel to the surface.

flood—The flow of water into an area because of high tide.

flutter kick—The most common type of fin kick. The flutter kick is an up-and-down kick that you can do facing down, up, or to the side.

fronds—The portions of kelp that appear to be the leaves.

gauge pressure—The pressure indicated by a pressure gauge that reads zero at sea level (this type of gauge displays only the pressure in excess of one atmosphere).

Gay-Lussac's law—This law states that for any gas at a constant volume, the pressure of the gas varies directly with the absolute temperature.

gyres—Large circulating currents that move clockwise in the northern hemisphere and counterclockwise in the southern hemisphere.

half-time—The amount of time it takes a tissue to accumulate half of the gas it can hold at a given pressure.

heat exhaustion—A medical condition that occurs when the core temperature of the body is above normal and the victim has become dehydrated.

heatstroke—An emergency medical condition that occurs when the body temperature becomes so high that the body's temperature-regulating ability shuts down.

Henry's law—This law states that the amount of a gas that dissolves in a liquid at a given temperature is directly proportional to the partial pressure of that gas.

hyperthermia—Higher-than-normal body core temperature.

hyperventilation—Rapid, deep breathing in excess of the body's needs.

hypothermia—Excessive loss of heat from the core of the body.

hypoventilation—Rapid and shallow breathing that does not allow you to expel carbon dioxide from your lungs.

ingassing—The process of gas diffusion into a liquid.

jumpsuit—A one-piece dive suit.

J-valve—A cylinder valve that was designed to maintain a reserve of air to permit a normal ascent. The introduction of submersible pressure gauges for scuba tanks has rendered the J-valve obsolete.

kelp—Giant algae that produce long strands that a diver can become entangled in.

Kelvin—The absolute temperature scale for Celsius temperatures. To convert a Celsius temperature to Kelvin, add 273 degrees.

K-valve—A cylinder valve that is a simple on-off valve that operates like a faucet. You turn the valve handle counterclockwise to open it and clockwise to close it.

lubber line—A reference line on a compass that indicates the direction of travel.

mediastinal emphysema—A lung injury in which air is present in the tissues in the middle of the chest.

middle ear—The air space behind the eardrum.

modified frog kick—A fin kick in which the diver rotates the ankles so that the tips of the fins point outward, slides the fins tip first in an outward direction, then pulls the bottoms of the fins together quickly in a wide, sweeping arc.

multilevel dive profile—A dive that progresses from deep to shallow during a given period of time.

neap tide—The twice-monthly period of lowest tides, which occurs when the moon and sun are at right angles to each other in relation to the earth.

neutral buoyancy—A state of buoyancy that a diver achieves when the diver neither sinks nor floats when holding an average breath.

nitrogen narcosis—A detrimental effect caused by the increased pressure of nitrogen that occurs at a depth of about 100 feet (30 meters).

nitrox—A nitrogen and oxygen mixture with a higher percentage of oxygen than is found in air. The mixture reduces the effects of nitrogen at depth.

no decompression stop limits—The maximum time that a diver may stay at a specified depth.

nonreference descent—A descent made vertically in water without any external reference.

octopus—A term used to describe an extra second stage.

open-circuit—Refers to a scuba system that permits a diver to breathe compressed air from a pressurized cylinder and exhausts the used gases into the water. Open-circuit systems are the safest and most popular form of scuba system.

open-valve ascent—A method for maintaining neutral buoyancy during an ascent by keeping the BC inflator-deflator valve open while holding the valve in a special way.

O-ring—A soft, circular ring that surrounds the outlet for scuba tank valves.

outgassing—The process of gas diffusing out of a liquid. For diving, it pertains to the diffusing of nitrogen absorbed under pressure.

overturn—The movement of water from the top of a lake to a depth of about 60 feet as a result of water circulation caused by winds. This water movement carries oxygenated water to the bottom and leads to what is called spring diving conditions.

partial pressure—The percentage of the total pressure exerted by each gas in a mixture of gases.

perfusion—The circulation in a tissue.

plankton—Aquatic life-forms that drift with the currents.

pneumothorax—A lung injury in which air is trapped in the chest cavity.

pony tank—A backup scuba unit consisting of a small scuba cylinder with a separate, standard regulator.

ports—The openings in the first stage of a regulator. One of the ports is for high-pressure air measurement with an SPG. The remaining ports are for low-pressure air.

pressure—Force (often weight) per unit area.

pulmonary barotrauma—Any lung injury caused by pressure.

Rankine—The absolute temperature scale for Fahrenheit temperatures. To convert a Fahrenheit temperature to Rankine, add 460 degrees.

reciprocal compass course—A course where the diver moves in a given heading for a given distance and returns to the origination point by reversing the direction of travel.

red tide—Blooms created by a type of red phytoplankton.

reference descent—A descent that the diver controls by following a line or the slope of the bottom.

repetitive dive—Any dive made within 6 to 24 hours (depending on the dive-planning device) of a previous dive.

repetitive group or repetitive group designation—The letter on a dive table that indicates the amount of nitrogen in a diver's body.

residual nitrogen—Nitrogen remaining in your system from a dive made within the past 12 hours.

residual nitrogen time—An amount of time that must be added to the actual bottom time (ABT) of a repetitive dive to determine the total bottom time (TBT). RNT compensates for residual nitrogen remaining in a diver's tissues from previous dives.

rest stop—A precautionary decompression stop during ascent.

reverse block—Discomfort that occurs when the pressure in the middle ear is above normal during an ascent due to blockage of the Eustachian tube.

reverse thermocline—The point of transition from a layer of cold water toward the surface of a lake to a layer of warmer water toward the bottom. This state exists in winter.

rip current—The narrow, strong current that moves away from shore as a result of water flowing back to sea through a narrow opening in an underwater obstruction.

sawtooth dive profile—A dive that progresses from deep to shallow and back to deep.

scissors kick—A fin kick that can be used as a resting kick. While lying on the side, the diver slowly extends one leg backward while extending the other leg forward, and then pulls the legs together quickly.

scombroid—A type of fish poisoning that can result if you eat fish that have not been kept chilled. It produces nausea and vomiting within an hour.

scrolling—A method used by dive computers to provide advance-planning information through a sequential display of time limits for various depths.

scuba—Self-contained underwater breathing apparatus.

semi-closed-circuit—Refers to a scuba system that combines the benefits of closed-circuit and open-circuit systems. Small amounts of used gases are released periodically.

set—The direction assumed by a current.

shallow-water blackout—The sudden loss of consciousness near the surface of the water.

shorty—A one-piece dive suit with short arms and legs used for diving in warm water.

sink—The area formed when the ground collapses into an underground cave system.

siphon—An opening where water is channeled from a sink back into the system.

skip breathing—An attempt to extend one's air supply by holding each breath for several seconds.

slack water—The period of time between flow and ebb when the water has minimal movement.

Spare Air unit—A backup scuba unit consisting of a small scuba cylinder with a special regulator integrated directly into the valve. A Spare Air unit is smaller than a pony tank and provides only enough air to permit an ascent from shallow depths.

spike dives—A dive with a short actual bottom time (ABT), such as a dive to free a fouled anchor.

spring tides—The twice-monthly period of highest tides, which occurs when the moon and sun are aligned with the earth.

square compass course—A series of headings that allows the diver to travel in a square pattern so that the dive ends where it began.

squeeze—A condition that occurs when the pressure on the outside of an air space in or on the body is greater than the pressure inside the air space. This condition may cause pain and injury and may be avoided by keeping the pressures equal (see equalization).

stages—The two parts of a scuba regulator that perform the two steps in the pressure reduction process.

stand—A brief period of time during which the tide neither rises nor falls.

step dive—A dive that is made in a series of steps.

stipes—Long strands of kelp.

subcutaneous emphysema—A lung injury in which air is present in the tissues under the skin. The air swells the tissues around the neck.

submersible pressure gauges—An instrument that measures scuba cylinder pressure.

surf—Breaking waves that occur when the water within the wave moves forward and gives up its energy. This occurs when the depth of the water is about the same as the wave height.

surface interval time—The elapsed time from when a diver surfaces after a dive to the time the diver begins the descent of a repetitive dive.

surge—The back-and-forth subsurface motion of the water within waves when the waves enter shallow water.

swells—The rounded, undulating forms that waves take as they move away from the area in which they were created.

tetrodotoxin—A type of fish poisoning that results from eating exotic fish such as puffer fish or blowfish. Tetrodotoxin is the most serious form of fish poisoning and can cause death within minutes.

thermocline—An abrupt transition from a warmer layer of water to a colder layer of water.

total bottom time—The sum of actual bottom time and residual nitrogen time.

Toynbee maneuver—A method of opening the eustachian tubes by blocking the nostrils, closing the mouth, and swallowing.

trail line—A long line with a float attached that is deployed from the stern of a boat. Divers use the trail line to pull themselves to the boat against the current.

trapdoor effect—A condition that exists when pressure prevents the Eustachian tube from opening. This condition may be overcome by ascending to reduce pressure.

trough—The bottom of a wave.

tsunami—Gigantic seismic waves caused by an underwater earthquake.

turbid—Water that is unclear or murky because of stirred-up sediment.

upwelling—The replacement of warm water at the surface with colder water flowing up from the depths as a result of a strong wind blowing along the shore for a sustained time.

Valsalva maneuver—A method of opening the eustachian tubes by blocking the nostrils, closing the mouth, and gently trying to exhale.

valve seat—The portion of the cylinder valve that closes and stops the flow of air.

vasoconstriction—Narrowing of the blood vessels.

vertigo—A subjective feeling of movement perceived as a spinning sensation.

wave height—The distance from a wave crest to the trough.

wave period—The time it takes two waves to pass a given point.

wave train—A long series of waves.

wavelength—The distance between waves.

Bibliography

Auerbach, P. (1987). *A medical guide to hazardous marine life.* Jacksonville, FL: Progressive Printing.

Barnhart, R., & Steinmetz, S. (1986). *Dictionary of science.* Maplewood, NJ: Hammond.

Bascom, W. (1964). *Waves and beaches.* Garden City, NY: Anchor Books.

Bove, A., & Davis, J. (1990). *Diving medicine.* Philadelphia: W.B. Saunders.

Divers Alert Network. (1989). *Medical requirements for scuba divers.* Durham, NC: Author.

Edmonds, C., Lowry, C., & Pennefather, J. (1981). *Diving and subaquatic medicine.* Mosman, NSW, Australia: Diving Medical Centre.

Foley, B. (1989). *Physics made simple.* New York: Doubleday.

Graver, D. (2004). *Aquatic Rescue and Safety.* Champaign, IL: Human Kinetics.

Lee, P., Lidov, M., & Tyberg, T. (1986). *The sourcebook of medical science.* New York: Torstar.

Lehrman, R. (1990). *Physics the easy way.* Hauppauge, NY: Barron's Educational Series.

Lippmann, J. (1992). *The essentials of deeper sport diving.* Locust Valley, NY: Aqua Quest.

Maloney, E. (1983). *Chapman piloting seamanship and small boat handling.* New York: Hearst Marine Books.

McGraw-Hill Professional Publishers (1998). Concise encyclopedia of science. Camden, Maine: McGraw-Hill.

Miller, J. (Ed.). (1979). *NOAA diving manual* (2nd ed.). Washington, DC: U.S. Government Printing Office, U.S. Department of Commerce.

National Association of Underwater Instructors (NAUI). (1991). *Advanced diving technology and techniques.* Montclair, CA: Author.

Professional Association of Diving Instructors (PADI). (1998). *The encyclopedia of recreational diving.* Santa Ana, CA: Author.

Sebel, P., Stoddart, D., Waldhorn, R., Waldmann, C., & Whitfield, P. (1985). *Respiration: The breath of life.* New York: Torstar.

Taylor, E. (Ed.). (1985). *Dorland's illustrated medical dictionary.* Philadelphia: W.B. Saunders.

Whitfield, P., & Stoddart, D. (1984). *Hearing, taste, and smell: Pathways of perception.* New York: Torstar.

Index

Note: The italicized *f* and *t* following page numbers refer to figures and tables, respectively.

About the Author

Dennis Graver has more than 30 years of experience as a scuba instructor and instructor trainer. He has authored 27 books and manuals on scuba diving, including three previous editions of *Scuba Diving* from Human Kinetics. In his position as director of training for the Professional Association of Diving Instructors (PADI), he designed the PADI modular scuba course and wrote the *PADI Dive Manual*, which revolutionized scuba instruction. During his tenure as director of education for the National Association of Underwater Instructors (NAUI), Graver wrote several diving texts, including the *NAUI Openwater I Scuba Diver Course Instructor Guide*. He has also contributed hundreds of articles on diving to such magazines as *Skin Diver*, *Sources*, and *Undercurrents* as well as several NAUI technical publications.

Since 1977 Graver has been photographing many wonders under the water, from the Red Sea off the coast of Egypt to the barrier reefs of Australia. He has won numerous awards from the Underwater Photographic Society, and his photos have graced the covers of numerous magazines and illustrated several diving texts and audiovisual educational programs.

Graver and his wife, Barbara, live in Camano Island, Washington.